A Chaplain at Gallipoli

WAR DIARIES

A Chaplain at Gallipoli

The Great War Diaries of
Kenneth Best

Edited by Gavin Roynon

IMPERIAL WAR
MUSEUM

SIMON &
SCHUSTER

London · New York · Sydney · Toronto · New Delhi

A CBS COMPANY

First published in Great Britain by Simon & Schuster UK Ltd, 2011
A CBS COMPANY
In association with the Imperial War Museum

Text copyright © the estate of Kenneth Best and the
Imperial War Museum 2011

1 3 5 7 9 10 8 6 4 2

Simon & Schuster UK Ltd
1st Floor
222 Gray's Inn Road
London WC1X 8HB

www.simonandschuster.co.uk

Simon & Schuster Australia, Sydney
Simon & Schuster India, New Delhi

The maps 'Operations at Helles' and 'The Theatre of Operations'
on pages viii and ix are reproduced from *Gallipoli* by Michael Hickey,
by permission of Watson, Little Ltd.

Every reasonable effort has been made to contact copyright holders
of material reproduced in this book. If any have inadvertently been overlooked,
the publishers would be glad to hear from them and make good in future
editions any errors or omissions brought to their attention.

A CIP catalogue record for this book
is available from the British Library.

ISBN: 978-0-85720-225-3

Typeset in Caslon by M Rules
Printed in the UK by CPI Mackays, Chatham, ME5 8TD

In memory of my great-uncle, 14989 Private William Roynon. A veteran of service with the Royal Wiltshires in India and the South African War, he volunteered to re-enlist in 1914 at the age of 45. He landed at Suvla Bay, Gallipoli, with the 7th Battalion, Royal Dublin Fusiliers on 7 August 1915. Nine days later he was killed in the bitter fighting on the Kiretch Tepe Sirt Ridge, which overlooks the Aegean. I was proud to see his name inscribed on the British War Memorial at Helles.

Contents

Maps   viii

Foreword: Chaplain Best's Journals and Letters
MICHAEL HICKEY   1

Preface
LIEUTENANT-GENERAL ANDREW GRAHAM   5

Biographical Note on Kenneth Best   9

Kenneth Best in Cairo and Gallipoli, 1914–1915
ANNE BROOKS   14

Crisis in Egypt and the Threat to the Suez Canal   25

Westerners, Easterners and the Dardanelles   34

List of Abbreviations   43

Chronological Diaries and Letters, September
1914 – October 1915   47

Evacuation   241

British Army Chaplains in the Great War   250

Epilogue – The 1967 Pilgrimage to Gallipoli
and the Reverend J.K. Best, MC
CHRISTOPHER FAGAN   265

Acknowledgements   271

Select Bibliography   275

Index   279

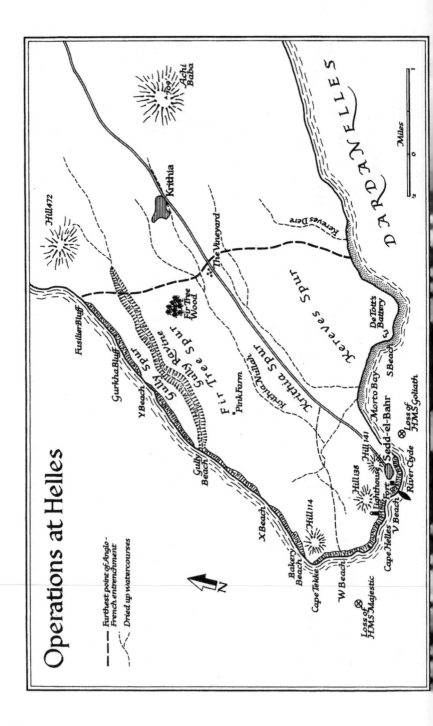

Operations at Helles

- - - - Furthest point of Anglo-French entrenchment
········ Dried up watercourses

N

DARDANELLES

Achi Baba
709

Hill 472

Krithia

The Vineyard

Kereves Dere

Fusilier Bluff

Fir Tree Wood

Kereves Spur

Gurkha Bluff

Gully Spur

Gully Ravine

Fir Tree Spur

Krithia Nullah

Krithia Spur

De Totts
Battery

Y Beach

Pink Farm

Morto Bay

S Beach

Gully Beach

Sedd-el-Bahr

Loss of
H.M.S Goliath

X Beach

Hill 141

Hill 138

Lighthouse

Fort

V Beach

River Clyde

Hill 114

Cape Tekke

Cape Helles

Bakery Beach

W Beach

Loss of
H.M.S Majestic

Miles

0

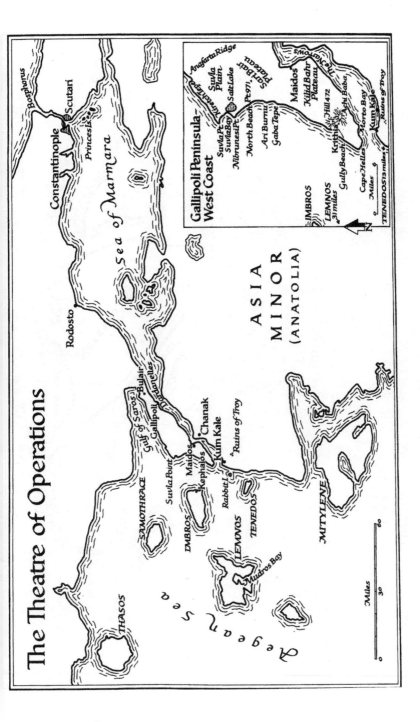

The Theatre of Operations

Inset: Gallipoli Peninsula — West Coast

Anafarta Ridge, Kuchuk, Anafarta, Suvla Plain, Salt Lake, Suvla Pt., Suvla Bay, Nibrunesi Pt., North Beach, Ari Burnu, Gaba Tepe, Sari Bair Plateau, Pt. 971, NARROWS, Maidos, Kilid Bahr Plateau, Hill 472, Achi Baba, Krithia, Morto Bay, Gully Beach, Cape Helles, Kum Kale, Ruins of Troy, IMBROS, LEMNOS 31 miles, TENEDOS 13 miles, Miles 0 3 6, N

Bosphorus, Scutari, Constantinople, Princes Is., Sea of Marmara, Rodosto, Gulf of Saros, Bulair, Gallipoli, Dardanelles, Suvla Point, SAMOTHRACE, Maidos, Kephalos, IMBROS, Chanak, Kum Kale, Rabbit I., Ruins of Troy, ASIA MINOR (ANATOLIA), LEMNOS, TENEDOS, Mudros Bay, MITYLENE, THASOS, Aegean Sea

Miles 0 30 60

Foreword
Chaplain Best's Journals and Letters

The Great War of 1914–18 was a watershed in British history. The nation that emerged from that conflict was no longer the same as the one that had entered it in the summer of 1914. Never until that point had war been waged on such a scale and at such terrible cost in materiel and blood. The seemingly enduring social life of town and country never regained its pre-war character. This was, in many ways, due to the traumatic war experiences undergone by men and women of all classes, which had propelled thousands of otherwise obscure and undervalued people into positions of responsibility to which they rose splendidly. Former bank clerks, farm workers, machine operators and minor officials were commanding battalions and warships with distinction by 1918, and a great army of women had replaced thousands of male workers to make munitions of war; they were never likely to revert to subservience once back in their pre-war communities. What they had experienced in those crucial years would settle the social order for generations to come.

Those who opted for non-combatant duties – or were obliged to do so by virtue of their profession or the workings of conscience – included the priesthood, whose volunteer members served in uniform as chaplains to the Army or the Royal Navy. One such was the Reverend Kenneth Best, aged 26, a brilliant Cambridge mathematics graduate who was ordained in 1913. On volunteering for the military chaplaincy, Best was accepted at once and was sent to Egypt, then Gallipoli, with the 42nd East Lancashire Division. At Gallipoli he found conditions appalling. He recorded what he saw in letters to his father and also in a journal. These have been edited by Gavin Roynon with all the sensitivity and perception to be expected from a historian who served in the army as a National Service officer.

Following the actual letters and diaries, Roynon describes the work of a number of army chaplains in the 1914–18 war. These included men who became legendary: 'Tubby' Clayton, the founder of TocH; Geoffrey Studdert-Kennedy, immortalised as 'Woodbine Willie'; Noel Mellish, VC, MC, and Theodore Hardy, VC, DSO, MC, who was killed in 1918. All were truly remarkable men, whose ministry differed widely in character.

Although Kenneth Best gained no awards, he soon decided that the only place for him was in the front line, conducting services whenever time permitted to small congregations, often under severe shrapnel fire. He also regarded it as his duty to rescue the wounded from no-man's land and to bury the dead wherever he could. These tasks were fraught with danger, as exposure above the trench parapet invited immediate death at the hands of the Turkish snipers.

Best's views on the conduct of fellow officers and chaplains are often virulent; he had no time for those who were not prepared to share the men's dangers in the very front line, and even less for staff officers lurking in their dugouts who were never seen in the forward trenches. His descriptions of living conditions for the infantry, whose lot he shared, are horribly realistic. The constant danger of death from artillery fire and the expert Turkish snipers, the frequent badly planned assaults on the Turkish positions, the apparent lack of consideration on the part of the staff, and dreadful unhygienic conditions due to the thousands of unburied dead on the battlefield – all are vividly brought into focus by the spare, often underrated prose of this sensitive man of God as he struggles with the cure of souls in a nightmare situation.

Four months of this resulted in his being evacuated with enteric fever, but after convalescence in Cyprus and Egypt (where again he encountered officers he castigates as shirkers) he was back at Gallipoli. By now, however, his health was seriously affected and he was sent back to England, but his sense of duty to the front-line soldiery – the PBI or 'poor bloody infantry' – compelled him to continue his ministry in France. There he served in a formation of Kitchener's Army, that great host of patriotic volunteers who flocked to the colours in 1914 at the behest of the celebrated national hero and War Minister. Kitchener's hypnotic stare on the justly celebrated poster would eventually lead so many to mass slaughter on the Somme, where Best was posted to minister to the 'Pals' battalions of the 31st Division.

Inured as he was to horrors of the front line at Gallipoli, Best was shocked to find conditions on the Somme battlefield even worse. He continued to carry out what he regarded as his Christian duty by venturing further into no-man's land with patrols and listening parties, and rescuing the wounded, frequently under fire and against the orders of his commanding officers. He continued to serve with infantry battalions until the armistice of November 1918, after which he returned to civilian life. By now, however, his faith had undergone such stress that he decided to revert to teaching and became a schoolmaster for twenty years; in the Second World War he felt the call once more and rejoined the Royal Army Chaplains' Department, serving in the sort of staff appointments for which he had expressed such scorn in his earlier journals. His later years were spent as an agnostic; given his horrific experiences in Gallipoli and on the Somme, this should not unduly surprise or shock today's reader.

Gavin Roynon's editorial sensitivity enables us to comprehend, if at a safe distance, the sheer bloody horror experienced by a generation that has now gone; a generation whose sacrifice ultimately went unheeded by the politicians who had promised them 'a world fit for heroes', only for them to trudge obediently to their deaths in tens of thousands.

How fortunate were those of them who had a priest like Kenneth Best to give them some consolation on the brink of eternity.

Michael Hickey

Preface

In the foreword to his essays[1] the Reverend Geoffrey Studdert-Kennedy CF writes, 'When a chaplain joins a battalion no one says a word to him about God, but everyone asks him in a thousand different ways "what is God like?". His success or failure as chaplain depends upon the answer he gives by word or deed. The answer by deed is the more important ...'

While Studdert-Kennedy's experiences, utterances and reputation are well chronicled, the diaries of the Reverend Kenneth Best describe a different theatre of war and reflect the views of a less well-known observer. The diaries of Padre Kenneth Best tell the tale first-hand of a chaplain who, very shortly after war was declared, found himself embarked for Egypt and, less than six months later, en route for the Dardanelles to take part in the amphibious landings at Gallipoli. Gavin Roynon's deft and informative editing brings to life the realities of that most desperate and bloody of operations. For four long months Padre Best ministered to the soldiers under his pastoral care with the bravery, self-lessness, commitment and compassion that characterises the work of the best Army padres.

It is impossible to underestimate the importance of a 'good' padre to the morale, well-being and effectiveness of

---

1 G.A. Studdert-Kennedy, *The Hardest Part*, Diggory Press, 2007.

a unit or a formation. The words of a private soldier in the Great War talking of the battalion's padre, 'He was always with us. He was always in the front line' stand the test of time and are as true today as they were in May 1915 when Padre Best sailed for the Dardanelles and four months service on the beaches and battlegrounds of Gallipoli. The whys and wherefores of the Gallipoli campaign will be debated for years to come. But the fighting on the Gallipoli Peninsula was nonetheless less horrifying in its intensity for the combatants, and demanding for the chaplains ministering to the spiritual needs of the men with whom they were deployed.

British Military Doctrine describes three components of fighting power: the conceptual, the physical and the moral comprising that which provides the motivation, leadership and management. For there to be an effective moral component, soldiers need a sense of well-being that enables them willingly to maintain their commitment. The body, mind and spirit must be in healthy balance so that the soldier can cope with the stress, danger, climatic and emotional challenges of the operational environment.

For the soldier of the twenty-first century, the pressures of culture, society, and media perception are increasing by the day. Achieving a healthy balance for the 'body' may be reasonably straightforward through the provision of sustenance, sanitation, healthcare and recreational facilities; so too for 'mental well-being' which can be assisted by facilities for personal development, relaxation and communication. Far more complex is achieving the healthy balance of the 'spirit' that is crucial for the generation and maintenance of morale.

High morale means that in battle men will persevere doggedly with pluck and a determination not to let one another down. The issue of morale revolutionised the role of chaplains in the First World War. Military leaders became convinced that religion was a crucial and sustaining force for the morale of citizen soldiers through the spiritual and material comforts that organised religion could bring. In Field Marshal Haig's words, *no-one could do more than a chaplain to sustain morale and explain what we're fighting for . . . a good chaplain is as valuable as a good general.* Since the ideals of loyalty, courage, discipline, integrity, and selflessness are the life of an army, then who better to explain the rightness of the cause and exemplify those values than a padre?

On or off operations, as every commander will testify, a trusted chaplain is invaluable as a critical friend and comrade, available to the men, sensing those individuals who need help, and providing gentle, purposeful, principled and disinterested (in the true sense of the word) support and assurance; someone with time just to spend time. Selflessness and friendship are at the heart of a good padre's approach – he is plucky, doggedly persevering, approachable, positive; he takes an equal share of the soul-searching and hardship that the soldier experiences and then, through quiet words, helps troubled souls make sense of the world around them in order that they can continue doing their duty.

The young trooper asking on the eve of Operation TELIC 1 (Iraq 2003) whether the padre was 'coming with them', and feeling just a bit more certain that things would be all right on receiving the answer 'of course', exemplifies the truism that in war or times of real difficulty, the time of greatest spiritual need is most likely to coincide with the time of greatest pastoral needs.

That articulate and compelling speaker and troubled soul Padre Geoffrey Studdert-Kennedy was known colloquially to the men he served as Woodbine Willie. He was asked for his views on the role of the military chaplain by the Reverend Theodore Hardy who, before his death by enemy fire in October 1918, was awarded the VC, DSO and MC for his repeated courage and devotion in the face not of the enemy but of the horrors of war itself. This was Studdert-Kennedy's answer:

> There is very little spiritual work, it is all muddled and mixed – but it is all spiritual. Take a box of fags in your haversack and a great deal of love in your heart, and go up to them, laugh with them, joke with them. You can pray with them sometimes, but pray for them always ... You can take it that the best place for a padre (provided he does not interfere with your military operations) is where there is most danger of death. Your place is in the line. The line is the key to the whole business ... The men will forgive you anything but lack of courage and devotion; without that you are useless.

Through skilful, informative and sensitive editing, Gavin Roynon has brought to life, through the diary accounts of an Army padre, the realities of the way in which human beings, soldiers and sailors conduct themselves in the face of enormous difficulties, where the threat of death or mutilation is a constant. Also, where the most likely outcome is negative – at best disembarkation and withdrawal, at worst death, wounding or capture. For four long months, Padre Best ministered to the soldiers under his pastoral care with the bravery, commitment and compassion that characterises the work of the best Army padres. His story is a compelling one and his circumstances are well summed up in the words of that private soldier writing of another padre:

'He was always with us. He was always in the front line.'

Andrew Graham

Biographical Note on Kenneth Best

John Kenneth Best, son of Julia and the Reverend John Dugdale Best, was born on 26 December 1887. His father, sometime principal of Chester College, was appointed Rector of Sandon, near Chelmsford, in the early twentieth century, and the Rectory became a base for his son when on home leave during the First World War. Kenneth Best was educated at Lancing College (1899–1900), Arnold House School (Chester) and Queens' College, Cambridge, where he was awarded a first-class honours degree in mathematics. After training for the priesthood at Egerton Hall, Manchester, he went as curate to St Cuthbert's, Lytham, in September 1912, and was ordained a year later.

Soon after the outbreak of war in 1914, Best was appointed a chaplain in the Territorial Force.

He joined the 1st/3rd East Lancashire Brigade, RFA (Royal Field Artillery)[1] and sailed with the unit to Egypt on 10 September 1914. He spent four months based at Heliopolis near Cairo, and was then sent to Ismailia to minister to troops stationed on the Suez Canal. Here he had his first taste of enemy action. He returned to Heliopolis in late February 1915 and embarked for the Dardanelles on 3 May.

The next four months were a testing period for Best, and he rose to the challenge magnificently. He held services

---

1 Royal Field Artillery, attached to the 42nd East Lancashire Division.

Kenneth Best's Certificate of Commission, issued by the
Court of St James
© the estate of Kenneth Best. Imperial War Museum. BestJK_010297_4_1

under fire, visited men in the front line, helped care for the wounded and buried the dead. Unfortunately, his determination was not enough to protect him against disease, and in July he fell sick with enteric fever. The following month, within a few weeks of his return to Gallipoli, he contracted dysentery and – to his displeasure – was ordered home. He was put on a hospital ship, the *Ausonia*, which sailed from Mudros, ostensibly for the UK, on 25 September 1915.

Despite the debilitating effects of dysentery, Best kept up his diary. He recorded the arrival of the *Ausonia* at Marsemuscatta Harbour, Malta, where the ailing troops were all unwillingly transferred to Cottonera. This was a makeshift military hospital, several miles from the harbour, where they were given a meagre supper.

However, Best felt well enough to visit Valletta, where he attended a service in the cathedral, of whose style he was strongly critical. The two-week delay before the invalid soldiers departed from Malta underlined the shortage of hospital ships (some of which had been used for transporting large numbers of horses to the Peninsula). They finally left Malta on 16 October, this time bound for England. They passed Gibraltar and Cape Trafalgar and arrived at Southampton on 23 October.

Best appears to have spent the first six months of 1916 in England, but in late June he joined the 13th Battalion, York and Lancaster Regiment (94th Infantry Brigade, 31st Division) on the Western Front. He was with the unit during the opening days of the Somme Offensive, defying orders to keep away from the front line. During August 1916 he regularly stayed overnight in the trenches and accompanied wiring parties on night work. By September he had taken on pastoral responsibility for the 14th Battalion, York and Lancaster Regiment, as well. He continued to go out at night with working parties and bravely attempted to rescue the battalion's wounded officers even when forbidden to do so. It was not surprising that he was asked to consider a combatant commission.

In January 1918, Best's gallantry and devotion to his men was recognised by the award of the Military Cross. The citation reads as follows:

> 'Best, J. K.
> Captain Best has been chaplain of the battalion for over a year and has from the first held an almost unique position in the estimation of the men. His absolute fearlessness and complete disregard of danger under fire is a by-word among them and many instances of his great courage and fine example can be quoted. On many occasions he has tended the wounded under very heavy shell fire.'[1]

1 As quoted by Edward Madigan in his recently published work, *Faith Under Fire, Anglican Chaplains in the Great War*, (Palgrave Macmillan, 2011, p. 140).

Kenneth Best was demobilised in 1919. During his last months in the Army, he had given his future much thought. He decided against returning to parish duties and instead joined Cheltenham College as a maths master in 1920. He remained at the school for twenty years and became the housemaster of Boyne House. In 1940, however, he resigned and became once more a Chaplain to the Forces, perhaps hoping to recapture in the Second World War the sense of fulfilment and adventure he had experienced during the First World War. Initially he seems to have been posted to an Officer Cadet Training Unit at Alton Towers, but in

Kenneth Best, 1914
© the estate of Kenneth Best. Imperial War Museum. BestJK_010297_3

November 1944 he was asked to join Supreme Headquarters, Allied Expeditionary Force. He served with SHAEF at Versailles then, after VE Day, was based in Frankfurt for six weeks before returning home for demobilisation at the end of June 1945.

During the postwar years Best lived in Devon with an unmarried sister, and became active in various local orchestras and musical societies. He had loved music all his life and was an accomplished violinist. It was said that on the Western Front during the First World War he would play his violin in the trenches and that even the enemy held their fire and listened when he performed pieces by German composers. His religious faith was not so enduring, however, and in his later years he was an agnostic.

Kenneth Best died on Easter Day 1981.

Kenneth Best in Cairo and Gallipoli, 1914–1915

The Reverend Kenneth Best began keeping a diary soon after his arrival in Egypt in late September 1914. He was also a prolific letter-writer, especially to his family. He had left Southampton aboard the Royal Mail Steamship Packet, RMSP *Avon* on 10 September, as chaplain to the 1st/3rd East Lancashire Brigade RFA, and disembarked at Alexandria. He then travelled by train to Cairo and on to a camp near Heliopolis, just south of the city. His initial impressions of the camp were not favourable. The place was in chaos, with no fodder or nosebags for the horses and not enough men to look after them. The animals stampeded and many died. Rations allocated to the ordinary soldier were inadequate, especially as the men were expected to work in searing heat. The treatment of native servants by British officers was often deplorable.

Eventually Best was apprised of his duties. In addition to organising services, conducting burials and visiting the sick, he was to help with the YMCA tent, and act as Mess secretary and treasurer. He disliked the idea of having to do accounts and thought the Mess subscription far too high.

The life of an Army padre was going to be entirely different from the existence of a country clergyman. In his diaries and letters, Kenneth Best explains where some of the differences lay. He refers to his frustration that, without hymn sheets, singing in services was bound to be a haphazard affair, as the men were not allowed hymn books in their kitbags. Venues for these services might be local churches, or a tent, or even the parade ground. In a letter dated 12 November 1914, he describes kneelers made out of sacks cut in two and filled with sand, communion rails fashioned from posts and some rope, and a makeshift altar, covered by a dark tablecloth.

By Christmas 1914, however, the chaplain's tent was quite an impressive affair, with a proper altar frontal, a gilded wooden cross, candlesticks from a native bazaar and a hired American organ. The kneelers had been replaced by horse blankets. Best held confirmation classes, carried out pastoral work and took part in discussions about providing wholesome recreation for the men. On 23 October, he conducted his first military funeral at Cairo War Cemetery. He described the occasion as 'impressive and memorable', partly, no doubt, because the service was held by candlelight – the cortège having got lost and thus having not reached the burial ground until after dark. Other funerals followed. At least one of the deaths was from dysentery, but others were the result of accidents; in late December 1914, for example, Best buried a pioneer who had fallen off a pyramid, and another soldier who had tumbled out of a train.

Off duty, the chaplain enjoyed riding and regularly helped exercise the unit's horses. He also did a great deal of sightseeing, noting down aspects of local civilian life as well as chronicling his visits to antiquities. When martial law was declared because of civil unrest, he prudently considered purchasing a revolver to protect himself on these jaunts. Relations between Allied forces and the local population probably worsened in early December 1914 with the arrival of the first Australian and New Zealand troops. Best describes the 'invasion' in his diary entry for 3 December, remarking that the newcomers were of fine physique, but a 'rough hardy undisciplined lot' who quickly got into fights in the town.

On 20 January 1915 Best travelled to Ismailia to replace a colleague who had been hospitalised and act as chaplain to the forces stationed on the Suez Canal. He was delighted with the appointment, which had gone to him partly because he was an experienced horseman and so could ride from one unit to another. In practice, however, fearing he might get lost, he travelled by rail or boat when conducting pastoral visits.

The British Government was well aware of the vital importance of the Suez Canal. It provided a crucial waterway link to India, the Far East and the Antipodes, hence the build-up of troops in Egypt. Towards the end of January, in a series of skirmishes, the Turks showed their intentions all too clearly.

Many of the troops at Ismailia were from India; Best noted that native officers did not dare to take responsibility for ordering their men to open fire, even when the Turks were spotted cutting through barbed wire. Both Best's letters and his diary refer to enemy gunfire and shelling which caused casualties and damage.

On 1 February 1915, the Turks attacked the Suez Canal. Best visited the wounded and eventually buried the dead, though his first funeral on the Canal was not for battle casualties but for two Royal Army Medical Corps (RAMC) men killed when a trench fell in on them. The severest fighting was between Serapeum and Toussum as the Turks advanced to cross the Canal. A few days later, on 9 February 1915, Best visited the battlefield and in his next letter home wrote a description:

> ... It was a gruesome sight – the Turks were slaughtered like cattle. Burial parties had to go out for a week before all the corpses were put under the sand. The ground was

littered with ammunition, rifles, bayonets, clothes and especially old boots. They evidently found they could run faster without them ...

According to his diary, sand had been blown away from some of the corpses in shallow graves, exposing hands and feet. The same problem occurred with the dead who had been pulled out of the Canal and interred, leaving Best to wonder why they had not been cremated.

Towards the end of February the Canal Defence chaplain returned to duty and Best was recalled to Heliopolis. For two months he resumed his duties at the camp, coping with a church tent which resembled a parachute in high winds, and grumbling at the innumerable requests from vicars in England to look after a particular parishioner apparently now amongst the thousands in his pastoral care. There were constant rumours of a move; indeed, one unit even punished the promulgators of such rumours with seven days of defaulters' parade. Late in April 1915, Best was ordered to Abassia Garrison in Cairo, and within a few days was preparing to leave Egypt altogether.

There were conflicting orders about whether the chaplain should be accompanying the 42nd (East Lancashire) Division to the Dardanelles, but the matter was settled by General Douglas and he duly embarked on the *Derfflinger* on 3 May 1915. The ship had just returned from the peninsula with a cargo of wounded and looked like a slaughterhouse. Best and his companions were given graphic descriptions of the ANZAC (Australia and New Zealand Army Corps) landings; Australian troops mentioned having to swim ashore from ships' boats, with many drowning in the attempt. There were tales of Turkish atrocities, and of enemy spies masquerading as British and Australian officers. Hearing of the danger posed by snipers, officers travelling with Best had their heads shaved and cut off their badges of rank to present less obvious targets.

The transport reached Cape Helles on 6 May 1915. Troops were taken by tender to within a quarter of a mile of land, and then had a three-hour wait for transport to the shore. It was two a.m. before Best reached the trenches, where it was too cold for him to sleep. Later that day he began his pastoral visits, calling at a casualty clearing station where there were too few medical officers and stretcher bearers. Hundreds, he recorded, were dying of exposure. He also mentioned meeting the Lancashire Fusiliers returning from the trenches, their morale low. Some had refused to advance, and at least one of the men, dreading the order to return to the front line, later shot off his trigger finger. The enemy's Maxim guns and well-camouflaged snipers, one of them rumoured to be a girl, were causing the greatest damage, and a common feeling was that 'It is perfect hell. The Turks are perfect demons.'

Best landed at Gallipoli on the opening day of the Second Battle of Krithia. His diary records the bombardment, and the constant stream of wounded men passing through the clearing stations and dressing stations to the hospital ships. Sunday, 9 May was *as usual a day of blood*, though at least religion was no longer scoffed at. He spent part of the day creating a cemetery and burying corpses. The heavy casualty rate had made the Australians *mad with fury and longing for vengeance.* Best felt rumours of Turkish atrocities were being spread to justify not taking prisoners. He observed that the Australians used burial parties as cover for bringing in reserves for a surprise attack.

The British, too, used subterfuge against the Turks, firing a volley and shouting as if about to charge, then targeting any of the enemy who raised their heads in preparation to meet the supposed advance. There was plenty of genuine heroism too, both on land and at sea. Best recorded the bravery of men in a rowing boat trying to rescue passengers from the water after a transport had been shelled. The comparative peace of Heliopolis must have seemed far distant. On 21 May he wrote 'Our playtime is over, we have put away childish things and got to business, real grim business'.

But he seems to have adapted quickly to the constant stream of bullets and shells. On 20 May 1915 he took his first service under fire:

> I managed to borrow (communion) vessels from a neighbouring padre. My altar was a pair of biscuit boxes. My vestments a khaki shirt, dirty greasy tunic and riding breeches, muddy brown leggings and boots. It was a wonderful service. We fixed it for 6 a.m. hoping to anticipate the usual morning 'hymn of hate' which the Turks play to us during brekker. Unfortunately they rose early. Perhaps our artillery had made them restless and they started up just as our service commenced. I felt very responsible but thought I would be there in case they should turn up. To my surprise, regardless of shrapnel, about 100 men were present. Never shall I forget my first service under fire. We all felt God's good providence watched over us, for not one was hit. We are all in excellent spirits.

Best's casual attire confused more recently arrived chaplains, who mistook him for an officer's batman. Towards the end of May he held a Whit Sunday service; he noted that he had a reputation for bravery because he did not take cover when shells burst – a conscious decision on his part in order not to lose face in front of the men.

He believed in setting a good example, and was contemptuous of those who shirked this duty. He mentions a staff officer who, although himself petrified of shells, court-martialled a boy of fifteen for losing his nerve. Regimental chaplains who sat reading in their tents instead of visiting their charges were also criticised. Chaplains were non-combatants, like doctors, but it is clear from his diaries that Best frequently visited the men in the front line.

Preparations for the Third Battle of Krithia on 4 June are recorded. News of the advance filtered back with the wounded, and initially morale appears to have been good. Best went up to the trenches in Gully Ravine and found them full of dead and dying. After a return visit the following day he wrote:

> All along trench am stepping over dead bodies. Some men, shot clean through heart or head, looked quite natural and peaceful except for yellow-green hue of skin. Most with look of agony or horror on their faces – if faces were not blown away. Nearly all mangled in ghastly fashion. Outside trenches, fields and open ground littered with dead and I fear some not dead – but sheer suicide to try to get them in ...

On 6 June he visited the Worcestershire Regiment in the firing line. He found the men exhausted, their nerves shattered; they were incapable of lifting a bayonet or defending themselves against an enemy attack, and too weak to remove the dying by stretcher. Best did what he could for the wounded, helped with the stretchers despite the heavy shrapnel, and buried the dead. He noted with disapproval that, though men were dying from exposure, exhaustion and loss of blood, their comrades in the Field Ambulance *still found time to play cards and read novels*. The lack of stretcher bearers seemed inexplicable, as did some of the orders from HQ which caused the heavy losses.

Best speculated that few staff officers had any experience of the trenches and that they cared more for the horses than the men. He wondered what knowledge of the campaign had reached England, and predicted as early as 8 May 1915 (less than a week after his arrival) that there would be a scandal, and perhaps the need for an official inquiry. A memorandum stating that the Turks were on their last legs was dismissed by him as childish, and an unworthy way to improve morale. One of Best's close friends was killed in the Third Battle of Krithia while serving with the Collingwood Battalion, Royal Naval Division, which was virtually wiped out.

There was another Allied attack on 19 June. It involved the 9th Battalion, Manchester Regiment but ended in panic and near disaster. Best spent twelve hours without food, burying the dead where he could at the side of the trench or in a dip in the land. His diary entries for June and July are full of references to wounded men and funerals. There is further evidence, too, of the decisions from GHQ which ultimately caused these casualties and meant so much misery for the survivors. The diary remarks on the madness of ordering reliefs to take place in daylight, and notes the lack of a master plan and the apparent inability of staff officers to understand the nature of modern warfare or the limits of human endurance.

He comments on the absurdity of sending an officer to Alexandria to procure delicacies for General Headquarters (GHQ), and the insensitivity of a staff officer who orders exhausted men to dig ever deeper trenches while he stays safe in his dugout. With such bitterness of feeling the rumour was not surprising that Major-General Sir William Douglas, who commanded 42nd Division, was only going to be killed by a direct hit of lyddite (an explosive) or by a bullet from one of his own men.

By contrast, Best had considerable respect and admiration for the Turkish soldier, the 'finest in the world'. He considered that, with certain exceptions, the enemy fought 'honourably' and in a 'gentlemanly' way. They were good marksmen with well designed trenches; it was unfortunate that the British troops opposing them did not have the peak of fitness such a formidable enemy warranted.

He notes that men in the front line were often exhausted or at the end of their tether; one man even deliberately attracted enemy fire by raising his head above the parapet. Patients in May were being returned to their units before they had fully mentally and physically recovered, and soldiers with a new draft who arrived in late June appeared weak and sickly, much to the examining MO's (medical officer's) disgust.

As the summer progressed, the cases of dysentery increased, and after a hospital visit on 27 May, Best noted that most of the patients were sick rather than wounded. By mid-July he was himself sick with enteritis, caught, he believed, from infected water, or from his proximity to corpses during the day and to the buried dead at night. Eventually he was evacuated to Egypt in His Majesty's Hospital Ship HMHS *Soudan*, but not before he had been left for a considerable period in the sun without food and drink. He was admitted to No. 15 General Hospital in Alexandria, then sent to a convalescent camp at Troodos in Cyprus.

The diary notes for his convalescence on Cyprus are confused, partly because of his illness, and some of the entries were made on loose scraps of paper. He appears to have returned to Egypt on 14 August 1915, and sailed back to the Dardanelles six days later.

The return voyage to the Gallipoli Peninsula was in SS *Huntsgreen*; the curious name indicated that it was a captured German steamer (hence the Hun component), initially spotted by someone called Green. German submarines provided a major threat, and on 13 August the Allied troop ship HMT *Royal Edward* had been sunk near the Greek island of Kos, costing the lives of 861 soldiers. This sinking was witnessed by Canon Donald Bartlett, aboard the *Alnwick Castle* en route for Mudros. Survivors told him that the *Royal Edward* had been hit by three torpedoes and sank in four minutes.[1]

On board Best's ship were survivors of the sinking of the *Royal Edward*, anxious for the voyage to be over. There were old hands returning to the Dardanelles, wisely trying to get as much sleep as possible, and new drafts, excited and full of anticipation. The *Huntsgreen* docked at Lemnos and Best continued his journey in the *Ermina*, arriving on 26 August at the Lancashire Landing Beach.

Within a few days of his arrival Best was receiving news of fresh disasters; he mentions how an unidentified battalion was wiped out when the nominal guard on watch over men cooling off in the sea was killed, and the bathers were picked off at leisure by snipers. A day of funerals followed, as the victims of a mine and some accurate sniping were buried. Four days later it was the turn of a soldier in the 9th Battalion, Manchester Regiment, tragically shot dead by his comrades when he failed to respond on being challenged.

Lack of fitness was still affecting Allied troops in the Dardanelles. According to a diary entry for 9 September, 75 per cent of the original 42nd Division had been certified medically unfit. Best himself soon felt below par again. When the pain and sickness worsened, he was sent to a casualty clearing station where all the other officers were sickness cases. He had dysentery and was evacuated in HMHS *Gascon* to Mudros, where he transferred to HMT *Ausonia*. It annoyed him to see young chaplains on the hospital ships when they could have been with front-line troops. He was also irritated to discover that three-quarters of the medical comforts were being siphoned off into the officers' mess. As the *Ausonia* sailed west, decisions were made as to which men should return to England and which would recover

1 Reminiscences of Canon D.M.M. Bartlett, ed. A.M. Wilkinson, 1969.

quickly enough to rejoin their units. Best was conscious that this meant life or death for some.

The *Ausonia* reached Malta at the end of September and Best was admitted to Cottonera Hospital. A week later he went before a medical board and was invalided home on the SS *Carisbrook Castle*. Before he left he had the chance to socialise, enjoy concerts and sightseeing, and had his camera confiscated by suspicious local police. On arrival in England Best was sent to a London hospital, then discharged to his father's rectory at Sandon, near Chelmsford. He remained in England for six months, initially serving as a chaplain near Weymouth, and then with the South Staffordshire Regiment at Catterick.

Nothing daunted by his grim experiences in Gallipoli, Kenneth Best joined the York and Lancaster Regiment in France towards the end of June 1916. He little realised that within a few days he would witness the carnage of the opening days of the Battle of the Somme.

Anne Brooks
Imperial War Museum

Crisis in Egypt and the Threat
to the Suez Canal

Egypt in the early years of the twentieth century was the most ambiguous of British possessions. It was neither colony, nor protectorate, nor a condominium like the Sudan – in fact, it was not a part of the British Empire at all. Its constitution was said to be one of the most complicated in the world. In theory it was an independent province within the Ottoman Empire, whose head of state (and chief Egyptian official), the Khedive, was answerable to the Sultan at Istanbul. Although it had its own parliament, government, military, and civil administration, the country had been run by the British since 1882.

The great French engineer Ferdinand de Lesseps supervised the construction of the Suez Canal from 1859 to 1869. Great Britain became the second largest share-holder in 1875 by purchasing the financial stake of the Egyptian Khedive. In 1888 the leading European powers agreed to declare the Canal a neutral waterway and to guarantee an unobstructed right of way to international shipping. The management of the Canal was vested in the hands of the Suez Canal Company. It was up to the British Government to ensure that it remained open in wartime and safe from possible predators.

Egypt had been acquired by the British when a nationalist

revolt against the Khedive and his Turkish henchmen broke out. This had been prompted by the state of bankruptcy caused by the vast debts to European banks accumulated by the Khedive Ismail. He abdicated, was succeeded by the Khedive Tewfik, and the British and French appointed commissioners to exercise financial controls. But this did not prevent the Minister of War, Colonel Arabi, leading a revolt from the ranks of the Egyptian Army. This led to the deaths of Europeans during riots in Alexandria, whereupon the British sent in naval and military forces to impose law and order.

The Battle of Tel-el-Kebir followed in August 1882, and Arabi's troops were defeated by the British Army under Sir Garnet Wolseley. British troops did not then withdraw, as had been envisaged by the Egyptian Government, and British officials took over the key departments in the administration. The Egyptian Army now had a British commander-in-chief and 6,000 British troops were stationed in Egypt.

Lord Milner, in his book *England in Egypt*, described the status of the country thus: 'It was a veiled Protectorate, of uncertain extent and indefinite duration, which we could not call on others to recognise.' By 1901, all was quiet on the Egyptian front, with the new administration providing career opportunities for enterprising young Britons, on a par with those available in other territories of the British Empire.

Control of the country remained in the hands of Evelyn Baring, Lord Cromer, who was the British Agent, Consul-General and self-styled Plenipotentiary from 1883 to 1907. He was said to have practically reconstructed the country with little or no interference either from the Turks or the British Government. But Cromer did little to take account of the nationalist agitation which was spreading through schools and colleges during the first decade of the twentieth century. When he appointed an ambitious politician, Saad Zaghlul Pasha, as Minister of Education shortly before he retired, he was unaware that he was promoting a man who strongly resented the British presence and would be an ardent leader of the nationalist movement.

One great bone of contention with the Egyptians was the fact that English and French were the two main teaching languages and Dr Douglas Dunlop, the fiery Scot who controlled the curriculum as British adviser on Education, strongly discouraged Arabic. This linguistic clash caused deep divisions in the way secondary examination papers were set and marked, sometimes with a bias against those who had not been taught in English or French.

However, Cromer's successor as Consul-General, Sir Eldon Gorst,[1] with encouragement from the Liberal Government in Britain, sought to pour oil on troubled waters by giving the Egyptians more responsibility for running their own affairs. In line with the 'Egypt for the Egyptians' movement, he strengthened the powers of local Egyptians and – despite opposition from British officials, who felt their own positions were threatened – he built up the numbers of Egyptians in the administration. He also improved relations with Khedive Abbas Hilmi II.

While this was happening, provinces within the Habsburg Empire were also seeking more independence. Beset by competing imperial ambitions and a naval armaments race, the European imbroglio was building up, and was finally triggered into war by the consequences of the assassination of the Archduke Franz Ferdinand in Sarajevo on 28 June 1914. Many major questions arose to be asked in the tense weeks which followed, but none more unpredictable than the allegiance of Turkey. Which way would the regime in

1 By training a barrister, Gorst was Consul-General of Egypt from 1907 to 1911. He launched a lenient policy towards the Egyptians, but the murder of his appointee as Prime Minister, Butros Ghali, caused him to adopt a harsher one. Gorst was not a popular figure among British officials. His time in Egypt was curtailed by cancer and he died in England in 1911.

Constantinople jump? Their traditional foe was Russia, their traditional ally Britain – as the Crimean War had shown. Unfortunately, the British Government lost this crucial diplomatic contest with Germany for the hand of Turkey.

Fearful of a thrust by Russia for the Dardanelles and skilfully wooed by the formidable German Ambassador, Baron Marschall von Bieberstein, the Turks signed a secret alliance with Germany against Russia on 2 August 1914. The wily, pro-German Enver Pasha had already started mobilising Turkish forces, and on the following day the first mines were laid in the Dardanelles.

Meanwhile, the British Ambassador to Turkey had been on leave during these vital weeks. Also, the British Government had alienated Turkish support by informing Constantinople that it was requisitioning the two modern battleships which Turkey had ordered and which they were expecting soon to be delivered. On 10 August, to the immense chagrin of the First Lord of the Admiralty, Winston Churchill, a pair of German warships, the *Goeben* and the *Breslau*, slipped past the British fleet in the Eastern Mediterranean, into the Dardanelles and up to Constantinople. By means of a fictitious sale, these German warships were transferred to Turkey.

More and more German soldiers and sailors filtered into Constantinople in August and September – though the country was not yet at war – and the Straits were closed. In October there were reports from Palestine that German officers were visiting frontier posts, and an unidentified group with explosives was detected moving towards the Canal at Kantara. As a riposte, the War Office stated that a substantial number of troops was being transferred from India to Egypt.

On 8 September 1914, Sir John Maxwell arrived and took over command at once.

Turkey entered the war on the side of the Germans on 30 October. It would be difficult to exaggerate the consequences of this – not only to the Western Allies, but also to Russia. Next day, Maxwell ordered a contingent from the 42nd East Lancashire Division to march through the streets of Cairo so as to underline their presence to the local populace. Following the declaration of war by Britain and France, the Sultan of Turkey issued a *fatwa* (decree) proclaiming a Holy War (*jihad*) against the Allies– a word nowadays with an all too ominous ring. Essentially this was a call to all Moslems to rise up in defence of their faith – but there was no instant uprising.[1]

For the British and French, by common consent, defence of 'their' Canal was paramount. On 2 November martial law was declared.

Once again, the convoluted position of Egypt's loyalties reared its head. It was being pulled one way by Britain and another by Turkey – and therefore her allegiance – since 70,000 Turks lived in Egypt – was uncertain. While Khedive Abbas Hilmi was predictably pro-Turkish, it was a relief to the Acting High Commissioner, Sir Milne Cheetham, that Egyptian officialdom put their resources at the disposal of the Allies. On the other hand, the *fellahin* and local populace felt a latent hostility to Britain as the occupying power, and a natural sympathy towards the Turks as a Moslem power.

Having lost the diplomatic battle over Turkey – a loss which would cost them dear in the forthcoming conflict – the British Government needed to clarify its ambiguous position, since Egypt was still technically a province of the Ottoman Empire. On 18 December, Egypt was deemed to be a formal Protectorate, thus replacing the 'veiled Protectorate' of the early 1880s. The Khedive Abbas, who was away in Turkey, was deposed and his uncle, Prince Hussein

---

1 The Sultan was also the Caliph of Islam and regarded as the spiritual leader worldwide. His *fatwa* was almost entirely ignored by Muslims in the Indian Army, except in Singapore, where the 5th Native Light Infantry mutinied and killed their officers.

Kamal, was declared the nominal ruler of Egypt in his place, with the title of Sultan. The British Consul-General was upgraded to High Commissioner.

It became instantly apparent to the British Government that the Suez Canal was under threat. Described aptly as the 'jugular vein' of the British Empire, the Canal, which goes straight through the province of Sinai, provides a vital link between Asia and Africa. It is also the linchpin for the bulk of trade between Europe and Australasia. If the Turks captured the Suez Canal, all the troops coming from India, Australia and New Zealand would be compelled to travel to Europe via the Cape of Good Hope – a very lengthy alternative route. The protection of the Canal from possible attack, either by sea or overland, was essential for the United Kingdom.

At the outbreak of war in Europe, a number of British cruisers passed through to the Red Sea and guarded the southern entrance to the Canal, which it was their task to protect and keep open. Until Britain went to war with Turkey, it had seemed that an overland attack was less likely, but precautions had been taken in August against possible acts of sabotage.

In the last week of September, the 42nd East Lancashire Division – the first Territorial Division in the war to serve abroad – disembarked at Alexandria. On board the RMSP *Avon* was a young chaplain, Kenneth Best. He was 26 years old – and had no military experience. Best had been appointed Divisional Chaplain to the 1st (Blackburn) and 3rd (Bolton) East Lancashire Brigades. He described to his family (in his letter dated 23 September) the last few days of his voyage to Egypt via Gibraltar, and his first impressions of Alexandria which *looks to me like the White City on a large scale*.

On 16 November, Indian troops destined for the defence of Egypt reached Suez and took up positions in Ismailia and Port Said. Four days later, the first clash occurred when 200 men of the Bikanir Camel Corps, under Captain Chope, were attacked by 200 Bedouins 20 miles east of Kantara. Reinforcements in the form of Australian and New Zealand troops – a willing but still only partly trained force – arrived in early December. By then the defence of the Suez Canal had been organised. It was primarily entrusted to two Indian divisions, but two field artillery brigades boosted the defences and much reliance was also placed on the presence of warships moored up in the Canal, which could be used as floating batteries in case of need.

The Turks attack the Suez Canal

The full length of the Canal from Port Said to the Gulf of Suez was deemed to be upwards of 100 miles, but the British had a somewhat shorter line to defend. Twenty-two miles was taken up by the expanse of water known as the Great and Bitter Lakes, and seven more miles by Lake Timsah[1] at the southern end. These lakes substantially reduced the frontage of the Canal that the Turks could attack. The general officer commanding (GOC) Canal Defences was Major-General A. Wilson, much helped by the Suez Canal Company, who stoutly supported his defensive measures and put all their available resources, including small craft, at his disposal.

The attack was expected to come from Palestine through Central Sinai from three Turkish divisions assembled close to the frontier near Beersheba. Trenches were dug on the east bank and barbed wire placed in front of them, mainly to protect the ferries and provide the back-up for a local counter-attack. Before long, these defensive measures were put to the test when, on 1 February 1915, the Turks attacked.

While the Turkish Fourth Army was nominally commanded by Djemal Pasha, the strategic decisions were taken

1 Now known locally as Crocodile Lake.

by his chief military adviser, the Bavarian-born artillery officer Friedrich Kress von Kressenstein, who had worked with Liman von Sanders as a member of the German military mission to Turkey. The Fourth Army headquarters were at Damascus, where there were 60,000 men and 100 guns available. It was Kressenstein who planned and orchestrated the attacks on the Suez Canal during that first week in February. Fortunately, he seemed to lack the inspirational powers of leadership which Mustafa Kemal was to display with such conspicuous success in the defence of the Gallipoli Peninsula a few months later.

At Kantara, a strong attack was made between five and six a.m. Twenty dead Turks were found outside the wire perimeter and 36 prisoners were brought in. These so-called surprise attacks failed utterly – and by daybreak next morning, the bulk of the Turkish troops seemed to have disappeared. Further South, some Turks even succeeded in crossing Lake Timsah and the Great Bitter Lake, but British and French fire from warships drove them back into the Sinai Desert. Taking into account other skirmishes, 238 Turks were buried between 30 January and 9 February and an unknown number had been drowned in the Canal.

One of the all too frequent tasks of Army chaplains was to bury the dead. In his diary for 4 February 1915, Kenneth Best describes the backdrop to one of the first wartime funeral services he had conducted, and his reactions to being in the enemy fire zone:

> Steady bombardment round Ismailia – we have no cover, but fortunately shells were bursting a bit high.
> ... Got to cemetery. Mohammedan funeral going on next door. Howls and sobs of hired mourners. Chant of **'There is no God, but God'** on one side and roar of battle on the other. Buried two RAMC men in their sleeping rugs. Some very reverent attenders present. No gun –

but Last Post, with its thrilling poignant, yet hopeful last note. Hear in evening that enemy has half-built bridge near Toussum, but lost 200 killed near Serapeum.

Stayed up late packing things, accompanied by the scream of shrapnel and boom of shells. One is bark, the other bite, but the bark is worse than the bite as regards the sinking in the pit of one's stomach. Went to bed expecting to be woken by scream of shrapnel and hail of bullets on the trees. It was a stormy night.

A week later, when the Turks had been driven back, he reports, on 10 February:

Went with Colonel to Serapeum. Arranged for needs of the wounded and confirmation of Smalley. Went out battleground and picked up a few relics. Hands and feet of dead sticking out of ground. Gruesome sight. This was the scene of the fighting a week ago.

Kressenstein's attack had failed. The successful beating-off of the Turks came at a timely moment for the standing of the British in Egypt. British prestige was enhanced, while that of Turkey dipped in the eyes of her former admirers. Kenneth Best, serving with the Territorials of the 42nd Division, had had his first, admittedly mild, taste of confrontation with the enemy.

The threat to the Suez Canal remained, but the attention of the British Cabinet was now primarily focused on a major strategical problem. In the west, a costly war of attrition had replaced the war of movement and a line of trenches stretched from the Belgian Coast to the Swiss border. Could the deadlock be broken and, if so, how?

The eyes of Churchill and Kitchener were already on the Dardanelles.

Westerners, Easterners and the Dardanelles

Further east, the preliminary bombardment of the outer forts of the Dardanelles which Churchill had ordered (against the advice of Admiral Limpus, former head of the British naval mission in Constantinople) had taken place on 3 November 1914. The British Aegean Squadron had achieved some success, including a strike on Sedd-el-Bahr which blew up an ammunition store. But the most significant effect was to give a wake-up call to both the Turks and their German advisers to expect another attack – and therefore to tighten up their defences with all possible speed.

The prime responsibility for decisions about the conduct of the war lay with Kitchener, who was Secretary of State for War and Winston Churchill, First Lord of the Admiralty. The First Sea Lord, the veteran Lord Fisher, was also closely involved with any strategy which deviated from the lethal and fruitless slogging match in the trenches.

In a letter to Asquith,[1] dated 29 December 1914, Churchill wrote in strong terms, '*Are there not other alternatives than sending our armies to chew barbed wire in Flanders? Further, cannot the power of the Navy be brought to bear more directly upon the enemy?*'

1 Vol. III of Martin Gilbert's biography of Churchill, William Heinemann, London, 1971, p. 226.

He went on to outline the advantages of invading Schleswig Holstein by sea, a move which would threaten the Kiel Canal link with the Baltic. Churchill was aware that, thus far in the war, the Army appeared to have been far more active than the Navy – and he was anxious to redress the situation. He was determined to launch an operation in which the Navy would play a key role. The naval scheme, which Fisher had described as hazardous a decade earlier, offered a tempting carrot in the form of Constantinople at the southern end of the Bosphorus, should the Dardanelles be successfully forced.

Yet in 1911, Churchill himself had written, '*It is no longer possible to force the Dardanelles and nobody should expose a modern fleet to such peril.*'[1]

Other prominent 'Easterners' who felt that a solution to the deadlock should be found other than in France were Lloyd George, not yet Prime Minister but about to play a key role as Minister of Munitions, and Sir Maurice Hankey. The latter was the influential Secretary of the Committee of Imperial Defence. But the Army chiefs were adamant: they were not in favour of any move that might take away troops from France and reduce what was still a worryingly small British Regular Army.

Then fate intervened in the form of an urgent message from the Grand Duke Nicholas in Russia, received by Lord Kitchener on 2 January 1915. The Russian Commander-in-Chief was under pressure from the Turks in the Caucasus. He asked for a diversionary attack, and his request did much to convince the Cabinet of the merits of the Dardanelles Expedition. If the Straits were successfully forced, then the Navy could open up the backdoor to Russia and enable desperately needed munitions to be delivered to the under-equipped Russian armies. Furthermore, neutral Balkan

1 Robert Rhodes-James, *Gallipoli*, London, 1965, p. 4.

powers such as Bulgaria and Greece might be encouraged to enter the war on the side of the Entente Powers.

Kitchener's reaction to the Grand Duke's appeal was to write to Churchill: '*We have no troops to land anywhere ... The only place a demonstration might have some effect would be the Dardanelles.*'[1]

This provided further impetus to Churchill, who had already shown his awareness of the potential of a naval attack by ordering the bombardment of the forts at the mouth of the Dardanelles in early November. By the New Year, the stalemate on the Western Front was all too clear to the Cabinet. On 3 January, Lord Fisher proposed a joint military and naval attack on Turkey, stating that only older battle-ships should be used and urging that the assault should be immediate. This gave Churchill the encouragement he needed. He set to work to muster a fleet of old battleships, both French and British, and within this fleet Fisher per-mitted the addition of one brand new super-dreadnought, the *Queen Elizabeth*, with its eight massive 15-inch guns.

The land forces in support comprised the 29th Division – who were regulars and might be summoned back by Kitchener to the Western Front – while Churchill had the Royal Naval Division available. The Australian and New Zealand Army Corps, commanded by Major-General Birdwood – the ANZACS – who had originally been des-tined for France were also standing by for onward movement from Egypt. Kenneth Best encountered some of the latter troops while he was stationed at Heliopolis Camp outside Cairo, and commented on their boisterous behaviour.

But the 'Westerners' held a contrary view. They were led by Joffre, the Commander-in-Chief of the French armies on the Western Front, whose main priority was to regain the ter-ritory lost by the French by waging a war of attrition (*la*

1 First report of the Dardanelles Committee, p. 15.

guerre d'usure). He was strongly supported by Sir John French, the C.-in-C. of the British Expeditionary Force. Both were convinced that the war in Europe could only be won on the Western Front. Any such alternative strategy as was now proposed by the Easterners was, in their eyes, a sideshow. They felt they could ill afford to detach any of their most experienced officers or units from France and were disinclined to make any move which might prejudice their efforts to make a breakthrough in France.

Clement Attlee, who served at Gallipoli in the 6th Battalion, the South Lancashire Regiment, confirmed that the attitude of the Army chiefs was a stumbling block. He had stringent criticisms to make of the leadership and stated that, with more wholehearted and prompt support from the military, the Gallipoli venture might have ended very differently.

In *As It Happened*[1] Attlee wrote: '*The Gallipoli Campaign will always remain a very strong memory. I have always held that the strategic conception was sound. The trouble was that it was never adequately supported ... Unfortunately, the military authorities were Western Front minded. Reinforcements were always sent too late. For an enterprise such as this, the right leaders were not chosen. Elderly and hidebound generals were not the men to push through an adventure of this kind. Had we had at Suvla generals like Maude,[2] who came out later, we should, I think, have pushed through to victory.*'

In his masterly book *Gallipoli*, Michael Hickey points out that naval gunnery was not the answer to the Dardanelles forts. He argues that in making their decision to execute a major naval bombardment 'the War Council were being swayed more by Churchill's eloquence than by practical

1 Clement Attlee, *As It Happened*, Heinemann, London, 1954, p. 41.
2 Major-General Sir Stanley Maude commanded the 13th Division at Anzac Cove and Suvla Bay, from August 1915. He was appointed Commander-in-Chief of the British troops in Mesopotamia in August 1916.

consideration'. Further, Hickey points out, the German guns used to reduce the strong Belgian fortresses relatively easily had been large howitzers, employing a high trajectory and causing shells to descend and detonate inside the walls of the forts. By contrast, naval guns employed a flat trajectory which could inflict substantial damage on the exterior walls of forts – but left the guns behind them relatively unscathed.

Despite these reservations, the possibility of taking the Dardanelles by naval assault was an attractive option. The next naval bombardment was duly planned in several stages by Vice-Admiral Sackville Carden. His strategy was to chip away with gunfire so as to reduce the inner forts and batteries to such an extent that the fleet would be able to sail from the Eastern Mediterranean, through the narrow Straits of the Dardanelles, up to the Sea of Marmara.

However, day by day the Germans were bringing up more batteries of howitzers and reinforcing the Turkish defences. Mines, both floating and moored, were a further hazard, testing the courage of the trawlermen who were dealing with them. Their converted trawlers moved at a snail's pace compared with the naval vessels, so their brave little craft were all too easily in the sights of the Turkish gunners.

Initially the assault went remarkably well. The Russians indicated they would attack Constantinople from the Bosphorus and the Italians made favourable noises about joining the Allies. The strategy of the Easterners seemed justified.

On 25 February, the naval attack was renewed. In addition to the warships involved, there was a force of 2,000 Royal Marines standing by on the island of Lemnos to assist the Navy in case of need. The forts of the Dardanelles were shelled by a squadron of warships under Carden, and the guns of the outer forts were put out of action. The assault was a limited success, but again it was clear to the Turks that another attack was in the offing, and they continued to stiffen their defences.

From now on Sir John Maxwell and his staff in Cairo were absorbed by this problem of the Dardanelles. He was ordered to prepare a force of about 30,000 Australians and New Zealanders to come under the command of Major-General W.R. Birdwood. Despite the opposition of Joffre, the French had mustered a division and had started to embark on 3 March. In addition to the ANZAC troops (two divisions), the force included a battalion from Newfoundland, as well as the Royal Naval Division and a contingent from India. Kitchener was still in two minds about sending the 29th Division but, one week later, decided to release them.

As late as 12 March Sir Ian Hamilton was appointed commander of the expedition. The circumstances of his departure next day were extraordinary: he left without his administrative staff and appeared to be armed only with out-of-date maps, a 1912 handbook of the Turkish Army and a guidebook to Constantinople! Nonetheless, he travelled out with all possible speed on a new light cruiser, the *Phaeton*, and took over command of the Mediterranean Expeditionary Force. He arrived on the eve of the largest – and last – of the purely naval assaults on the Dardanelles forts.

One of Hamilton's first discoveries was that Lemnos was unsuitable as a base, largely owing to lack of water and a limited number of piers in Mudros Harbour. Another was the shambolic loading which had taken place in Alexandria, so that guns had been stored separately from their ammunition, wagons from their horses, even shells from their fuses. Thus the troops were far from being equipped for a landing on a foreign shore. Reloading of stores was a time-consuming operation and Hamilton was compelled to change his base from Lemnos to Alexandria. This muddle was probably a reflection on the lack of administrative staff. It was an inauspicious start to a highly complex operation, in which speed was of the essence.

These were all signs that the expedition was ill-prepared and lacked the necessary back-up resources. Not only would munitions prove to be in short supply, but staff officers also did not visualise the vast scale of casualties which ensued. As a result, the medical teams were chronically ill-equipped and overstretched – as Kenneth Best makes all too clear when he becomes a victim of dysentery himself.

On 18 March the Navy launched a major assault on the Dardanelles. Commanding the fleet in the absence of Vice-Admiral Carden, who was on the verge of a breakdown, was Vice-Admiral de Robeck. The armada of sixteen battle-ships – twelve British, four French – which followed the serried ranks of cruisers, destroyers and minesweepers, must have been a magnificent sight, and all went well at first. In two and a half hours, from 11.30 a.m. to 2 p.m. the vessels advanced almost a mile, overcoming each and every fixed and mobile battery as they moved forward.[1]

Then disaster struck. The *Bouvet*, an old French battle-ship, blew up and sank remarkably quickly. The *Irresistible* was damaged and sank later – as did the *Ocean*. Several other vessels, including the *Inflexible*, *Suffren* and *Gaulois*, were damaged. These body blows had been delivered by a line of twenty mines laid parallel to the shore in Eren Keui Bay, which had eluded the minesweepers. The fleet withdrew, the nerve of the naval high command was shaken, and the Dardanelles remained closed.

Would a second assault in the next few days have succeeded, or would it have resulted in more sacrifices to the unswept mines? De Robeck was under pressure, notably from his subordinate, Commodore Roger Keyes, to renew the attack, but refused to budge. Perhaps he lacked the Nelson spirit. At a joint meeting with Sir Ian Hamilton and his senior staff on 22 March, de Robeck made it clear he

1 John Keegan, *The First World War*, Hutchinson, London, p. 258.

would not commit his battleships to another attack without substantial support from the Army in the form of strong landing parties. Neither Hamilton nor Churchill was able to persuade him to change his mind.

Delay was inevitable. Combined operations always require lengthy preparations and there were important decisions to take about where the military landings should be made and in what strength. It was the Turks, half-expecting the Allied battleships to return to the fray, who benefited most from the delay and were able to strengthen their defences.

In his finely researched historical novel, *Birds without Wings*, Louis de Bernières reveals through the eyes of the young Karatavuk the emotions of the Turks after their naval victory of 18 March:

> At the end of the day we knew that we had won a victory and no one was more surprised than us ... All the same, we knew that we had no chance at all when the enemy came back with his ships in the morning ... We knew that soon the big ships would be in the harbours at Istanbul and the war would be lost ... The fact is that the artillery at the Narrows had only 30 shells left and the Franks [the British] could have sailed straight past us in the morning.

De Robeck would not be persuaded to change his mind. The Allied Fleet never came back.

On 25 March, Enver Pasha[1] formed a separate army under the command of Liman von Sanders to defend the Dardanelles. 'If the English will only leave me alone for eight days ...' said von Sanders to his subordinate Colonel Hans Kannengiesser, after examining the existing defences.

---

1 The volatile War Minister who handed over control of the Turkish Army to the Germans.

In fact they gave him four weeks. This breathing-space enabled him to increase the strength of the Turkish troops in the area six-fold, compared with the manpower available before the naval attack.[1]

On the European side of the Narrows, Liman von Sanders feared most a landing at the Bulair neck of the Peninsula. At this point, the Gulf of Saros is separated by a mere three-and-a-half-mile strip of land from the Sea of Marmara. Hence the Bulair beaches were strongly prepared for defence, with two Turkish divisions.

By the time the military landings were made on 25 April, the Turks outnumbered the Allies. Their troops under the command of von Sanders consisted of 84,000 men deployed in six divisions and responsible for the defence of 150 miles of coastline along the Gallipoli Peninsula. By contrast, Hamilton had 75,000 men in five divisions. These comprised the 29th and Royal Naval Divisions, the 1st Australian and Australian and New Zealand Divisions, and the divisional troops provided by the French, namely the *Corps Expéditionnaire d'Orient*. The ensuing month saw high-level planning as objectives were decided upon and assigned to the five Allied divisions. This coincided with frantic activity on the island of Lemnos where, in Mudros Harbour, the stores were being prepared and landing craft assembled to transport the troops to the various beaches.

Today, visitors to Gallipoli can observe for themselves the justifiable pride with which the Turks regard their victory of 18 March. They successfully repelled a fleet representing the greatest imperial powers in the world, and were paving the way for a historic victory in the military campaign that began one month later. It is not surprising that, with the benefit of hindsight, 1915 is considered to be the year in which modern Turkey came of age.

1 B. Liddell Hart, *The Real War*, Faber, 1930, p. 174.

List of Abbreviations

ASC	Army Service Corps
CEMS	Church of England Missionary Society
CF	Chaplain to the Forces
FA	Field Ambulance
GHQ	General Headquarters
GOC	General Officer Commanding
HC	Holy Communion
HE	High Explosive
HMHS	His Majesty's Hospital Ship
HMT	His Majesty's Transport (ship)
IMS	Indian Medical Service
KOSB	King's Own Scottish Borderers
MEF	Mediterranean Expeditionary Force
MO	Medical Officer
QMS	Quartermaster's Stores
RAMC	Royal Army Medical Corps
RE	Royal Engineers
RF	Royal Fusiliers
RFA	Royal Field Artillery
RHA	Royal Horse Artillery
RMLI	Royal Marine Light Infantry
RMSP	Royal Mail Steamship Packet
RNAS	Royal Naval Air Service
RND	Royal Naval Division
SCF	Senior Chaplain to the Forces
YMCA	Young Men's Christian Association

Gallipoli! Who in Lancashire, in England, before the year 1915, knew where or what it was, or had even heard the name? Bitter was the dispelling of ignorance; hard indeed the road that led to knowledge! A name of death, of affliction, of suffering almost too heavy to be borne; but also a name of heroism and endurance and of high endeavour. A name of Failure, but no less of Glory.

Frederick P. Gibbon
The 42nd East Lancashire Division, 1914–1918

Chronological Diaries
and Letters

September 1914 – October 1915

1914

Bolton Station
Wednesday September 9

My dear Father,

Much to my surprise and delight I received a telegram from the Bishop saying he had sent up my name for an Army Chaplaincy. Also a telegram from General King suggesting I should apply at once at County Association for commission.

I am now on my way to do so. If I am accepted I go as Divisional Chaplain to 1st and 3rd East Lancashire Artillery Territorials. My present Vicar agrees and future Vicar S. Chapman will keep my place open as long as necessary. Will write again tonight.

8.45 pm. Still at Bolton Station! You will have about finished your sermon by this time. I fancy we are really off now. We struck camp in a regular downpour. I have been exceedingly fortunate in getting my kit through in 24 hours because I did not go to the authorised depot, but went to Beatty Bros. The last piece arrived only 15 mins before leaving Turton. I don't think it worthwhile any of you trying to see me, but if we have a moment at Southampton I will try to see Elsie.[1]

I am afraid I shall not be much of a hand at addressing Tommies, but I may get used to it. I travel in great comfort with Brigade Staff, 1st Class, sharing carriage with Doctor and Lieutenant Garnett, some of whose relatives I have met at Lytham.

Best love again to all. I hope you won't get many bills to pay.

---

1 Elsie Best, Kenneth's younger sister.

(Later) Sorry I shall not be able to see any of you. We leave tomorrow. Address will be

Chaplain, 3rd East Lancs. R.F.A., Egypt.

Love to all,
Ken

On board RMSP *Avon*
Thursday September 10

My dear Mother,
We started last night at about 9 p.m. and arrived at Southampton Dock this morning at 7 a.m. We are probably sailing in a few minutes. I have had no chance of seeing Elsie for I have had the job of apportioning out the money necessary for the salaries of the Tommies to the various Batteries; then finding out the boat on which they were sailing and where it lay. I shall be qualified to be a Bank clerk when I return. I don't think I'm 6d out of my reckoning yet. We are living like Lords. 1st class cabin – outside, very roomy, with *beds*, not berths. The doctor and I share a room, which is handy for he is an excellent sailor and can attend to me when I go green.

I must now rush around and enquire if our last battery has turned up, and what is their boat. If they don't come soon I shall be off and there will be no pay for them. Hope you will continue to hear no news or else good news from Herbert.[1]
Heaps of love,
Ken

1 Kenneth Best's younger brother, Lt. Herbert Best, was serving on the Western Front.

On board RMSP *Avon*
Trafalgar Bay
Wednesday, September 16

My dear Father,

I was meaning to write a long letter and send it from Gibraltar, where we are not stopping, but are signalling a small boat to take off letters. I have made short notes of what has happened from day to day, but unfortunately I was inoculated against typhoid yesterday, and it has given me rather a bad time, so that I have to lie in bed and scribble a short note in pencil.

The notes which I have made will have to wait till I get to Egypt, to be incorporated in a letter. Rumour says we are bound for Khartoum. Today we saw an amusing sight, a whale spouting and floating about while porpoises gambolled round about it. I have asked the officer on guard to wake me so that I can catch a glimpse of Gib. We should pass it about 4 a.m. tomorrow.

On Sunday, as there are nearly 2000 men on board, I held three short services. Each time I spoke much in the same way, about patriotism – the difference between patriotic feelings and practical patriotism. I don't know how I shall keep on addressing men Sunday after Sunday if we stay in Egypt a year, giving out constantly and taking nothing in.

I hope news from Herbert is good. From wireless messages we gather that the Germans are steadily retiring.

I am feeling very stupid just now with the beastly dead typhoid germs playing the fool inside me, but I wanted to write a line at the first opportunity to assure you that all is well and that we are having a most pleasant journey.

I feel heartily sorry for the Tommies. They sleep in a
sort of Black Hole of Calcutta, while we live off the fat of
the land. Yet many of the Tommies in better regiments
e.g. Westminster Dragoons, are superior in every way to
some of the sloppy conceited babies to be found among
the Territorial Officers. There are parades and exercises
all day long. Fortunately I only have to attend the parade
at 11 a.m. There is much musical and dramatic talent
among the men. They gave us a great entertainment
Monday evening.

On board RMSP *Avon*
Wednesday, September 23

My dear Elsie and family in general,
So sorry I could not see you before I sailed from
Southampton. We had about 12 hours there, but I was
very busy dividing up and distributing money to different
sections of our Brigade, who were told off to different
transport boats. We arrived after a ten hour journey from
Bolton at Southampton 9 a.m. September 10th.

On Wednesday before we left from Bolton one of the
Subalterns, Lieutenant Garnett, had a nasty attack of flu.
As the doctor with whom I share a tent had to go and see
him, his father motored us over to his Grandmother's.
This was some 7 or 8 miles from camp (where Garnett
was recovering) and we had a memorable last dinner. A
welcome change from camp fare.

I travelled in a first class compartment with the
doctor – a Manchester Owens College man. Also with
Lieutenant Garnett was Lieutenant Drewry who was a
contemporary of mine at Cambridge. He was a Caius man
and we found mutual friends. He actually remembered
having seen me at Cambridge.

We are now approaching the end of our voyage which will take us to Alexandria, the port for Cairo – our destination. We have had a glorious time and been living most luxuriously – A ship's officer says it would ordinarily have cost me £120 at least.

I don't think I should choose a sea voyage for a holiday under ordinary circumstances. The Atlantic roll which lasted till we got into the Mediterranean, wasn't pleasant. I did not suffer from malaise, but it gave me a nasty headache. Then – this over – I had three unhappy days after my first inoculation against typhoid. The last few days, however, have been plain sailing.

Gibraltar is a most striking place, especially from the sea. We had been moving slowly through the fog when suddenly it lifted and we found ourselves right under the fortified hill of Gib. We spent a day outside, not going into harbour. A pilot boat took away some letters.

The town looks unpleasantly dry and ugly and the hill behind simply bristles with guns. Up to that time, there had been 14 boats in our flotilla, escorted by the *Ocean* and *Minerva*.

At Gib. a Middlesex Regiment and one horse boat landed. The *Ocean* also left us and went back. We next passed Morocco clearly visible on our right. Next we passed various islands, Galeta north of Tunisia, then Pantellaria on our right, Gozo and Malta on our left. On Sept 21 we met a squadron of 23 transports mainly BI[1] and P and O boats under escort of a cruiser. They must have been the Indian troops – about 50,000 of them. We exchanged cruisers, the *Minerva* sending a wireless message wishing good luck to the General, officers and men, whom she had had the honour to escort thus far.

---

1 British India (Shipping Line) and Peninsular and Oriental (Steam Navigation Company).

We are now making much better headway. Shall probably do about 300 miles today. We came in sight of Africa again yesterday – an unbroken line of mountains gradually dropping as we sailed Eastward until at last they ceased to be visible.

I am playing cricket for the 18th Battery and we have actually got into the final. We had drawn a bye in the first round and won the next three matches. One team we got out for 0 and our bowler did the hat trick twice in an innings. Each Sunday I have held three services for the men and officers. There are about 3000 on the boat, so we divide them into three batches.

I generally give them two more or less similar addresses at the first two services and then, if one goes distinctly better, I repeat that one again at the third Service. If there is nothing to choose I combine them. I am very busy learning Morse and Semaphore. Also when we get to Egypt I have to act as Mess Secretary and Treasurer. I have to buy furniture etc. for the Mess and keep accounts.

Our orders at present are – 3 months training in Egypt round the Pyramids, then off to the Front. I wonder if any of the West Lancashires are in our squadron and whether I shall meet any Lytham men. I hear the West Lancs could not form a division and so have been left behind.

Here there is a break in the letter. Kenneth Best resumes it a few days later, after the Avon *has docked in Alexandria.*

On Friday September 25th, we arrived at Alexandria about 8 hours earlier than we expected. Last night lights in the port state cabins fused and so I was stopped in the middle of my packing. It therefore gave me a shock when my orderly roused me at 6 a.m. and I found we were sailing into Alexandria Harbour.[1] I had a great scramble to get into my togs, leggings and riding breeches and pack my things in time, only to find that we are to sit tight in the harbour for 3 days before going ashore.

Alexandria looks to me like the White City on a large scale. All the buildings look brand new and so clean and yet so quaint and old fashioned in form. I can hardly believe it is real. The ship is surrounded by Egyptians after baksheesh. I have ordered 100 Egyptian cigarettes from a villainous looking old dragoman.

I am sweltering at present in leggings and uniform. I hope helmets and lighter uniform will soon arrive. The old dragoman trying to do business says England is going to leave Germany like a small village and he prophesies that the war will end on October 8th. Moses Mohammed Salem is his name. He will take any one on. 20 sovereigns to a single sovereign.[2] I don't know where he would be when the time comes to pay up the quid ...

I hope you are all keeping fit and cheery. What news of Herbert? I hope all goes well with him.

Heaps of love to all

Your affectionate brother

Ken

P.S. Do pass this round as a general letter to all the family, as I may not be able to write again for a bit.

1 Alexandria, named after Alexander the Great who founded the city in 332 BC, is the chief port of Egypt and once a major centre of Hellenistic culture.
2 A gold coin then worth one pound sterling or twenty shillings.

Young Men's Christian Association
Cairo
October 5, 1914

My Dear Family,

What a life! I feel as if I had been suddenly hurled into a new world, and a pretty strange one too. I think I wrote to you last as we arrived at Alexandria. Well! We were ordered to stay in the harbour for 3 days until the other troops were landed. Hurrah! We thought, now we can have our second inoculation while comfortable beds are still to be had. We were inoculated and immediately word followed to say we were to leave the ship. In a few minutes we had to pack and get into full marching kit. Not much fun when you are feeling cheap and feverish. We were pushed into a train Saturday evening at 7 p.m. (Sept 26, I believe, was the date) and travelled until 3.30 Sunday morning when we reached the Palais de Koubbeh, a station just outside Cairo.

I had a 1st-class carriage with 3 other officers, but the 1st class are not quite equal to English 1st class. We could none of us sleep as the heat was stifling, our arms painful and our heads aching. The only amusement we had was at the stations. There were crowds of Arab hawkers, crying out their wares in a whining chant. Then arrived the officials on the scene – whips whistling through the air and coming down with a whack on the backs of the hawkers. I bet they felt it, wearing only their thin sort of night shirt dress. There was a lot of excited chattering (they always talk in a high pitched voice as though they were quarrelling) and they retired like sheep, rubbing their bruises. I wonder what would happen if English folk were so treated.

The Colonel (C.E. Walker of Bolton), the doctor and myself trudged off to find our way to the Heliopolis Race Course camp,[1] while the rest of the company brought up the luggage. It was dark. Nobody about except a few squatting figures of Mohammedans at prayer, over whom we kept stumbling. They of course could not understand us, and, if they had, they would not have answered, for they had got into a holy state and to speak would mean starting all over again. To our joy, at last we deciphered a large board directing us to the camp.

We arrived 4 a.m. Sunday morning and flopped down exhausted on the race course. It was a foot deep in dust and creeping things. These conditions combined with a high temperature rather spoilt my rest; yet I did sleep for an hour or so. It was Sunday. Never have I spent a less sabbatical Sunday. I was not sorry that there was no church parade, as I don't think I could have got through it.

Also the horses had broken loose at the station, as so few men had been detailed off to take charge of them. They were running wild all over town, villages and desert round about, then dropping down dead in dozens from heat, hunger and thirst. I felt it was quite lawful to do good on the Sabbath even if it meant cancelling a formal parade service. It was an awfully sad sight because even when horses were caught there was no fodder, or head ropes for them.

The organisation has been atrocious and the blame lies mainly with the Regulars who have just gone. The men also had a vile time. We landed during a short spell of very trying heat – even the native ponies were dropping owing to excessive heat. Yet our Tommies were made to work the whole day non-stop, even from 12 – 3 which are always regarded as off hours. All this on a crust of bread

1 Just north of Cairo, now an upmarket suburb.

and cup of tea. Yet they came through it, got the camp straight and caught most of the horses. How they did it I don't know. Of course they grumbled, as they always do, it is their habit even when things are comfortable, but they never shirked.

There is something radically wrong with military organisation. But still, one cannot expect everything to run smoothly at such a time. Matters are improving now, but the expedition is by no means a picnic. We are camped on the edge of the desert. The heat, the flies and ailments due to strange food and conditions are trying. I am getting used to them, and though I perspire all day long, I now feel wonderfully fit. The dry air suits me grandly.

I am running the Officers Mess and learning elementary book keeping from one of the Officers of our battalion. You would not recognise me as the same person who but a few weeks ago was a humble junior curate at Lytham. Now in full kit I ride or swagger through Cairo, escorted by a corporal and an interpreter. My arm aches merely returning the salutes of police, Egyptians, Indians, Australian and English soldiers. I drove through the native quarters with Garnett the other day trying to find the man with whom his father deals in cotton.

The streets are very narrow with all sorts of dirty rags hanging from upper stories which project further out than the bottom storey. How we escaped killing the people who sat and strolled about the streets I don't know. The driver kept up a continuous chant which means 'clear off to right or left'.

I have been kept pretty busy as Mess Secretary, getting native cooks and haggling with them. Also buying cooking utensils, crockery and so on. It is a pity we are messing on such a grand scale. It is costing us 4/6[1] a day

1 Equivalent to 23p in today's currency.

in addition to heavy initial outlay. Most of the officers want to draw rations which are more in accordance with being on active service. But our Colonel and Senior Major grumble if they have to dive into bags for their lump sugar, instead of taking a lump out of a basin with silver tongs! I get quite impatient with them. It does not to me seem soldierly, but babyish to be so fastidious.

Last Sunday I had a full parade service at 7 a.m. before the heat of day. There were about 2000 or 3000 men with their officers and General King and his Staff present in this formation:

Band

Chaplain

Piled drums

Men   General King   Officers

Officers   Staff   Men

Officers
_____

Men

The Service only lasted about half an hour, yet two men fainted. My text was 'What is your life?' This was prompted by the deaths of two soldiers during the last week of our voyage – all ship's flags being at half mast. The service was a hopeless failure – a dreary formal affair, because the men had neither service books nor hymn sheets. Not allowed because it adds 'weight' to kit. Have you ever heard such nonsense? As if a slip of paper could make any difference. One of our officers, a very good fellow, said how nice it would be to have some hymn sheets. The Adjutant replied, 'Why dammit, do you think I am going to provide playthings for the ——- men?' That type of soldier makes my blood boil.

The YMCA are doing a lot for us and may help us in
this matter also. They have put up one large marquee,
supplying writing materials and good literature free, and
selling post cards at cost price. Men were getting horribly
cheated by Arabs and this ought to prevent it. They are
adding another marquee for the sale of non-intoxicants
and sing-song evenings. I was asked by the General to
consider it as my child.

At 10 a.m. I was down at Kasrel Mil[1] taking another
parade service in the barracks church. How different – a
most hearty cheery service, plenty of books. I spoke again
about having a purpose in life. We had to have large
rectangular fans hanging from the roof. It was very hot. I
looked like a wolf in sheep's clothing, my brown boots and
leggings protruding below a very short cassock. We had a
good collection of nearly £3: the usual collection seems to
be about 6/-.[2] A lady, daughter of Admiral somebody or
other, helped me to count it, as I was rather confused with
foreign money. Her husband is probably going to call on
me. Met a jolly little English boy scout on my way back.

In the late afternoon I walked with a missionary to the
Obelisk of On. A most glorious walk through quaint
native villages and fields beautifully green with maize
and cotton plants. The Obelisk is older than the Pyramids
or Sphinx. Joseph, they say, must have seen it on his
wedding day.[3] The patriarch of course I mean. It looks
only a few years old and is wonderfully preserved. On the
way back we visited the tree under which our Lord and
his parents were supposed to have rested during their
flight from Herod.

The Missionary tells me that if you bid a Moslem *Good*

---

1 Slang name for former huge barracks, where the Nile Hilton now stands.
2 About 30p today.
3 Because it was here that he took his wife the daughter of Pa-ta-pa-Ra, priest of
On. *The Man Who Loved Egypt*, Bimbashi McPherson, Ariel Books, 1983 p. 33.

Morning or *Good Night*, he is bound to offer you hospitality. We greeted an old Moslem sitting in his shop, and he invited us to sit down and take coffee. If they really want you, they will come and catch hold of your garment. The invitation is a formality – yet, if you do accept, they are bound to give you coffee. They salute you by touching first the forehead and then the heart.

Just received yours and Margery's second letters. The address is sufficient and only a penny stamp is required. What grand news from Herbert! I do hope they let him have a rest soon. He must be half dead with the strain. I do hope we shall shortly go up to take his place. It is grand to hear the turn affairs are taking. According to our paper Germany seems to be making another stand.

Cheerio everybody. The mail is just going. Very best love to all

Your affectionate son

Ken

P.S. I am trying in odd moments to keep a rough diary.

Heliopolis Camp
Cairo
November 12, 1914

My Dear Father,

It is jolly good of you to write so regularly and so frequently. I hope now to be more systematic with my correspondence. The first few Sundays I found very heavy. Also running the officers mess proved a burden, till I got things working smoothly. The last Sunday in October my programme was:

7 a.m.   Parade Service with address at Heliopolis Camp
8 am   Holy Communion at Heliopolis

10 and 11.15 am Parade Service at Kasrel Mil (suburb of
Cairo) Barrack Church with address
3 pm   Bible Class at Heliopolis
7 pm   Evensong with Address at Heliopolis

Now an Assistant Chaplain has been appointed to
Kasrel Mil so that things are easier and I can devote all
my attention to Heliopolis. I have now got two decent
sized tents and made them into one. The Camp
Commandant, General King, is a very good fellow. He
lets me get anything I consider necessary – giving me
carte blanche to order chairs, tables etc. to furnish the
tent and books to form a library for the men. I have got
60 cane bottom chairs and a table.

There are a number of CEMS[1] men in camp. I have
set them to work to find sacks, to cut them in two, sew
them up and fill them with sand. They ought to make
good kneelers. For Communion rails I am having four
posts knocked into the ground and a rope stretched
across. A dark table cloth reaching to the ground in
front and a linen cloth over the top makes a very
neat altar.

The evening service is held in a huge YMCA tent
which holds about 800 sitting. I am running rather low as
regards addresses and your notes will prove very useful.
It must be a horrid fag copying them out for me, but if
you don't mind and can find time to do it, it is a great
boon to me. I can get a certain number of books here, in
fact there are one or two quite decent English bookshops
including a CEMS shop but the prices are increased
anything from 30% to 50%. We are living in a most
civilised part of the world, in fact I had a game of tennis
this afternoon.

1 Church of England Missionary Society.

Everything is delightful except the sand. We have not seemingly surfaced upon the Egyptian winter, which resembles the period at home when springtime turns into summer. The heat of course is as great as the middle of summer, but the atmosphere being so dry it is much less oppressive. The water is very good and plentiful. I keep a native water bottle which is made of porous earthenware. It keeps the water delightfully cool by means of evaporation.

As you have seen, the authorities have been locking up many Germans and none too soon either. They have been busy stirring up a rebellion for some time. We are expecting trouble. When we go out exercising horses each morning I take this opportunity of practising riding. Though we only go a mile or two out of camp and take some guns with us. The state of affairs here is rather curious. The Turks are not popular with the Gyppies but they are the leaders in Mohammedanism and therefore have considerable influence. The Copts[1] are the real Egyptians who refused to accept Mohammedanism at the point of the sword and are very disturbed in mind at present. They anticipate a massacre.

Martial law was declared here a week ago. Pickets are out each night patrolling the desert. I sometimes wonder what would happen if our camp was attacked by night, the artillery would of course be helpless – they have but few rifles and no bayonets. The infantry probably would not wake before their throats were cut – the Bedouins quite possibly may make a raid – the troubled times are their opportunity. They will not side, I fancy, with Turkey, but are out for loot and plunder. It may be the fighting will not come near us – it is only local and

1 Native Egyptian or Ethiopian Christians.

negligible at present. The latest report states that we leave for the Front on December 26th – a still later one that we move within a fortnight. I believe we shall still be here in six months time. The latest joke heard in the Mess is that the Esquimaux have declared war on Germany! They heard that the Kaiser, after celebrating one of his pseudo-victories was found 'up the pole'. The Esquimaux considered that their neutrality had been violated.

I brought a small 'vest pocket Kodak' a few days ago and hope shortly to send you a few photos. It seemed better to get a small one than to send home for mine. The photos are minute, but they are advertised to make good enlargements.

I must toddle off now to Chaplains' meeting at Abbassia, which is held each Monday at 11a.m. Will write again very soon.

Your affectionate son

Ken

After spending two months in Cairo, Kenneth Best expresses his frustration at having to endure the continuing round of training exercises and the lack of real action. As yet, there is no sign of any fighting. He is mystified that thousands more troops have been sent to Cairo – to what purpose? In fact their raison d'être is the global significance of the Suez Canal to the British Government, for whom its defence at all costs is a top priority.

3rd East Lancs Brigade R.F.A.,
Heliopolis Camp,
Cairo, Egypt
December 10, 1914

My dear Family,

I am reduced to writing to you en bloc for Xmas. There is nothing Christmassy about our surroundings out here though the nights are certainly becoming chilly. Life is not romantic, but rather monotonous. Each day is more or less the same – toddle round the camp seeing a few odd fellows – going into Cairo on personal or Officers Mess business. We all want to get down to business and do something for our money.

This at present is a land of shams. The church parade is a sham. It is no more a religious service than a field day; all relics are shams – made in Birmingham. The Christmas weather will be a sham. I have seen some warm Christmases, but this will be my warmest. The fighting so far is a sham. On an exercise, I was killed today – when I was with 20th Battery. We stayed in our position too long and had to gallop out through heavy machine gun fire. However as I was very hungry I forgot I was dead and rode back to camp!

So far there is no fighting worth mentioning here – no signs of the Turks – it will take them 2 or 3 months now to get to Suez. The Bedouins don't count – they are just vulgar bandits.

Why are so many troops congregating in Egypt? There are about 100,000 here now, Indians, Egyptians, Ceylon Teaplanters, Australians, New Zealanders and now one hears the Japs are coming in great force. I hope it means we are moving, though, not if Herbert really is coming here.

I begin to distrust rumours entirely – this camp is simply buzzing with them, but they never come true. I know just what Herbert must feel about both men and officers when not in action and yet separated from the refining influence of good women. Preaching is no good – may the Front or Home soon be our lot for the sake of the men.

I am going to take a day off soon and wander round Cairo taking snaps of quaint scenes and local dress, all being well. I shall not miss Christmas at home as much as Herbert will, as I have already spent two away from home.

Yours affectionately,

Ken

1915
Suez Canal

Monday January 18

Hear rumours of a move – called to see GOC RA – he is holding a meeting of OCs and Battery CO's. From me he only desires information regarding property of YMCA and C of E in camp. Telephone message to Headquarters. Little, who is our SCF, wishes to see me concerning matter which cannot be communicated by telephone. I ride round camp to arrange evening programme for Farewell Concert and then on to SCF.

Hear Turks are quite near Suez Canal and forces need chaplain. Most of the infantry on canal are Indian. I am to go (1) because I am Chaplain to the Artillery and (2) because I am the only chaplain who can ride a horse. Concert great success. Go round to Sergeants Mess of 10th Manchesters, where I have spent many happy evenings, to say goodbye and sing Auld Lang Syne.

Tuesday January 19

Financial business – go round Cairo in Arabeyah settling up accounts. Lunch with Grindon – last enlisted boys class at Heliopolis Camp. Start to pack. See part of boxing competition in evening. Smalley put up plucky fight against experienced boxer. Pack till 2 a.m.

Wednesday January 20

Up at 6 a.m. – go on packing, making arrangements for confirmation and finish packing in a desperate hurry – tent down and off by noon. Leave Palais de Koubbeh 2.15. I share a first class carriage with medical GOC RA and staff of 18th Battery and 3rd Battery staff on the train.

We pass endless number of cemeteries – sheep and goats inseparable. Wireless station and not far beyond a convict settlement. Men in rough blue clothes. Armed sentries posted among them and around them in sentry boxes. The men are stone quarrying – many manacled and in chains. Cultivation turning to desert. I am overcome with sleep.

Wake up at Zagazig[1] – where ammunition column will be stationed. Later passed a small Christian cemetery where the soldiers who were killed at Tel el Kebir are buried – the trenches are still visible. From now onwards, many Indians and Gurkhas guarding bridges. I noticed white and blue lilies in flower, then back we went into desert again.

Arrive at Ismailia 6.30 p.m. Go to club and dine with Walmsley RAMC. Come back to station 11 p.m, get into wrong train to sleep, just as it was moving off. Got into another with GOC RA and Staff, Brigade staff and Rankin. We have to turn out at 6 a.m. as it goes to Port Said. I get a first class compartment to sleep in by myself. Ismailia seems to me the most beautiful spot in Egypt.

Thursday January 21

Turn out 6 a.m. Spencer came and sat with me up to midnight and then again at 3.30 – he could not sleep, so came to chat. Waited till 8.30 watching to see where luggage went to, so as not to lose any. Then getting tired and hungry and hearing that GOC RA has refused to go to appointed place because it stank, we sloped off to the Club – knowing it should take time to select fresh site. After breakfast I saunter back to Station. Aeroplane flies

1 Town in the delta of the Nile, north-east of Cairo.

low overhead. Go into RC Church, '*Respect Saint Luke and don't let in dogs.*' The Saint is carved large on high altar.

In early morning one might have been in India – nothing but Sikhs and Gurkhas. Captain Dickinson keeps finding sites and getting ousted. Ismailia has two distinct sections – native and European, mainly Greek. We find a delightful spot, thick wood of very tall and graceful firs, interspersed with palms and small trees. Among them were tents and Gurkhas. They were sitting wrapped up in blankets, red and brown and looked just like American Indians round the camp fire. Glorious flowers especially bougainvillea. Went down to edge of Lake Timsah and collected some rather curious shells – then back to help with horse lines and tents.

We are with the Brigade Staff near CRA Headquarters. Men on look out everywhere for Turks. Bugbears so far have been Arabs under Turkish Officers, next we expect Turks under German Officers. Lunch 1.30 with 53rd Sikhs officer. Down to Club with Rankin for tea.

Wonderful how abruptly luxuriant vegetation becomes arid desert. Native cooks very careful we should not touch food. Flocks have to be driven up so that Indians may kill them in their own fashion. Wonderful night. Lights twinkling in wood and here and there a camp fire. From behind leafy palm comes from time to time a gruff challenge – '*Who goes there?*' Moonlight is making sand look like snow.

Friday January 22

Took exercising party over to 18th Battery. Found them very busy digging and removing crest from hill. Left them to dig. Six men from 20th detailed to carry provisions in mule cart were stuck in soft sand. Came home with the rest.

Afternoon see Porter who has been running short of C of E Services on Sunday evenings. Went round to tea with him and also saw Lewis. He wants to hand over the service to me. Ordered a native mattress eiderdown.

Saturday January 23

Arrange work at Canal Defence HQ. 8 a.m. celebration and 5 p.m. service at Culte Evangelique. Rode over to 18th Battery in afternoon. They are working hard, and expecting action soon.

Sunday January 24

8 a.m. H.C. 20 men present, mostly officers of Indian Regiment and one General. 5 p.m. 30 present, including General Wilson who likes to read lesson. To 18th Battery in morning where General King is inspecting. Then Service at 12.30, just before lunch. The men are grumbling, but I think well and happy. Had lunch with them and tried to find 20th but got lost. Had dinner with Lewis. Played some music on tinkly old piano and Mrs Limpus tried to sing.

I have arranged to have this notice put in Orders:

The Chaplain will be at the under mentioned places each week:

18th Battery	*Ismailia*	*Sunday 11 am*
19th Battery	*Serapeum*	*Friday noon*
20th Battery	*El Ferdan*	*Tuesday 11 am*
4th Battery	*Kantara*	*Wednesday noon*
5th Battery	*El Kubri*	*Thursday 11 am*
6th Battery	*Kantara*	*Wednesday noon*

He will be prepared to hold a short service or a celebration of Holy Communion.
Also he will be glad to see any who desire it, especially with regard to confirmation.

In the following letter to his mother, Kenneth Best describes his last duties before leaving Cairo – and his rail journey to Ismailia. He is delighted to have been posted to the 'Egyptian Front', where he will be continuing his pastoral work visiting the troops – many of whom are Indian soldiers – who have the essential task of defending the Suez Canal. An attack by the Turks is known to be imminent and within a few days the young chaplain has his first experience of being under fire.

Suez Canal Club, Ismailia[1]
Tuesday January 26 1915

My dear Mother,
I fear I have just missed the mail as is my custom. However, here is a dry and unsatisfactory record of my movements since I last wrote. On Wednesday Jan 20th I saw the last of Heliopolis. It was simply ripping that the privilege of going to the 'Egyptian Front' should fall to my lot. It was partly because I was connected with the Artillery (the Infantry being still quartered round Cairo).

On Monday I was told to stand by for a move. On Monday evening I arranged a farewell concert in the YMCA tent. The 10th Manchester Band formed the foundation of the concert. They are a top-hole lot and I have seen a good deal of them. They came over in the

1 The club is still used by Suez Canal pilots and Company officials.

same boat, and have been in the same camp, providing
the support for our Services. The concert ended with a
hearty '*Auld Lang Syne*' in which singers and band tried to
drown each other. Some of the best evenings out here
have been spent in the Manchesters' Sergeants Mess.

On Tuesday I helped to arrange a Boxing
Competition – much to the disgust of the pious section of
the YMCA who regard boxing as a brutalising, wicked
sport. The event was a great success. The trumpeter fully
maintained his reputation as a thorough little sportsman.
One of the more experienced boxers could find no
opponent. So this little chap, to prevent the item being a
washout, volunteered to take him on. He lost of course,
but not till the 4th round. He is a mere lad, but the way
he stuck to it simply brought down the house.

These two functions left me little time for the
unpleasant job of packing up. By 3 a.m. I was well on the
way, but overcome by sleep I had to finish with a great
scramble next morning. I had not only my personal
belongings, but also a certain amount of equipment
connected with my tent church.

At noon we left for Ismailia. The Doctor and myself
had a First Class compartment to ourselves. The train
runs through alternate patches of fertile land and arid
desert, the sudden changes being caused by the
presence or absence of water. Everywhere in cultivated
parts were the inevitable camels, cemeteries, palm
groves and sakfrs (wells). Out of these water is drawn by
a gamoose (sort of ox) working a series of buckets to be
used for irrigation.

In the desert we passed a convict settlement. Most of
the poor wretches seemed to be in chains. One half of
them were dressed in bright red, the other in bright blue.
Round them hovered armed guards in sentry boxes.
Their work seemed to be stone quarrying. A little later

we passed a small Khan cemetery, where the soldiers who were killed at Tel el Kebir were buried.[1]

About 6 p.m. we arrived at Ismailia. Ismailia is quite small. It does not boast any shop worth mentioning except a Co-operative Stores, which cannot cope with the demands of the Military. I cannot even get a pair of stockings. So I should be very glad of 3 pairs of stockings and 3 pairs of socks. Fortunately Ismailia has this club patronised by the Canal Company servants and here we got a good supper.

Then back to the station to find a train in a siding in which we could spend the night as the tents were not up. My first choice was a poor one. The train moved off and I had to clear out double quick. However I later found the right one. We were out next morning about 5.50 and tents were pitched outside Ismailia, near the Artillery HQ.

We are in a beautiful spot on the edge of a wood of palms and firs. At night it is like fairyland. All over the wood flicker bright spots of light and here and there the ruddy glow of a camp fire, with Indian soldiers huddled round it. Many of them in red blankets. The desert round us looks like snow in the bright moonlight. Nothing could be more picturesque. The only drawback is the number of salutes and challenges one receives on passing through.

On Saturday I went to the 18th Battery, whose position is about 2 miles up the Canal north of Ismailia, to arrange services on the following day. Found them very busy digging in the guns and making trenches. Aeroplanes fly to and fro all day long, reporting changes in position of the Turks. On the other side of the Canal are a lot of Indian troops. Sikhs, Gurkhas, Pathans, Punjabis, Infantry and

1 During the battle in 1882, when the uprising led by Col. Arabi Bey was put down by the British.

Mountain Batteries. Also many Imperial Forces sent out privately by Indian Rajahs.

On this side there are 6 British batteries and many more Indian troops. Our own Infantry are in reserve at Cairo and elsewhere. On Sunday we had a celebration at 8 a.m. in a Mission Room in Ismailia. There were present some civilians and about 15 English officers attached to Indian Forces, including a General. I then rode to 18th Battery and did an hour's digging. Held a short service and had bread and cheese lunch.

In evening held a service in the Mission Room. Again a good gathering of Indian Army Officers. This time another General present, who likes reading lessons. Monday all horses were busy, so I went in a launch to El Ferdane, 20th Battery. It was a dirty little boat, but I managed to find a comfortable seat on a coil of ropes. The party was rather mixed. A Sikh in charge of flour and provisions which we were towing alongside. Arabs in charge of engines with a Gordon Highlander, cheery little fellow called Jock. One Brigade Sergeant Major and myself.

This was my first trip on the Suez Canal. I was dismayed to find how narrow it is. On both sides we kept passing Indian Camps. We passed a French gunboat, but could see nothing of interest. High sand banks on either side of the Canal blocked the view. When we got to El Ferdane we could not get anywhere near the side and had to be carried to the shore by natives. It was nearly dark. We tramped for some time without finding the Battery and then when we thought we were lost we suddenly found ourselves right on top of it. Found that things were stirring. Attack by Turks imminent, so I managed to miss the only train back,

The night's rest was broken up – as we spent most of it digging and carrying ammunition. What was left of the night was spoilt, first by the wild dogs, which kept prowling round and howling as we lay on the sand, and later by mosquitoes. Nothing happened except a constant flow of refugees carrying all their worldly goods tied up in a large handkerchief on their backs. All women have been sent inland. So far only a mountain battery has come into contact with the enemy and exchanged a few shots. I fancy there will soon be a move forward by the Turks, as the desert water will shortly be unfit for drinking.

We are having a great time. The men are working like Trojans and never stop grumbling like bears. It is a quaint habit they have. The British soldier may be perfectly happy and contented and yet he grumbles continuously. I want to get round to all the other batteries this week by launch, train or horse.

Heaps of love to you all.

Your affectionate son,

Ken

Thursday January 28

Wrote to mother and SCF. In evening, after news of day had been read and movements of Turks traced on map from aeronauts' information, Rankin and I went out to Arab quarters to see the Zikkars[1] which I heard were taking place. We thought soldiers would not be popular on last day of the great feast – especially when we noticed a number of Turkish flags flying.

We called for Porter who is in charge of a mission school here. He came round with us. Owing to shortage of money the feast was a comparatively small one. One rich

---

1 Traditional mystic rites practised by the Arabs after dark, continuing until the early hours of the morning.

man had provided a tent with native tapestry all round and flags hanging from roof. Numerous candelabra. Fortunately this meant that all sects had to join in one Zikkar, instead of each his own. About 150 men joined in large tent.

First we went to buy some pipes which we saw made for us. Poor native policeman in fearful funk came and begged us to deal with a large drunken soldier. The town picket arrived and relieved us. A party came along headed by a man bearing lamp containing 4 candles. They were chanting and at intervals forming into a circle while swaying from side to side and continuing to sing. Then we went into the large tent. Men sitting round drinking coffee. They got up, formed two lines facing each other. Verses of Koran read – prayers were offered.

Then they started to sway, reciting Creed '*There is no God, but God*' then livening up saying '*Allah*' – emphasis on first syllable after side to side motion – head flopping about like that of dead man they move head and upper trunk back and forward. Then back to old transverse movement with emphasis now on second syllable *Allah*. It is all a kind of mysticism – there is no connection with original Mohammedanism and Zikkar mysteries are often held in supreme contempt by true Moslems.

They try to lose themselves in God and get out of themselves into deity. They call this stupefied feeling divine ecstasy and sometimes cut themselves and put hot coals in their mouths without feeling it or doing any damage (power of mind over matter). Violent exhalations on first or last syllable till it sounds like a huge gas engine at work. Some did not let themselves go – others entirely lost themselves. Only articles for sale are red sugar dolls in paper, native sweets and panpipes which sound like bagpipes.

From 10 pm – 3 am Zikkar mysteries continue. Mystics

practise from verse of Koran which says *'Using the name of God is beneficial'*. As a matter of fact the motion and violent exhalation is the important thing in producing the state of ecstasy.

Friday January 29

Left Ismailia by launch *Robuste* at 9.45. Arrive Tessorum 10.45 after passing many liners cheered by each in turn. 'Any news, any scrapping?' Sat on Captain's steer box. At Tessorum got off. Turks 3 or 4 miles away. Saw Bedouin prisoners under quarter guard. They had a pass and bayonet – dirty clothes in rags and patches. Engineers putting up entanglements of barbed wire. Punjabis make capture, the men are blindfolded and hands tied together. Passed AE2[1] submarine hurtling along. After getting lost trying to ride to 20th Battery last Sunday, I decided that where possible it is better to visit batteries by train or boat.

Today was a terrifying experience. After riding for about half an hour, daydreaming I suppose, I suddenly became aware that I had lost sight of the trees along the Canal. There was no landmark only a wide featureless expanse of sandy desert. I rode for some time in the direction, as I thought, of the Canal, but still nothing but empty desert. My heart sank. I was really frightened. No possibility of being found. I saw myself dying miserably of hunger and thirst. Feeling desperate and without hope

---

1 HMAS *AE2*, Australia's Gallipoli submarine, penetrated the Dardanelles at 2.30 a.m. on 25 April. Passing through the Narrows, she entered the Sea of Marmara next day. After four days of attacks on Turkish shipping, her engine room was fatally damaged by the guns of the Turkish torpedo boat *Sultan Hissar*, and the *AE2* sank on 30 April. The entire crew was rescued and spent the rest of the war in a POW camp. In 1988, a Turkish wreck diver, the director of the Rahmi Koc Cultural Foundation, successfully located the famous Australian submarine lying in 72 metres of water.

I let the reins go slack. Without hesitation my horse which was fortunately a battery horse, began to trot. About 20 minutes later I found myself back in the horse lines of the 18th Battery.

Saturday January 30

Went out for tramp across desert at dusk. Feeling of isolation – quiet, and absence of care is wonderful. Away from the noise of camp life. So I was meditating on my sermon.

Unfortunately I was not so far away from mankind as I had fancied, for dusky forms appeared all round me and I was summoned to halt – which I did promptly. Then two armed Sikhs approached me cautiously. They could not speak English and I did not care to risk moving on – for I could not tell whether I had leave to do so and if not I should have had the same fate as a woman a few days back. However an interpreter was fetched and after some powwow I proceeded on my way.

Sunday January 31

8 a.m. – At Holy Communion, two generals again, one a Brigadier the other a Major General. 15 communicants. Changed into riding breeches and in accordance with desire of Nall, caught train to El Ferdan. The train had been put 20 minutes late and was further delayed by New Zealand troops on their way to El Ferdan trenches this side of Canal. When I got to camp they had just finished. Orders had got to Nall saying I was at 18th Battery at 11, so he assumed I would not come. Got on horse Sarah belonging to Lt Knowles and arrived at 18th 1 p.m.

Held a small service. Lunch and then back to Ismailia

for 5 p.m. evening service. Spoke on Habakkuk 3:17. The test of real religion is power – power to overcome sorrows of life. Receive letter from Bishop which somehow had got into hands of RC Community. Fortunately I met the RC Chaplain and he of course knew RCs at Ismailia and about this letter, which they knew not how to handle. The Bishop promises to hold confirmation here and see about those left behind.

Monday February 1

Tramp across desert for 4 hours – had a glorious sun bathe – came back brown as a berry. Heard of death of two of 18th Battery who – not caring for their tent went to sleep in a trench and got buried alive. Must go out and see what has happened to them.

General Watson was having lunch when I stumbled in to find out if I could get to El Ferdan. He was affable and kind, sending a captain off in the middle of lunch to find out when commissariat boat was leaving and arrange that it should take me. He told me I could have General Younghusband's private launch as a rule, if I advised them when I should need it.[1]

Left for El Ferdan 4.30. Saw Gurkhas fishing with string and bamboo cane. Gyppy natives loading firewood and corn with usual Allah sing song. The day before Jock (Gordon Highlander and Sergeant in charge of boat) informed me they had been fired on by a Maxim belonging to Indians.

We carried, lashed to the side, a lighter bearing firewood, horse fodder and flour to Indian troops opposite hospital between Ismailia and 18th Battery. Water kept

1 To enable Best to visit the troops dug in along the Canal Defence Line more easily.

splashing right over lighter. Their bread will be a trifle salty I fancy. On board a varied assortment of men – Sikh on lighter, Jock a cheery old Scotty. Gyppy Engineer and 3rd Brigade Warrant Officer and self. Boat very dirty, but found comfy seat on coil of ropes.

Near hospital passed two small boats, each armed with pair of 5 pounders. Hospital being dismantled in view of probable attack. As we continued, on either side the Indians and natives all busy digging and fortifying banks. Saw two of 18th Battery by side of Canal as we passed. Canal very narrow. Could not see much as banks were high though gradually becoming lower as we neared Ferdan coast guard station.

Passed *Requin* – out-of-date French battleship with two good guns. Passed coastguard station from which all women had been sent away. Reached spot opposite 20th Battery and found Captain Brown waiting. Could not get near the side so hailed a dinghy belonging to native sailing boat – then punted part of the distance – carried rest of the way by natives. Tramped in direction indicated, but could not find tents. Just when giving up found ourselves on top of them, hidden in hollow.

Went to Officers Mess. They had just received message of probable Turkish attack either that night or at daybreak. I therefore decided not to go back by boat and managed to miss train. Had scratch meal. Tents were dropped. Most of night spent digging our trench and carting ammunition brought up by train – the intervals of rest were spoiled by barking of wild prairie dogs and buzzing and stings of mosquitoes. No attack.

Along the railway line proceeded a stream of refugees (natives) carrying all their worldly possession on their backs. Armoured train proceeding up and down. Yet ordinary Suez Express passed with all lights blazing and windows up. Chilly sleeping in open, but managed to dig

myself a fairly comfy trench. English Officer in Indian
Regiment says he's jolly glad no attack was made before
20th Battery arrived, as they were weak and under
equipped. Sound of firing further north.

Returned to Ismailia by 10 a.m. train, leaving all very
cheery. Got on train to go to Serapeum in afternoon, but
had to get off as train refused to stop there. My sort of
native eiderdown arrived, so I had a pleasant night
though somewhat troubled by mosquito stings.

Rankin returned from Kantara reporting brush with
enemy. Casualties: 2 killed and a few wounded. Enemy
losses not known. Only a scrap with outpost Mountain
Battery and infantry in action. Two shells fall near
`````ine of retreat – thinks strength of enemy
underestimated.

## Wednesday February 3

8 a.m. – Rode off to 20th with telegram for Nall. Very
heavy going. Passed General Watson who asked me to
report movement of Camelry and Cavalry from Ismailia,
lest Battery should fire on them. Did so, walked back to
El Ferdan Station and just caught train on to Kantara.
Considerable firing during last ¼ hour at El Ferdan. Went
to Kantara with Rankin, where firing still going on
spasmodically, even after our arrival.

Go up to Major Birtwistle's[1] observation post – a
platform about 30ft high in fir tree. I spot through his
telescope what looked like a gun on horizon – probably
Turks nearest to our Indian troops are digging trenches.

Had a drink at Officers Mess with Stoll – back for 1.15
train, seeing Clarke who was receiving message saying

---

1 Major Birtwistle commanded the 1st Brigade, Royal Field Artillery.
`````

5th Battery had been in action and their gunboat *Cleo* had been firing on camelry and cavalry coming from Ismailia – so that accounted for firing. The *Swiftsure* was just north of 6th Battery.

Rowed out to launch with a Sergeant fitter who took oars first, but I had to show him how I used to do it at Queens'. Met Trumpeter Smalley over the other side of the river who is horseholder to Major Dobson. Major comes back with news that Turks are entrenching at Moya Halat and that another 3000 are coming up. Also some 6 or so wheeled vehicles. Return to pick up prisoners at Tussoum.

1st Lieutenant IMS gets on board and starts chatting about difficulties confronting a Brahmin entering Army. He had to keep up two establishments at home – did not want to offend either party. His father and uncle very high in Civil Service, and remained also orthodox, but conceded some immaterial principles. His cousin had been first to break way and leave India – but was outcast. He had followed. I said – *was not Maths an Indian subject*? He rose at once. All his family for generations had been great mathematicians. Some of their books on wave motion and astronomy had been printed in England and Germany. His first cousin turned out to be the last Senior Wrangler whom I had met at Cambridge.

Situation developing as surmised yesterday evening. At 10 a.m. there was a considerable fusillade and booming of guns amid which I had to leave for El Ferdan. Nothing happening at El Ferdan except that they could see something of enemy movements, some 7000 yards away. They expected a night attack for they had seen some officers summon several others, hold a pow-wow and verbal message sent out.

However it probably had reference to action at Ismailia. The Turks are probing to find out disposition

of our forces, at El Ferdan. After lunch at 1.30 I hold
celebration of Holy Communion in Sergeants tent. 10
present. The service was very reverent, though tent was
lowered so that I could not stand upright and men knelt
throughout in one corner. Outside a regular gale was
blowing, the air thick with sand. I then got on to
Brown's horse and rode back blinded by sand and
almost thrown off – clinging to reins in one hand and
bag in other.

Before I reached 18th Battery the gale had somewhat
abated. I could not wait for train, as I was expected to
take funeral of 2 RAMC who were buried alive through
sleeping in a trench, instead of in their lice and flea-
ridden tent. Got back and found a note, so jogged Major
Pritchard's memory. He put blame on Canal Defence
Headquarters. The two men, Private Lorimer and a
Sergeant, were both professional footballers and nice
quiet fellows.

Have tea with RAMC. IMS man comes in and
reports five casualties in what was merely an outpost
foray. Indians had come to test and discover enemy's
position. This done they retired in orderly fashion and
mountain guns covered their retreat, doing some
damage in Turks ranks. A Turkish officer gave himself
up: *he was fed up with not having enough food* (sic). The
Indians let Turks cut barbed wire entrenchments and
come quite near. Their native officers dare not take
responsibility of ordering 'Open Fire'. If all battles are
like this, then war is an '*affaire comique*' unless you
are hit.

A fierce and sanguinary battle is raging up to the Suez
Canal in the east – while on road and railway to the west
of it rolls on the world's commerce. Most amusing of all
are the eternal feminine cycles proceeding serenely down
the road.

6.30 A good deal of gunfire, later accompanied by rifle-shots and Maxims. The enemy were firing strongly and apparently accurately for when they had sighted an object, the other guns got right on the spot. Half a dozen shells fell all round our evacuated hospital – many in the canal. These were directed especially on a tramp steamer and dredger.

The workmen and natives left boat and scuttled for their lives along road which is parallel to and just this side of canal. Funnel knocked off gunboat, but propped up again. Our guns don't seem to have located theirs or perhaps encouraging them to come on. We are within easy range of their guns, but they prefer to direct fire on trenches 1000 yards east of canal and on canal itself in hope of getting gun boats. The cookhouse of 18th Battery has been struck.

Thursday February 4

Saw 19th Battery wounded. Bombardier Hart seemed worst, but all very proud of Battery and officers at Clapham up in tree observation post under heavy fire. Trouble expected at Toussoum again. Moreland is sent down there. There is a lull in fighting at Ismailia. Spencer sallies forth with all horses at his command to fetch back enemy gun. He finds a dead horse. Bombardier Nightingale seems to have had a hot time holding two horses without cover.

At 5 a.m. Turks attack Kantara outposts, but are driven back. Daybreak finds enemy with bridge built at Toussoum. Some get across, but gunboat and 19th Battery get on to them. A good many killed. 300 taken prisoner in entanglements. Turkish OC killed leaving on himself valuable papers, which his staff did not take away. Looks as if they were in a hurry. British officer killed in white flag episode.

Steady bombardment round Ismailia – we have no cover, but fortunately shells were bursting a bit high. We had been watching shot land in canal all round hospital. Sheep and goats trot off together for safety when our horses came over the ridge and probably attracted fire. We found ourselves not spectators – but passive actors – shrapnel bursting before and behind.

Packed up traps and removed into wood. Lunch in peace. Got to cemetery. Mohammedan funeral going on next door. Howls and sobs of hired mourners. Chant of *'There is no God, but God'* on one side and roar of battle on the other. Buried the 2 RAMC men in their sleeping rugs. Some very reverent attenders present. No gun – but Last Post with its thrilling poignant and yet hopeful last note. Hear in evening that enemy has half-built pontoon near Toussoum, but lost 200 killed near Serapeum.

Stayed up late packing things properly, accompanied by the scream of shrapnel and boom of shells. One is bark, the other bite, but the bark is worse than the bite as regards sinking in pit of the stomach. Went to bed expecting to be woken by scream of shrapnel and hail of bullets on the trees. It was a stormy night.

Friday February 5

Morning bright and clear. All quiet as death. Had swim in Lake Timsah.

Sunday February 7

Celebrations of HC at Serapeum and Toussoum. Ask them to wait for me. Return at 9.30 and go off with Post Major. A bomb lands miles from Ismailia, but no one hurt.

Four Turks wandering for hours on the side of canal

looking for someone to capture them. Pass *Requin*, *Ocean*[1] (Chaplain on board looking exactly like Swann-Mason) and *Swiftsure*. Between Toussoum and Serapeum saw many zinc boats used for making the pontoon absolutely new.

Tuesday February 9

In evening Staff Officers come to our Mess. They say Australians are being sent back as absolutely impossible. No discipline. They obey commands, turn up on parade only if it suits them. They go out for route march, take towels and go swimming whatever the objective of the route march may have been.

The Staff Officers also say many of our men on the Western Front had to be shot on retreat from Mons, to prevent retreat from becoming a panicky flight.

Wednesday February 10

Went with Colonel to Serapeum. Arranged for needs of the wounded and confirmation of Smalley. Went over battleground and picked up a few relics. Hands and feet of dead sticking out of sand. Gruesome sight. Had a glorious hour or two galloping over the desert. This was the scene of the fighting a week ago.

Thursday February 11

To Hospital – only Hart and Gallagher left. Went by train to Kantara. No service as Generals King and Douglas were there. Walked from 6th Battery to 4th Battery with Major Clarke. He is of opinion all is over and that we shall

1 The battleship *Ocean* hit a mine during the naval offensive on March 18 and sank in Eren Keui Bay. *Swiftsure* participated in – and survived – the great naval assault on the Narrows forts, described in 'Westerners, Easterners and the Dardanelles'.

leave here mountain batteries which are of no use at Front (being supplanted by new pattern).

Australian half-seas over with drawn knife follows French sister into hospital, grapples with officer just recovering from enteric – at last he is overcome and ejected. Whatever be their orders, the march ends at bathing sheds. General Maxwell desires not be left alone with Aussie troops. Source of anxiety to medics, despair to officers and menace to Egypt and yet papers are full of their loyalty and efficiency. Why not put them in the front line, as David did to Uriah?

Friday February 12

Arranged Confirmation Service and rooms for Bishop and SCF.

Saturday February 13

Funeral of another boy from the Hondinge. Dead March from 'Saul' played all the way from British Hospital. Firing party came first – then band who inward turn and march to rear to allow coffin to come through. Sailors and also retinue of sailors and NZ troops bear coffin. Naval and staff officers surrounded by all sorts of nationalities, Natives follow, lazily interested. Poor boy – yet he now knows more than the wisest sage on earth. The sailor seems so much more reverent and appeals to me more than the Tommy – particularly colonial Tommy.

Get Dainty and ride to Herts Yeomanry and Westminster Dragoons to see 2 confirmees. Dainty was an old beast who reared and bucked because she thought it was time for food. Desert walk to sermonise in afternoon. Saw there an Indian who spent his half holiday in

Moslem devotions. Wonderful example to us 'superior'
Christians.

Children play same games as at home, footer with
small ball, hop, skip and jump, marbles etc. Dropped in
at RC Chapel and saw monk and sister at devotions. Also
school children finish there each day – business men also
present, in the quiet calm of the chapel. Through
windows drifted martial music of NZ band at club
nearby.

How much the RCs exceed us in reverence. I think
their frequent services and some even of their rather
superstitious beliefs help to make God's presence very
real to them. They give children medal of Virgin which
they say will help to protect them. When I go back I shall
try to work on stiffer church principles – the religion of
the broad Churchman tends to become just a code of
morals – an ethical system.

Sunday February 14

Holy Communion 8 a.m. Again General Wilson with
about a dozen or so men present. Ride to 20th Battery on
Dainty with Knowles. Saw Sergeant Major and Doctor,
then back to 18th Battery for lunch then off with Higgins
and Brown to Ismailia. Nice congregation in evening,
preached on casting all your care upon Him. Confirmation
class 6.30 to 7.30.

Monday February 15

Tons of lead falling around us, but only one man killed.
Turks say, if their main body had come up as prearranged, they would have been well on the way to Cairo
by now. Hear that Yeomanry did not follow up retreat. But
it is recognised they could have done more effective

work, because General M. heard from secret service of
strong reinforcements and General Wilson dare not give
command on his own responsibility.

In morning see the confirmees. Receive letters from
SCF saying I shall probably be recalled, as Canal Defence
Chaplain will soon be out of hospital. Wrote back saying
it was discouraging to chop and change and keep starting
de novo among strangers. Met Bishop at 1.45 and went up
to the Lyddons, who were putting him up. Lyddon is a
canal pilot, who had a very narrow escape on *Cleo*. His
straw hat was filled with shrapnel.

Confirmees to tea at Lyddons. Two Indian CEMS
present. I arranged they should meet Bishop – they made
obeisance and kissed his hand. I fancy Bishop a bit
embarrassed, Confirmees very earnest especially
Sergeant Major Rancy. Bishop very nice and simple.
Talks mainly about sacrament: what is received and how
men faced up to realities of life and death. He had hands
recently laid on his head by Archbishop of Canterbury.
No magic *passe-partout*, but grace received by faith of
Bishop, candidate and witnesses. He emphasised power
of prayer.

We should be on lookout for manifold gifts of Holy
Spirit. We each need one or two and should strive to find
out which we have. He expressed his belief in personal
devil as next strongest and wisest force after God. Life
will not be easy after confirmation, maybe because devil
wants to take us off guard. But we are given strength,
which if used, increases – otherwise it shrivels up. Short
preparation is needed before each Service.

In the evening went to Lyddons where we had music. I
sang and played accompaniment to Lyddon's violin.
Rotten piano. Then looked at draft of Crusaders Society.

Cercle du Canal de Suez
Ismailia
February 16, 1915

My dear Mother,

Since the little fracas on February 3rd and 4th, life has resumed its normal course and we have felt rather flat. Strange to say there is a sort of fascination about being under fire and hearing the shriek as the shell passes through the air and the bang as it explodes. It feels like a very realistic display at Belle Vue. It is very good to have had the experience of being under fire, an experience which I fancy few chaplains are privileged to have, for even on the continent I gather the Chaplains remain for the most part at the base[1] – holding services and visiting hospitals.

One of our batteries was never found and escaped without a shell. Another was under a hail of shrapnel bullets for some hours, the guns and carriages bespattered all over. Yet not a man was touched. It is amazing how much lead – even when fire is well directed – is required to kill a man. It was estimated at about a ton in the Boer War. The last of the 3rd Brigade batteries got it hottest, not only heavy shell fire but also rifle fire, the Turks came down right on to the bank of the canal and were sniping them all day. They had seven casualties but all are doing well.

I rode over the field of battle a few days later. It was a gruesome sight. The Turks were slaughtered like cattle. Burial parties had to go out for a week before all the corpses were put under the sand. The ground was littered with ammunition, rifles, bayonets, clothes and especially

---

1 Kenneth Best felt strongly that this was not the place where chaplains on active service should be.

old boots. They evidently found they could run faster without them.

The enemy's advance guard made a very plucky fight and if their main body had come up as prearranged things would have gone badly with us, methinks. As it was the advance force just failed to push home the attack and lost heavily trying to return. The enemy have now retired and it seems doubtful if they will return. They have gone back some 50 miles and left no outpost.

Time is precious for in a few weeks the desert is supposed to be impossible for a large body of troops because of sandstorms and lack of water (water can be got almost anywhere by digging for it). I fancy the retreat is genuine, but we have to remain prepared.

To my sorrow I hear the Canal defence chaplain will soon be here and so I shall have to go back to the Division at Heliopolis. It is a sad disappointment to me – but I have been rather lucky to get up here at all.

The socks arrived safely on Saturday – nothing to pay – thanks awfully. I was so sorry to hear of Daddy's collapse – the weather must have been atrocious. I hope the constabulary work won't be too much for him: '*a policeman's lot is not a happy one*'.

I am afraid it looks as if you too may come under fire. Have one of the cellars ready prepared in case it should come to pass. It is the only possible way of escape.

Heaps of love to all

Your affectionate son Ken

Saturday February 20

Issued RAMC magazines and also twitched the men about Sunday services. A very pleasant bunch.

Sunday February 21

Had breakfast before service, as no time afterwards.

8 a.m. 25 Communicants. General Wilson present in riding togs. Off to El Ferdan on Dainty. Dainty wants to stay in camp and slack. We have an argument in which Dainty has the advantage, until I ride back and deposit bag in camp, telling orderly to take it to station and send it by QMS. Taking a stick in exchange, the debate turns in my favour and we arrive just in time for parade.

I speak on how to bear anxiety. Hearty singing, best service up to now I think. Following on we have Holy Communion to which 12 came. 4 newly confirmed men and Major Nall. Lunch there and then back to Ismailia, carrying bag and haversack which broke. Very wearying.

At evening service some stood in road, as room was so full. I spoke on the impact of Christ crucified among us. This is an eternal fact, not just a tragic event in past history and how this should comfort and inspire us. Supper and music with Kenneth Lewis.

Receive order after Evensong to return to Heliopolis next Wednesday.

Monday February 22

To Serapeum. Corpses pulled out of the canal and buried as we passed.

12 noon Holy Communion. 12 men with Lieutenant Garnett, 2 RE Officers, Signalman Gregory and Trumpeter Smalley joins Crusaders. Later there is much stuff to be unloaded from lighter, so did not get back till 4.15. Found Crookham waiting. We go to GOC and then to station about luggage. I escort him round and introduce him to men. He dines with us in camp.

He has been with home troops in East Anglia. He tells

us of events in England – the expectation of invasion in East Anglia – of the air raids, of fear of traitors and spies at home. Also of failure of Indians at the Front. Officers gone. Men sit in heaps in spirit of Kismet and refuse to budge until our men at bayonet point force them to move. He relates how East Anglian Division marched through villages round my home. One village looked very glum, because, at end of march, our troops looked weary and dispirited. Village thought they were fleeing before enemy and final battle was to be fought out round village.

Wesleyan Padre coming tomorrow. Why? Just to look after 3 or 4 Wesleyans or to say he has been on Canal? Went and saw Crookham established at Headquarters bungalow. Sand blowing off corpses. I dragged one out of water and buried him. Surely cremation would be the best way?

Tuesday February 23

Went to fetch Crookham and hand over to him, describing disposition of troops. In afternoon, missed train to Kantara. Wired to OC details to send wagon to meet my luggage and tent on morrow. Lose Lilley as servant. He goes back to Brigade Office, loss of a good chap. Had Kenneth Lewis to tea and did a little packing. Lloyd joins Crusaders.

Get picket to call Bombardier Nightingale, Dr Hilton, Trumpeter Lloyd and self for Holy Communion at 5.30 am. Dinner at club with CF. I remember I had met Leach and Lancaster once at Heliopolis with 10th Manchesters machine gun.

Read in paper of bombs at Chelmsford . . .

Wednesday February 24

Holy Communion at 5.30 a.m.. Luggage off 10 a.m. Great
rush, porters don't help or care whether one goes or not.
Get books brought down and dropped them at Kantara.
CF sees me off. On to Port Said. Meet Thorn in church
who had just had Wedding. He gives me lunch.

I wander round and take photos of lighthouse, fishing
and de Lesseps.[1] Visit Government School. Head monitor
recites 'Soldier'. School full of fun but discipline a bit lax,
I fancy. Back to Thorn, find out he is nephew of Mrs
Chapman. I have faint recollection that Canon C
mentioned him to me.

Heliopolis Camp
Cairo
March 6, 1915

My dear Father,
I have changed my quarters so frequently lately and as
many times started to organise my work afresh that
letter writing has been sadly neglected. I am now back
again from Ismailia and installed at Heliopolis as before.
Only now I have cut myself off from all 'Messes' so that
I may be more of a free man and less hampered by
Brigade rules and regulations. The reason for my return
is that a chaplain has been sent out by the War Office
specially for Canal Defence work. His name is
Crookham and he comes from some Parish near
Cambridge. I was rather fed up on receiving orders to

---

1 Ferdinand de Lesseps, who was primarily responsible for the construction of the
Suez Canal. His statue used to stand proudly at the Port of Suez, until it was pulled
down by Egyptian nationalists after the Suez War in 1956. Today only the pedestal
remains.

return, but on reconsideration I see I have been greatly favoured by fortune. I was the only Chaplain down there when the Turks attacked and the only one under fire.

There is, I fancy, very little chance of the Turks returning and not a very healthy chance of our leaving Egypt till the war is over. When will that be? I see Lloyds are laying 10 to 1 that peace will be declared by September. I hope they are correct. We are none of us appreciating Egypt as we should and wouldn't mind a change. Of course I had a glorious time down on the Canal, travelling about by horse, launch or train.

I fancy I know the Canal pretty well by now. Each night the narrative would be received after dinner was cleared away. The big map was brought out and the movements of the enemy, as reported by aeroplane and camel and cavalry reconnaissance, marked on it in pencil. It was a most absorbing game wondering what their tactics were leading to. It was all so clear and simple that we could follow the whole campaign. Whereas in France I fancy even the Generals only know their own sector and have not the vaguest idea what is happening all along the Front.

I must try early next week to record a few incidents from the Canal. On returning to Heliopolis I found the two Battalions of Infantry had changed and that now the 9th Manchesters were there, under the command of Lt Col. Wade, a former Chester student.[1] He has been very good in sending me men to put up tents etc.

The mail is just going – so goodbye and love to all.
Your affectionate son, Ken.

---

1 Kenneth Best's father, the Revd John Best, had been Principal of Chester College, before retiring to Sandon Rectory, Chelmsford, where he was Rector from 1910 to 1926.

Heliopolis Camp
Cairo
March 15, 1915

My dear Father,
The only Church Tent which I have is uninhabitable
when a wind springs up. Last Sunday it looked for all the
world like a parachute. Then some well meaning old
Vicar writes to ask why I am not looking after dear
Tommy Jones. If Vicars want their pets nursed, they
ought to provide the nurses. I cannot manage a thousand
or two young rascals.

I am pretty irritable. It is the khamseen.[1] Perhaps in
your travels you have not been to a land where such things
breed. Let me introduce you to him. A most obnoxious
fellow. A strong south wind brings with it swarms of
locusts and flies and a suffocating heat, burying oneself
and one's possessions in sand and dust. One feels sand
everywhere – breathes sand – eats sand – till one vows he
will never look again ever at an advertising poster of a
seaside. At home with rain and slush I dare say you would
enjoy a khamseen. We should like a little sleet.

The men are sticking to their work like heroes. Having
been with both I don't know which to admire the more –
the fellows who worked their guns as cool as cucumbers
under heavy fire (their first engagement, too) or the men
who were left behind and doggedly went on with their
exhausting field days across the soft dusty desert with no
hope of meeting a real enemy to spur them on. The
Lancashire lad is a pig-headed, narrow minded and
conceited fellow in most cases, but he has got grit.

1 An oppressive hot southerly wind, which prevails in Egypt in the spring.

At the Canal I was kept on the move. Walking or travelling by launch, train or in the saddle most days. Sometimes we had a short service. But often I doffed coat and dog collar and set to work with a shovel. Officers and men worked like navvies. The men thought their officers brutal taskmasters until the Turks came – then they understood. If they had slacked, they would never have escaped in the marvellous way they did. Seeing the huge numbers of dead and wounded which the Turks left behind, I sometimes marvel that we lost so few.

Did I tell you of a rather humorous incident? A General spotted a black object left in a hollow. Hurrah, he said, we have collared <u>one</u> gun. So he sent for a gun team. Off started the gun team escorted by a Battalion of Infantry and some Cavalry – a noble sight. They crossed 3 miles of desert and found – a dead horse. This did not appear in the daily narrative!

Thanks awfully for book of addresses and whole family for the letters. The mail is just going and so will continue in my next.

Heaps of love to all,
Your affectionate son
Kenneth

News of the heavy toll of casualties on Gallipoli now begins to reach Egypt. In this letter home, Kenneth Best reflects the surprise of the troops in Cairo that reinforcements are needed so quickly. By April 30, the four Fusilier battalions forming the 86th Brigade of the 29th Division had lost 68 officers (out of their normal muster of 104) and only 1830 men (out of 4000) were there to fight another day.

Frederick Gibbon, whose history of the 42nd Division received the accolade of a foreword by Field-Marshal Haig, wrote, 'The story of Gallipoli might have been very different had General Hamilton been granted the support of the 42nd East Lancashire Division one week earlier.'[1]

Abbassia Garrison
Cairo
April 28, 1915

My dear family,
It is becoming quite warm again. Between 11 a.m. and 4 p.m. one perspires continuously no matter what one does. Even if one lies on a bed in bathing costume it's all the same. Yet having become acclimatised one does not feel it oppressive. At home one would think it strange to see a big burly policeman marching along with a flimsy and gaudy parasol over his head, as I saw this morning, but here nothing seems strange.

I have now moved down temporarily to Abbassia. Heliopolis Camp is taken over by Australians. For next few days I have joined 5th Manchester Regiment but I think they will move tomorrow. Everything is in a state of flux and it is generally believed that Ian Hamilton has ordered the Division to assist in the Dardanelles Operation.

Things do not seem to be quite so successful at Dardanelles as anticipated – at least it is surprising that reinforcements should so speedily be required. Perhaps we shall know better how things stand in the course of a week or two [...]

One order follows another in lightning succession. It is now an open secret that the Division has been ordered to proceed with all possible speed to the Dardanelles. Whether the artillery go with them I can hardly say, but

---

1 *The 42nd East Lancashire Division 1914–1918*, Country Life, 1990, p. 20.

they will go or else remain on the Canal. If they remain on the Canal, the Canal Defence Chaplains will look after them so that in any case it would seem I shall be free to go.

There will be some tough work without doubt. The Turks are renowned as brave soldiers and they will fight desperately and to the death in defence of their home. I don't believe they are seriously suing for peace – the conditions demanded are impossible. Also all Mohammedans realise defeat would be a serious blow to their religion. It was founded by force and force can do much more even than missions to bring about its downfall. They will fight like demons and fight to a finish for Home and Allah.

There is much singing and movement in the camp today. I must now buckle to and prepare suitable sermons for Sunday. I fancy we shall only be allowed 35lbs luggage so I shall see if I can leave the rest with the Senior Chaplain in Egypt.

Yours affectionately

Ken

Departure for the Dardanelles

Kenneth Best, 1914
© the estate of Kenneth Best. Imperial War Museum. BestJK_010297_7

Sunday May 2

Sudden orders came through on Saturday to entrain for
Alex on Sunday night and consequently everyone
amazingly busy – yet at 6.30 and 7.30 services we had a
good muster of communicants. Again at night a nice
congregation. Maxwell, whom I knew at Cambridge, was
sitting in front row. Just out for mission work among the
Jews.

Have received so many conflicting orders that at Col
Cummings' suggestion I went to Heliopolis HQ and saw
Gen Douglas personally.[1] I received direct orders from
him to accompany the Division to Dardanelles. This was
at 5 p.m. I had to prepare for a service, take it and then
pack. Remainder of my belongings went into 35lbs valise
and 100lbs into kitbag and box left with my batman
Philpott until sent for. Had just filled one box, found it
too small and was in despair when P came and helped me
out. All squared up by 1 a.m. Leave 4 a.m.

Pale dawn breaking over Cairo which put on its best
appearance for farewell. It was a moving sight to see boys
silently marching away in darkness. At last they were off
to the Front. Arrived Alex: 10.30 a.m. Embarked on
HMT,[2] formerly a prize German boat of *Norddeutscher*

1 Major-General Sir William Douglas commanded the 42nd East Lancashire
Division, which had the distinction of being the first Territorial Division to leave
the UK. As the diarist later records, he was not regarded with undiluted affection
by all ranks.
2 His Majesty's Transport. The captured German vessel was the *Derfflinger*. Best
describes it as 'like a slaughterhouse', as she had just landed 550 casualties a few
hours before she was boarded by the 5th and 6th Manchesters – with Best among
the passengers.
    In *The 42nd East Lancashire Division 1914–1918* Frederick Gibbon writes (p. 17):
'The gory clothing and stretchers which littered her decks were sufficient evidence
of war's brutality to sober the irresponsible and to banish all ideas of a panic expedition.' Best said later: 'I used the *Derfflinger* life jacket as my pillow for the
remainder of the war.'

Lloyd. It was like a slaughterhouse, having just returned with wounded.

Went to get brekker. By mistake I got into Tommies' cookhouse. They gave me potatoes and bacon – a greasy mess and tea in a dixie. I listened especially to their stark descriptions of the Australian and New Zealand Corps landing at Ari Burnu (Anzac Cove) on April 25 and subsequent fighting. A gruesome and fearful affair it was. Cruelty perpetrated by Turks, eyes gouged out, tongues cut off. The Australians give no quarter now. Spies get out in transport boats and in other ways inform the Turks of our movements and plans of troops. That explains why our landings have met such stern opposition.

Likewise the Germans have mingled with our troops disguised as officers, and given false orders leading troops to disaster and death. All's fair in war they say. Australians

A view of V Beach, taken from SS *River Clyde*, showing
horses being unloaded
© Imperial War Museum. Q13234

had to wade out of the sea. Found barbed wire in the water and met by deadly fire. Once on land they charged with fixed bayonets uphill. Turks don't like cold steel, though they are very clever snipers.

An R.C. chaplain[1] led a batch of men and got killed. They drove the Turks before them, but their losses were very heavy – 60% it is said. They admit themselves that they were too impetuous. At one place *Little Lizzie*[2] had dropped a shell into a Turkish trench. The Anzacs dashed in to finish off the havoc wrought when it dropped another shell, annihilating them. Later they found themselves without ammunition. The other landing parties had a bad time, but did not suffer so severely.

Tuesday May 4

Rumoured that we are to reinforce the 29th Division (Dublin & Munster Fusiliers, Lancs Fusiliers, Scottish Borderers etc.). A high honour as they are a crack division. We feared we might join Colonials and be sacrificed by their recklessness and lack of discipline. The casualties among officers have been so great owing to snipers that officers were busy all morning removing all distinctive marks – stars and braid.

Then we had a hair cutting parade and came out as bald-pated a lot of cut throat convicts as you ever saw. It was a bit chilly and gradually cooling atmosphere made it worse. Wish I had managed to get my parcel before leaving Abbassia. Went to Gym: in afternoon arranged

1 The Revd William Finn, RC padre to the Dubliners, was the first man ashore. He was the first Chaplain to the Forces to be killed in the war.
2 *The Queen Elizabeth* was firing her 15-inch guns over the Peninsula from the Aegean side.

with the Dean of Sydney[1] who was on board to hold a communion service tomorrow. Got into archipelago towards evening.

Wednesday May 5

Cooler and breezier today. Talbot celebrates, I assist 105 communicants in library. Sang '*Just as I Am*',[2] most inspiring reverent service despite awkwardness of situation. Brigadier and 20 officers present.

6.45 – Passing numberless islands. We follow a devious course to lessen chance of striking a mine. Pass two dummy cruisers on look-out for torpedoes. They signal 'all well'. Our return signal fails – pulley gets jammed and rope breaks. We sight various transport boats, some towing lighters or pontoons.

In afternoon, arrange concert at both ends of boat. Dean of Sydney takes one. I take the other. Both a great success. Taylforth & Valentine, Sergeants in 6th Manchesters of great assistance. Hearing of a few who could not attend HC this morning I arrange for evening communion – 8.30 in Nursery. Find room crammed full and men outside. Adjourned to Smoke Room. Take whole service straight through, then only Dean and self communicate. Then, after blessing, give communion to 101 Communicants. Only possible arrangement.

Chatted with Talbot afterwards. He has very broad

---

1 The Very Revd Albert Edward Talbot, 1877–1936, had been Dean of St Andrew's Cathedral, Sydney, since 1912. He had been married for only one month when he enlisted in the Australian Imperial Force and embarked for Egypt as Senior Anglican Chaplain in October, 1914. A tall, athletic and outspoken figure, Talbot made a great impression on Kenneth Best on this voyage. Later he struck up a close rapport with the troops on Gallipoli, but was wounded at Lone Pine in August 1915. *Australian Dictionary of Biography*.

2 Popular Anglican hymn, by Charlotte Elliott (1789–1871).

views. Says we fall behind the RC's every time, e.g. burial services and discipline. T. considers HC should be taught as essential – the service of absolution and forgiveness of sin – take place of curricular confession. Teach congregation to put on hold certain non-essentials, e.g. Virgin Birth, bodily resurrection of Jesus, etc. Teach modern critical view of inspiration of the Bible. T. says he himself swears, but avoids blasphemy. Why not curse devil and say 'by the D ...'? He would run parish mainly for men – women do without much care. He would take Matins and HC and football in the afternoon, leave Sunday School to lay people and Evensong to curate.

He was a great scholar – Double First in Theology. He says his parish for some time has been expecting their Precentor to retire. If I cared for post, would I communicate with him once a month.

Men of the Lancashire Fusilier Brigade, 42nd (East Lancashire) Division, before disembarking at W and V Beaches, 5–6 May 1915
© Imperial War Museum. Q13219

Thursday May 6

We stop off Fisherman's Hut[1] – probably to report to Ian
Hamilton. Then return to Cape Helles. Turkish shells
bursting on ridge and all down side of hill searching our
trenches. In bay, 30 or more transports and gunboats lie
quietly and peacefully at anchor, as though nothing was
happening. Troops continually moving about on land.

Suddenly about noon *Little Lizzie* and *Swiftsure* begin
blazing away and keep it up till about 4 p.m. Our troops
begin to land about 5 p.m.

> *This was the start of the Second Battle of Krithia. It was pre-*
> *ceded by a heavy artillery and naval barrage. Allied troops*
> *outnumbered the Turks by about 20,000. Hamilton had*
> *around 50,000 men and 70 guns at his disposal. Next day*
> *Kenneth Best deplores the absence of the RAMC and the lack*
> *of stretcher-bearers, which cost hundreds of lives.*

Sent letter home and to Little via the Chief Steward. *Auld
Lang Syne* and *Loch Lomond* favourite farewells. Firing
resumed until sunset. The first transport narrowly escapes
being sunk. Shells from battery on Eastern side of
entrance to Dardanelles drop round her. I leave with last
one at 8 p.m. on what was once a tender to a lighthouse in
Ceylon. She takes me to within ¼ mile of landing and
then we wait for small boats for about 3 hours.

Just when we expect to be there for the night and have
stowed ourselves away, the boats arrive. It is miserably
cold. About 2 a.m. we get to our quarters which are
shallow trenches. But it soon becomes so cold that we
spend rest of the night walking about. All our kit had to

---

1 Isolated stone hut on extreme left of ANZAC beachhead, an area controlled by
the New Zealanders.

be left behind. Throughout night continuous rattle and roar of infantry and artillery with naval guns booming at intervals. It's the Turks who make the night fighting.

The King has named the bay where we landed Lancashire Bay in memory of the heroic self-sacrifice of Lancs Fusiliers.[1] Their namesakes in the Territorials are worthily upholding their reputation. Poor fellows, they have lost heavily, I fear.

Friday May 7

Had some tea and ration biscuits and went off to the Casualty Clearing Station, to see if I could find any of our boys. It is hard to trace any. They are shipped off pretty fast. The deaths are multiplied enormously because there are not enough stretcher bearers or MOs.

Hundreds die from exposure who might be saved. Why does our RAMC not arrive? Meet some chaplains of the 29th Division. Senior CF Hall thinks I ought to be attached to RAMC of East Lancs Brigade, who are now arriving. I go in search of 5th Battery and get lost wondering whether a sniper will get me or whether our sentry thinks I am a sniper. Shells dropping in sea just near me. Get back and shells drop in camp, where troops are congregated, thick as bees. Transport wagon blown to smithereens yet nobody touched. I put bit of shell in pocket. Met Fletcher and see the M/C Brigade off to firing line. Sad leave taking. I feel very much attached to officers and men and some of course I shall not see again.

1 The 1st Lancashire Fusiliers who landed early on 25 April on W Beach were dec-imated by deadly Turkish machine-gun fire. Many soldiers were killed while still in the boats. As a tribute to their supreme courage, 6 VCs were awarded to the Lancashire Fusiliers 'before breakfast' and to this day W beach is known as 'Lancashire Landing'.

Get a shake down for the night with Hardy (Wesleyan
C.F.) as his mate, an RAMC officer, is out for the night.
Made up last night's loss of sleep.

Saturday May 8

Went to see Fusiliers on their return from first few days
in the trenches. They were most of them depressed and
dreading the order to return. Poor fellows. They don't
like it, but they stick to it like men when they get there.
Some I believe refused to leave trenches and advance –
but small wonder, it was suicide. Full of respect for cool
nonchalant way in which Inniskillings stroll about under
heavy fire. It seemed to them pointless to go out and
rush from trench to trench, and sometimes to what
proves to be no trench at all, and so have to retire and
lose one quarter of their men without firing a shot. It
looks like sacrifice of life for nothing – yet it is ground
gained and we hope the Navy and Artillery are doing
the killing.

Maxim guns and snipers are a great fear. Snipers
appear to have Maxims. They have been taken prisoner
with hands and faces painted green – dressed up in
branches like woodland demons. 'It is perfect hell and
the Turks are perfect devils' is the normal description.
Our men just having roll call. Unspeakably sad to hear
no answer, as the roll was called. I went out in the
afternoon. Trying to find RFA. I got close to French
lines. Evidently too much to the right and so returned
and just in time for shrapnel and high explosive to
drop on road.

Heavy shells from gun boats roll past like thunder
which accompanies forked lightning. Slow heavy work.
The troops have not retaken what was taken soon after
landing, but had to be evacuated, owing to lack of

ammunition. Batteries, howitzers and naval guns make a perfect concert of howls and shrieks overhead. Met four parties of Fusiliers trying to find missing enemy. Shrapnel bursting very high. Wonderful sight was the aeroplane with shrapnel bursting all around it. Beautiful country – hilly and verdant rather like Devon – glad sight after Egypt. But oh, those sad sights at collecting stations and the continuous long solemn procession of stretcher-bearers and wounded hobbling back home.

5 p.m.   Battle increasing. Shells following me like rain in the Irishman's gig. Evidently trying to find battery.
5.30   Terrific bombardment of Achi Baba. Hill covered with smoke and pillars of dust. Krithia (a beautiful little village with white hills) on fire. Periodically it is on fire from shelling. Looks as if a determined effort to take it is to be made tonight.

The Second Battle of Krithia lasted three days, but only a few hundred yards were gained. Meanwhile Sir Ian Hamilton, out of touch with events, was still at sea on the Arcadian. *Casualties were heavy, the village of Krithia was not captured, and the high ground of Achi Baba – vital to the Allies – remained in the hands of the Turks. Their defence was shrewdly directed by Liman von Sanders and other German officers.*

8.30 p.m.   See the Lancs. Fusiliers off once more. They are to be in support. What wonders a square meal and a good rest does. They are ready and keen to go. In the morning they asked pathetically 'Do you think we shall have to go to the trenches again'. Some said they would sooner shoot themselves. One at least shot off his trigger finger – court martial. What mere boys they are, to go through such cruel experience.

10 p.m.   Ominous silence. Heard only rifle fire. Wonder if it is true that KOSB located machine guns and informed gunboats. French – especially natives – very jumpy and difficult to work with. All through the night wounded men coming in – especially NZ's. Fortunately one gets hardened to it. But as RAMC man said 'It hurts' to see these poor battered relics of humanity. Hospital ships, dressing stations and clearing stations are all full. Men lying in the open all over the place. May there be a lull in the fighting for a bit. There will be a scandal over this.[1] Celebration of HC cancelled.

Sunday May 9

As usual a day of blood. During brekker five shells from Asiatic fort fall round us. I then strolled off to left wing. Went up Krithia road to Pink Farm and then cut off to the left to Y Beach. Chatted with veteran who considers that we have bitten off more or as much as we can chew. This Gallipoli venture seems to him a sort of brilliant notion occurring to the mind of some general after his sixth glass of port. Started with few gunboats and naval landing force which served to give due warning to Turks. When real land force arrived, they were cut to pieces.

Went up the Nullah.[2] Stray bullets spattering in sand, cracking twigs or singing past. Streams of NZ wounded coming down and being shipped off. At top of gully we formed a cemetery and buried a number of poor fellows. No one scoffs at religion now. Valley full of Fusilier caps.

1 Within a few days of the initial invasion, it had become clear that the medical support for the troops was grossly inadequate. This was the 'scandal' to which Best refers.
2 Dry river bed or ravine.

Came back with some Munster Fusiliers, practically wiped out. Do you want 87th Brigade? You won't find them up there or anywhere. *Non est.* They had a cheery word for everyone. Said stretcher bearers were slackers. Doctors waiting for you with a heavy stick. Three times in two days they went out on a desperate task. Each time cut off or failed, but they came back without a murmur. Revelation of manly heroism.

Congestion in a communication trench during an action, with walking wounded and stretcher cases going down
© Imperial War Museum. Q13325

Down the valley and had a bathe. Came back with Staff Colonel Earle. He said 'If you want poached eggs you must break them, but why break them all for breakfast?' Needless sacrifice of life. Solution seems to be night advances. Fusiliers made 400 yards without loss in this way. The East Lancs Brigade arrive. I walk up with them

and return with signal party. Star shells and heavy fire
from French 75s.[1]

*On that same day, Best writes home in characteristically
cheerful vein, shielding his family from his gruesome experiences of the previous two days.*

c/o 5th Manchester Regiment,
1st East Lancs. Brigade,
Mediterranean Expeditionary Force.
Sunday, May 9, 1915

My dear Family,
We have been rather rushed with the result that I have
nothing but what I stand up in. Perishingly cold after
Egypt. I dig myself a hole for night quarters. I have found
the best way of spending a night is to devote 10 miles to
hard exercise and then sleep an hour or two till the effect
wears off. If I lie down all night, I become too cold to
sleep. Wonderfully healthy life. The naval guns and
artillery kick up a deafening row, but one gets used to it.

Except for the sad side of war I am enjoying this
experience immensely. One sees wonderful deeds of
heroism and amazing pluck and cheerfulness. At times it
is absolutely uncanny. You see an Irishman with an arm
off and full of wounds dragging himself to the Regimental
Aid Post – a man offers to help him: '*Nay, get thee off to
trenches laddie, they need thee there more than I do*'. He has
even got witticisms for those he meets.

I am not of course allowed to tell you what is going on.
Weather is good and I am well, only I should like to get a

---

1 75mm field gun, known as the Soixante-Quinze. The rate of fire could exceed 20
rounds a minute and the French had 4,000 in service at the start of the war.

change of clothes or pick up a razor. I had a grand swim in
the sea yesterday, which was very refreshing. Cheerio – will
send Active Service P.Cs from time to time, I am trying to
get the last parcel you sent as I badly need a woollen
helmet now I have lost the protection afforded by nature.

Heaps of love.

Ken

Monday May 10

Buy large knapsack and then go with Lt. James to 5th
Manchester trenches. Go round and have a chat. Lunch
on own rations and tea, lead rations supplied by Turks. I
was just going off to post officers' letters when shrapnel
began to fly. So stay in trench and write letter home.
Regular as clockwork, two or three men a day are bowled
over, but only in the 3rd line of trenches. Among the
victims were a Sergeant opening a tin of biscuits and a
man bringing water – long distance sniping. I have come
off very well so far. My only ailment is a very bad cold. I
came back on mule cart at a gallop. I felt safer under shell
fire. Sometimes in ditch hurled feet in the air and came
down with bump. How the wounded must suffer.

*The following day the disembarkation of the 42nd East Lancs.
Division was almost completed – but not as planned. The 5th
Battery, Royal Field Artillery, and two guns of the 6th Battery,
had been landed, under the command of Lt.-Col. Birtwistle.[1]
But as the area occupied by the British was so small, the rest
of the artillery – as Kenneth Best records below – had to be sent
back, via Lemnos, to Egypt. This mortified the other batteries,
who had to turn tail before they had had a whiff of action ...
Three companies of the ASC were also sent back. More serious*

1 Formerly Major Birtwistle.

was the absence of the medical and surgical equipment of the
3rd Field Ambulance, lost somehow en route. These vitally
needed supplies did not arrive for another two weeks.

Tuesday May 11

Feeling feverish. Go up to trenches in afternoon. Part of
RFA landed, but they are to go back to Lemnos. So I lie
doggo lest I should be sent back with them. Capt. S. finds
he must go to dentist in Alex: his battalion go up to firing
line. Exciting walk to trenches, plenty of fire. Arrange to
attach myself to Brigade Staff of E. Lancs at Brown
Cottage. Come back to get tackle. Rains hard all night and
I am without shelter – homeopathic treatment for cold.

On that same day, Best wrote to his soldier brother, Herbert.

c/o 5th Manchester Regiment,
1st East Lancs. Brigade
Mediterranean Expeditionary Force.
Tuesday, May 11, 1915

Dear Herbert,
I wonder how things are going with you. I have left Egypt
and am now enjoying far more interesting work. You owe
this letter to the fact that I have just visited the 5th
Manchesters and when I arrived there the Turks began
to shell them so that I had to sit tight in their trenches
for a bit.

I have never felt so fit in my life. I live a vagabond
existence, wandering hither and thither at will. Fortunately
provisions are plentiful so that I can always pinch some grub
and tea. When night falls, I roll myself up in some handy
dugout. When shells fall I dart for the nearest trench.

On Saturday night I witnessed from a good vantage point one of the most terrific bombardments I could imagine possible. A mass of artillery and a fleet of battleships all bombarding a hill. I could not imagine a living thing left. Yet there was, as we found later. The Turks must have been well dug in. The *Little Lizzie* shells will wipe out a whole battalion if it hits them fair and square. The Turk on his own ground is a tough proposition. I am feeling a frightful tramp. We were not allowed to bring any kit on shore. Consequently, I am out at the toes and my clothes would do well to go to the wash. I managed to get a dip in the sea yesterday. Never have I enjoyed a swim more. I am acting postman and the Turks seem to have got sick of shelling us, so I will bolt while things are quiet.

A most amusing combination of sounds yesterday. On land a great battle in progress, at sea a naval band playing variations on Three Blind Mice! Now my boots are through, I am making a desperate effort to trace my horse. Everything seems to be common property. If you need a thing, that constitutes your right to it. The weakness of this arrangement is obvious, that it devolves upon the individual to adjudicate on the necessity or not.

Hope you are going strong? Are you yet in ASC[1]? Or are you too much in love with your motor bike? Heaps of love. Ken.

Wednesday May 12

Go off to forward supply base. Place inundated. Find dug-out only half full of water and sleep there behind 5th E. Lancs supplies. Drew blanket and waterproof from 4th

---

1 The Army Service Corps received the Royal accolade in 1918. Two members of the Corps were awarded the Victoria Cross in the Great War.

E. Lancs next door. Go to field dressing stations on right wing. No Terriers there.[1] The Territorials got into firing line with very small losses. No great advance. Turkish officer taken, says to try to take hill is madness. Is this bluff? Those who have tried suggest it is true. The naval landing gave warning and preparation for defence.

Girl of 14 taken sniping, in full sniping war paint. Things quiet in firing line except the hymn of hate each evening, when reliefs are taking over in trenches. It is said that naval brigade when first landed got right to top of the hill with little or no opposition. Now 100,000 men cannot get half way up, and thousands of lives have been sacrificed. Looks like serious blunder. Mystery of Dardanelles.

Surely there will be an enquiry in House as truth and casualties will come out.[2] What wonderful stories we heard of British success when we were in Egypt. It looked like a walkover. Does England think it is a picnic? The Regulars say that the Retreat from Mons was less terrible than this.

Thursday May 13

Go to 2nd line of trenches and visit East Lancs Brigade Headquarters. They are losing their daily toll through sniping and stray shrapnel, but nothing serious. At midday go to forward base again. Big shells whistle overhead. On way to hospital I pass Plymouth Brigade and find one shell fell there, killing 2 and wounding 7. Australians have their muster roll. Most have lost brothers, cousins or dear friends. They are mad with fury and longing for vengeance.

---

1 The Territorials.
2 Best was right. The first report to Parliament of the Dardanelles Commission was in early 1917.

Evening: Large shells dropping round W beach. Try to find divisional HQ and fail. Shells perhaps from *Goeben*[1] or one of the elderly Turkish pre-dreadnoughts, seem to be after aeroplanes or howitzer battery on top of bluff overlooking W beach. Still full of cold. Boy Ferguson rigs me up a nice shelter of blankets. Sleep clock round and then should probably not have woken, though sleeping in water, had not a terrific bombardment awakened me. We had over 100 shells landing in a space of about 100 yards by 20. The ground simply ploughed up, but only one RAMC man wounded.

Friday May 14

At noon I move off down to beach. Get instructions to join first Field Ambulance. Have a bathe in Bakery Bay, but have to take refuge under cliff. Heavy shells fall for about an hour. Some RE ASC and mules hit. A most appalling scene as day was closing. The heavy battery switched off to right. After a sighter or two she got on to a transport with sickening accuracy. She dropped shell after shell on to deck and first one hit boiler.

Fortunately little white boat alongside, though hit, her engine room escaped and after about 10 long minutes slowly towed her away. To us it appeared a miracle. We were waiting to see her sink. She appeared doomed, never have I seen greater pluck shown than by the little row boat which coolly rowed round her, shells missing by inches only – picking up men who had jumped overboard. Destroyer also steamed right into the midst of shells. Never shall I forget thud, rattle, bang as shells hit her ...

1 German warship which (with the *Breslau*) had eluded the Royal Navy in the Mediterranean and slipped through the Dardanelles, in August 1914, to Constantinople.

Saturday May 15

Significant that last Saturday, when there was no accommodation for wounded, who had to lie out in perishing cold nights – hospital boats being full – our transports were lying idle. Evidently our position on Gallipoli is not secure.

Two beautiful swans sweep overhead. Little muddy streams full of tortoises – frogs croaking all night. Real bluebird. French batteries clear trench. Infantry may have it for asking and Turks fled, yet days pass before we do take it. Aeroplanes (English) drop papers with Turkish writing on. Perhaps to inform them that transport fired on contained some Turkish prisoners who were killed. German *Taube* aeroplane circles overhead and drops bombs on aerodrome – nothing hit. Our guns cannot catch her. Find my valise. Continue to dig hole in cliff. The most secure position I have yet found. Heavy firing in trenches. I fear heavy casualties on morrow – Sunday the day of blood.

Sunday May 16

Gully Beach and Nullah. Turks firing at large birds thinking they were aeroplanes. Major Clark tells me Italy was to have declared war at 2 p.m. yesterday.[1] Developing into siege warfare. Engineers sapping our trenches within 200 yards of Turks. Impossible to advance. Hospital in afternoon – only a few slight casualties and a number of dysentery cases.

1 Italy declared war on Austria-Hungary on 24 May 1915. She did not declare war on Germany until 28 August 1916.

Monday May 17

Tried to get to East Lancs Brigade HQ, but shrapnel so heavy that I had to crawl into ditch and eventually return home. Went to Divisional HQ in afternoon and was told to take up my quarters with Brigade. Rotten idea.[1]

Tuesday May 18

Go to see Hall re Communion Wine – like a stupid old woman he showed a bit of temper. Meet Chaplin, who is also after wine. We go together to French hospital and a dear old curé supplies us with two bottles of red. He fairly bustled around to find bottles, corks etc.

Afternoon: Go to East Lancs Brigade HQ. Find man just killed by shell. Take corpse (R. Pinder) to W Beach Cemetery. Meet cart there and bring luggage from 1 Field Ambulance. On what a thin thread life hangs. Shells were getting near direct road. I still wanted to take that route, but gave way. Matter hardly settled before half a dozen shells burst on road just where we should have been. Got back to HQ and had a grilling from very hot shrapnel.

Wednesday May 19

As I was getting up – more heavy shrapnel fire. Considerable number of casualties in the camp. I seem to have joined them at the hottest time. They have lost more men in the few hours that I have been with them than in a whole week in the trenches. Curious fact that swearing is more noticeable just at present than ever before. Probably in the main a matter of nerves. Arranged for HC – went to borrow

1 Best deplored any orders which would detach him from the troops in the front line.

communion vessels. Eventually ran Chaplain Clowes to earth at RND Field Dressing Station. Coming back took refuge in 5th Lancs QMS in which fragments of shell fell. Did not sleep well – too anxious not to be late for 6 a.m. HC.

Thursday May 20

4 am: Bits of shell hit my dug-out. Lie looking up into blue sky. Birds twittering in trees on which the sun is brightly shining. Shells seem so out of place in such perfect surroundings. HC amid shell fire in open field. No vestments – use a pair of boxes as Altar. About 100 present. Buried Arthur Ogden 1st/10th M/C[1] and J. Miller 1st/8th Battalion, Lancashire Fusiliers. Shell hits signallers dug-out while breakfasting. Men's hair perceptibly turning greyer under strain. I think my hair would turn grey if I had any to turn – clippers have done their work well. Several times a day one has a narrow shave from shell or bullet.

It is sad to see the little white crosses peering up through the grass and woodland flowers scattered on cliffs, valleys, sea shores . . . The whole area is covered with trenches and dug-outs. '*Requescit en parce*' was the effort of a pseudo-scholar soldier. Most put RIP or Anglice for safety. Went to borrow set of HC vessels from Chaplain. Discovered 5th Battery and went with Colonel Birtwistle to forward observing station. Had to cross high land covered with gorse under rifle fire. New and exciting experience. Round observing station there was continuous ping and whiz of bullets. Got back to Gully Beach safely, but then lost way and did not get to camp till about 11 p.m. (pip emma). Big white Gurkhas have done great work at Gaba Tepe (7000 Turkish casualties).

1 Manchester Regiment.

Friday May 21

Under pretext of burying dead, Australians brought up forces for sudden attack. Officer saw through white flag and refused armistice. Slaughter among Turks.
Discovered rest of my kit at Transport Depot. Sent letter home.

c/o 1st East Lancs Brigade,
Mediterranean Expeditionary Force
Friday, May 21

My dear Father,
Our playtime is over, we have put away childish things and got to business – real, grim business. It came very suddenly in the end as everything in the Army does, and though we almost expected it, it took us by surprise. There was no working up gradually, no warning and suddenly the boys were plunged right into the thick of it. One cannot of course write a word about the operations here or our whereabouts or progress.

What can one say which the vigilant hawkeyed censor will pass? First, that we all are longing for a glimpse of the old country and our homes. It is such a long time since we left Southampton. Perhaps our hope will soon be realised, but whether or no, we are ready to carry on here so long as we are required.

The new life is by no means lacking in excitement. We are becoming quite expert in anticipating bullets and shells. Yesterday I had a celebration of Holy Communion. I managed to borrow vessels from a neighbouring padre, my altar was a pair of biscuit boxes, my vestment a khaki shirt, dirty greasy tunic and riding breeches. We fixed it for 6 a.m., hoping to anticipate the usual morning hymn of hate, which the Turks play to us during brekker.

Unfortunately they rose early. Perhaps our artillery had made them restless and they tuned up just as our service commenced. I felt very responsible but thought I would be there in case any should turn up. To my surprise, regardless of shrapnel, about 100 men were present. Never shall I forget my first service under fire. We all felt that God's good providence watched over us and nobody was hit. We are all in excellent spirits. Who could help it in such a glorious country and with such a perfect climate?

I ran into a chaplain with a familiar face yesterday. It turned out to be Failes of Queens', a year senior to me. I am not sure whether his father was not up with Daddy. He tells me that Edwards, whom you would not know is also here, and one whom you would remember, Waggle Andrews, is out here as a private in the Australian RAMC. He would not wait for offer of a Chaplaincy. He landed in a different place so I shall not see him yet awhile. I have had 2 or 3 glorious bathes. Otherwise I have not had my clothes off for a few weeks. I think if I were to return home I should spend my first week in bath and bed alternately. I have written this enveloped in an atmosphere of smoke and lead. It is rather pleasant to pose as a fire eater.

Heaps of love to all.

Ken.

P.S. Owing to change of address, letters have not reached me for 3 weeks.

Saturday May 22

Heavy shelling when darkness had fallen and in morning woke up with rain pouring down. Had to pack up in damp and go off to trenches. Found a grand dugout used once by some RAMC also as latrine. Made ourselves (South African officer and self) very comfy. Roof looks rather unsafe. Buried 4 East Lancs in valley hillside which was old Brigade Headquarters.

Whit Sunday May 23

Some shells ploughed into earth a few yards from our dug out – only one exploded properly – fraudulent manufacturers. Had a delightful evening service at twilight in 4th East Lancs lines. The OC childishly indignant because I did not call on him and leave him to make what arrangements he liked. Would not allow men to attend before dark, i.e. 8pm. Impossible. Could not read hymn sheet. Compromised at 7 p.m. with about 200 men present and dozen officers lying in dugouts.

I stood before them, spoke of joy and peace which accompanies true repentance. A number of shells burst just overhead. I had not the courage to get down or take cover for fear of appearing a coward, so I got a reputation for courage when my action was really due to fear of public opinion. Officer suggests I should be provided with shell proof pulpit!

Monday May 24

Little rain early morning making 'home' slippery and uncomfortable. The medics are sending wounded back to the firing line long before they are physically or mentally fit. Glorious day. Played with tortoise which I found and watched a gorgeous pair of bright blue birds – outer part of wings brown (NB protective colouring). Confirmation of Italy's declaration of war.

Tuesday May 25

Went up to firing line, fairly safe route. Bullets against sides of trench sound like explosive. All along the line one hears of deeds of heroism – bringing in wounded comrades or attempting it under heavy fire, tracking down snipers. Men cheerful – but tired of bully beef which they use as sandbags. First line trenches safest part of the Peninsula, except for spot marked out by sniper and enfiladed.

Got lost trying to get back along communication trench and then heavy rain. I huddled under a ground sheet with a Tommy, his pal giving me his place, but still got wet through with mud that splashed off the trench. Then horrible scramble home through mud knee deep. Had to keep at bottom of trench or should have been hit by Turks. Back 2 p.m. changed boots and socks, swallowed some bully beef and stewed tea and off to bury Captain H. Bolton of 5th East Lancs, nephew of Miss Allen of Lytham. His two brothers present, both of the same battalion. He was buried between two oak trees, near drinking water spring. A lovely spot. No salute at his burial. The Turks did that, firing a regular salvo over our heads. Got back about 5 pm when there was a regular cloud burst. Never have I seen such rain. Most of the trenches 4ft deep filled to the brim in a few minutes. I packed most of our things on Captain Richardson's bed (lucky he had one) and lay on top watching the water rise.

When it was 2ft deep within one inch (carefully measured) of the bed, rain providentially ceased. I took off shoes and socks and bailed out water solidly for two hours to see what was beneath. We recovered a few oddments. Then orders came to move. It was nearly dark. We put on everything we could feel, though sopping wet. We had an inkling of what France was like, though it was warm here. Fortunately rain storm was local and when we got back to old quarters we found dugouts quite dry. Shovels had by good luck been sent down early, so that floods of water had been diverted from our bivouac. Ration of rum and a good sleep.

Wednesday May 26

We are to be divided up for instruction and attached to 87th and 88th Brigades. Terriers said to be lacking in dash. Buried Lieut Clegg of 10th M/C. Had a glorious bathe on X Beach in afternoon.

Buried Lieut. Clegg of 10th M/C just by well – notorious as a favourite spot for sniper's deadly work. They generally choose wells to direct fire on. Sentry hit just by my dugout in mysterious fashion. No shell had burst anywhere near. Owing to increase in shelling and bullets, nerves get right again and I mind them less than shower of rain at home. Probably because I now have definite reason for running risk on duty.

The battleship Goliath *had been torpedoed on 12 May, while at anchor off Morto Bay, by a Turkish destroyer, the* Muavanet-i-Millet. *The daring German captain, Lt.-Com. Rudolph Firle, was awarded the Iron Cross (First Class) and the Turkish Order of Privilege, as well as receiving a tumultuous welcome in Constantinople. From a crew of over 800 officers and men, only 570 were saved.*

The sinking had serious repercussions in London. Despite the angry protests of Kitchener, Lord Fisher recalled the modern Dreadnought, Queen Elizabeth, *to home waters. Two days later Fisher, refusing Churchill's request to devote further naval support to the Dardanelles, resigned as First Sea Lord and slipped away to Scotland 'to avoid all questionings'.*[1]

1 Memo to Asquith on 15 May.

The sinking of the aged battleships, Triumph *and* Majestic, *on 25 and 27 May, had a demoralising effect on thousands of Allied troops, as they watched from the shore the dismal spectacle of both vessels capsizing. These dramatic events provided a double coup for the enterprising Kapitan Otto Hersing, in command of the German U-boat U21, who had knocked out two British battleships within two days of each other.*

Thursday May 27

Visit hospital. Very few wounded. Mostly sick, swellings and rheumatics. Saw what looked like small green yacht upturned. Found it was *Majestic,* torpedoed last night within 200 yards of shore right amongst transport. She fired at torpedoes almost simultaneously but doubtful if any were hit. A dozen stokers or so drowned. *Majestic, Triumph, Goliath* – all lost in a few days. Last time I was down, the sea was swarming with gunboats and shipping of all kinds – now it is practically deserted.

Lest troops should lose heart, GOC issues report stating object of operations. Twice gallantry of troops would have taken Peninsula, had not Turkish reinforcements (130,000) arrived. Object is to harass and demoralise Turks, till they feel their position hopeless. Turks have had 120,000 men on Peninsula and 55,000 casualties – an optimistic estimate. Troops advancing by 50 yards or so, mainly by sapping. In one place our sap met a Turkish one. Both retired in a hurry. Steady flow of casualties. Had a refreshing bathe on X Beach. Swam out to lighters, which soon afterwards, when I was dressing, were shelled.

At night I was called up to bury officer of 5th M/C. There found Fletcher had already taken the burial. We

Men bathing, south of X Beach, Helles Front. A dangerous pursuit if
the Turkish guns opened up, but heat drove them to take the risk. On
the cliff top are the tents of No. 87 Field Ambulance, 29th Division
© Imperial War Museum. Q13283

have to walk past sentry with hands up. Much questioning,
but necessary after a recent case of German officer
spying.

Friday May 28

Buried Pte Neville Lewis of 5th M/C at 1st FA Dressing
Station. Ride to hospital. Find Bugler Barrow was killed
by shell falling in his dugout just where I was before.
Take part in burial service at W Cemetery. Evening stroll
to Fusilier M/C HQ. Some say hill will be taken in a few
days. Very few Turks in trenches – but keeping up
fusillade to deceive. Others say months will be needed
for us to get anywhere and large losses inevitable.

Saturday May 29

Asiatic Annie[1] dropping lyddite in next field, Turks seem to be respecting RAMC Flag. But artillery and troops are forced by constriction of space to be near and so they get shelled. I believe Turks all fighting honourably and gentlemanly – except snipers and a few others. Australians have spread most of the rumours of cruelty to prisoners, perhaps to excuse their own practice of not taking prisoners.

Tramped round to Manchesters, Lancashire Fusiliers, 87th and 88th Brigades and Indian HQ to find out whereabouts of our Brigade – now split up to reinforce depleted ranks of regulars or for instruction and infusion of regular spirit. Only a few remnants in reserve and available for services. Found regular officers as usual sympathetic and helpful.

Hardly any officers left in the units. Lieut. or Capt usually in command. Came back via 3rd Field Ambulance. Escorted them to a fairly secure place for Advanced Dressing Station near Capt Bolton's grave. Unfortunately we were shelled directly we got there. They were ready to turn back, but I assured them Turks were after a battery (French) a quarter of a mile beyond us, and these were just range shots. So it turned out and they adopted position, though rather unhappy.

As I suspected, Major Clarke tells me 55,000 Turkish casualties is a fictitious estimate. The figure is calculated on no sure data, but intended to keep up morale of our troops who are having a trying time, losing men steadily and gaining nothing – except a few yards of Turkish soil.

1 Turkish batteries installed on the Kumkale side of the Straits constantly bombarded the Allied positions at Helles. Asiatic Annie was the nickname for one of the large Turkish guns there which caused many casualties.

Sunday May 30

At 7 a.m., 8 men from 1st & 2nd Field Ambulance attend early service.

Brekker with Lt Rosser, Adjutant of Hants.[1] He waited for me till 8.45. Topping soldier. We went together to Gurkha Bluff under considerable fire and then I went on to Y Beach. I rode Tommy (Signal Co. horse) part of the way, but got too hot and so did rest on foot. Found few 5th E Lancs. At 1.30 found myself alone on Gully Beach – having come back by cliff road. Horses buried at sea floating made disgusting odour. 87th Field Ambulance give me some lunch.

In evening fail to find 5th Battery. Driven back by rainstorm. Wells are named Dun Cow, Pig and Whistle respectively. KOSB led by piper and E. Lancs by mouth organ. How cheering is a little music. Why not more of it? It cannot give away position, except pipes actually in firing line. Hear a rumour that French squadron is at Lemnos having been relieved by Italian troops and will soon be bombarding Achi Baba. Cheers.

Monday May 31

Letter home. Rode on Tommy to Chaplains' meeting – found four new arrivals – who landed during night from England. One face I seemed to recognise. On questioning, he turned out to be Kinloch of Eccleston. Played with him for Eaton Hall Cricket XI. He does not relish this life – different from France, as *everyone* here is under fire. He is attached to our 42nd Division to look after small units. Peace reigns in our camp.

1 The Hampshire Regiment.

Tuesday June 1

One of our E. Lancs Brigades advanced too far. Cut off for 2 days. Many more casualties. Rode an obstinate old grey beast of a mule. If in a hurry I should walk. After kicking it along most of the way, I gave up in despair – let it walk wheresoever. Lo and behold! He fell down in front of the supply depot. Must have gone to sleep. Every day we are expecting a big attack, preceded by bombardment. No battleships yet seen. Casualties mounting rapidly.

Wednesday June 2

Turks busy shelling again, whistling over in batches. Ride down to base to see Lt. Griffiths, 10th Manchesters, dangerously wounded. Came back with Lt James and got very saddle sore. He hopes to ride soon up Achi Baba. Something big in the air. Austria collapses in the South[1] – probably only a natural consequence of invasion by Italy. HQ know nothing of it. Had a swim – sea choppy – did my soreness good.

Is this whole campaign a fearful blunder? Despite the naval attacks and after sacrifice of thousands of lives, we are still miles from summit – not even into Krithia. Go to 1st RFA Regimental Command Post in evening. Wounded coming in steadily. Clapham Junction a very hot corner.

Thursday June 3

Strolled up to reserve trenches at Clapham Junction – got into deep gully as informed I was taking a very risky course. It was a regular Ordnance gully, full of equipment.

1 Austria was not collapsing – but the Italians crossed the border on 24 May and were steadily advancing in the Trentino region, towards the Zillertal Alps.

I took what I fancied might prove useful. I hear our men have a new dodge. Fire volley – then shout. Turks, thinking a charge is coming, bob up. Our men expecting this and pick them off. A Turk officer lying dead in front of the trenches – displaying a fine wrist watch. An Inniskilling[1] announces intention of fetching him in, then I try to dissuade him – courting death – certain to be wounded – all for a wristwatch. No! he is after cigarette papers. I take refuge in trench and observe insect life. Wonderful variety of bugs and creeping things in dug outs.

Afternoon go with Walker to Gully Valley – leave him and climb the stiff ravine to communication trench leading to 5th Battery Observation Station. Had narrow escape at top. Men experimenting with hand bombs. Fortunately for me they were not very effective – though I was temporarily deafened. After a breather I go back to Battery. Back to bivouac – transports hung up, owing to heavy shelling on road. I dare not show white feather, as battery was watching. Regular death trap where Gurkha Bluff dips into valley.

Heaps of troops, gun boats and transport at Lemnos. We have only a mere foothold here and are not very secure. Lose many from shell fire when in reserve. Yet need them here – awkward problem. Hill must be taken soon. Find considerable stir – preparation for demonstration. I volunteer to go out with Signals Officer at 9 p.m.

Heavy fusillade begins which makes the gully impossible for anyone to go up alive. We stay in bivouac. All at once a large fire blazes up in direction of Krithia. Whether Turkish trench or beyond, it is hard to say. Our shells seem to be bursting in it. Therefore hope for the best. It is a terrible, awesome sight. Huge sheet of flame and in front of it we see figures. Possibly gorse on fire and

1 A soldier from the 1st Royal Inniskilling Fusiliers.

yet it seems to burn for periods, die down and then burst
out again. Flames running in opposite direction to wind at
a tremendous rate as though there were fire trails
specially laid. We shall have to wait for explanation of
mystery. Star rockets and guns busy.

I fear Turks had got wind of tomorrow's demonstration
and were out to forestall us and break through. Hear plan
is to bombard hill heavily, then our men in trenches will
shout, put up bayonets over parapet and Turks will flee or
send up reinforcements. Then second bombardment.
New troops to be landed between us and Gaba Tepe
behind Turkish lines and Achi Baba.

Making bombs from empty jam tins, filled with old nails, bits of shell
and barbed wire, and other scraps of metal, and an explosive charge.
This highly risky operation reflects the dire shortage of munitions. A
fuse was fitted through the top of the tin, which had to be lit by a
match. These bombs were first issued in very small quantities about an
hour before the Third Battle of Krithia, 4 June 1915

© Imperial War Museum. Q13282

Friday June 4

Up early. Bombardment timed for 8 a.m. We hear it is the King's birthday.[1] Is this coincidence or is it intentional? Probably as exact time is immaterial it is in part intentional. Achi Baba would be a nice birthday present for His Majesty. We should like to give it to him. It would be literally more blessed to give than to receive.

A 60-pounder battery in action in the open on top of the cliff. Up to July 1915, there were only eight of these guns in action at Helles, and by the beginning of August all but one had broken down
© Imperial War Museum. Q13340

In my morning peregrinations I meet Fusilier Officer who says action begins at noon. 10.30 guns registering targets – final preparation. Two gunboats – also the

1 King George V was born on the previous day, 3 June 1865.

Swiftsure[1] (she has done excellent work here and on the Canal) and nine destroyers looking after them. One gunboat looks as if she would cover landing party. French gunboat steams up Straits. A Scottie says Turks attacked *en masse* last night. They let them get within 60 yards and then blazed. Thousands of casualties, he said.

11 a.m. Huge bombardment mainly, it would appear, by land batteries. Terrific noise. Achi Baba enveloped in smoke. Rifle fire soon joins in. Some regular volcanoes, perhaps ships' shells.

1.30 Bombardment slackening.

1.45 Stream of wounded come down road – most cheerful and bloodstained. Young boys tell you how they bayoneted a Turk. Take two trenches and still going strong up the hill. Boys keen as mustard. Regulars (Hants) say never seen such a glorious charge. Shout – then rush – no holding them. General Noel Lee knocked out.

Cannot wait longer – so go up to trenches – Gully Valley. Meet Dr Henry and Dr Maloney of Worcesters. Go and see a few dying cases and have glances over parapet to see progress of battle. Trenches filled with dead and dying – ghastly sight. Clearly our boys will have a fearful time tonight. They made 4 lines of trenches. Sikhs on left – but Naval Brigade and French on right made little or no progress – therefore leaving our boys at mercy of a murderous enfilade fire. They will have to retire.

6 p.m. Strong Turkish counter attack. Dr Henry

---

1 Both *Swiftsure* and *Triumph* had been purchased from Chile in 1903. They were typical of the elderly battleships deemed unsuitable for Jellicoe's fleet in the North Sea, but seconded to the Dardanelles. They were nonetheless useful for static firing and each had 14 x 14-pounder guns. Each of these old ladies consumed, at top speed about 12–13 tons of coal per hour. *Jane's Fighting Ships, 1914*, p. 48.

wounded. I take him down to Y Beach and get back in dark. *Goeben* sailors among prisoners.

Anxious not to be behind the lines, Kenneth Best made his way up Gully Ravine. He gives a graphic description of the heartrending scenes he witnesses in the trenches. This battle, in which 24,000 Allied troops took part, was the Third Battle of Krithia – and the third attempt made by General Hunter-Weston, British commander of the 29th Division, to capture the key objective of the village of Krithia. The attempt failed. Very little ground was gained, except on the left where 88 Brigade advanced and was able to dig in only a few hundred yards south of Krithia.

Major-General Sir William Douglas, GOC, 42nd Division, finds a novel observation post, perched on a ladder up a tree, during the Third Battle of Krithia, 4 June 1915
© Imperial War Museum. Q13253

Best deplores the heavy toll of casualties – the Collingwood Battalion in the Royal Naval Division, for instance, was virtually destroyed and had to be disbanded, losing 25 officers and 600 men, out of a total strength of 850, in less than

ten minutes. Two days later, as the fighting subsides, Best con-
fides to his diary his pity for the exhausted survivors, his
anger at the shortage of stretcher-bearers and his scorn for the
staff officers, who are safe in the deep dug-outs, well clear of
the front line.

Saturday June 5

Hear 5th Manchesters were so thinned out that they
could not hold Turks and had to retire on to 1st Turks
trench – and hang on to it by teeth – perfect hell. Went
to Gully, 4th E.Lancs doing well, but heavy losses. 5th
E.Lancs trenches – gone to Y Beach. 10th Manchesters
horridly stuck. I somehow got lost, took left turn instead
of right and encounter once more Dr Maloney. All along
trench, am stepping over dead bodies. Some men shot

Lieut-Colonel H.G. Parker, O.C. 1/1 East Lancashire Field
Ambulance, 42nd Division, dresses a Turkish prisoner's wounds at the
Advanced Dressing Station at Clapham Junction
© Imperial War Museum. Q13258

clean through heart or head, looked quite natural and peaceful, except for yellow-green hue of skin. Most with looks of agony or horror on their faces – if faces were not blown away – nearly all mangled in ghastly fashion.

Outside trenches, fields and open ground littered with dead and some I fear not dead – but sheer suicide to try to get them in. Poor Hornby not found. He wrote a pathetic note to Dr Henry and doctor with orderly were hit trying to reach him. Found some of his belongings. Fear the worst. In some places one has to tread on corpses. In middle of a heap of bodies, one moves. It is the most gruesome ghastly experience I can imagine. Two armoured cars are stuck out between Turkish trenches.[1] Also a big drum with a hole in it. Two German officers, one dead – one badly wounded, but quite conscious and very surly.

Our poor boys behaved like heroes, but are sadly cut up. No clear orders. Told to make for unidentified objective. They went over trench after trench till they had a mere handful of men left and could get no further. Faced by a mass of Turks, they had to retire, losing nearly everybody. Heaps of mementoes, but one had not heart to take them away.

Blood, flies and smell – I shall never forget it. As one crawled along the trench, hands and legs of the dead hanging over the edge would strike one's face. Here and there a familiar face, cold in death. Heartbreaking work. One group of 4th E.Lancs, some very badly wounded, have been lying out for a day or two. To avoid losing all hope they formed themselves into Darwin Debating Society. Wonderful fellows – no funking a charge, no

---

1 None of the eight armoured cars tried as an experiment reached the Turkish trenches before the infantry.

complaining, despite fearful suffering. Some knocked
over just cried a bit and then died. Men full of Hornby's
pluck – cool and calm as on Field Day and yet sensitive. I
wonder where he is now. Those nearly dead greet one
with a ghastly ghost of a smile.

Sunday June 6

Went to Worcesters' firing line. Most of 4th E. Lancs
withdrawn early in morning before Turks made a heavy
and determined attack. Poor old Worcesters nearly done
for. Went round to Manchesters' Dressing Station and
then to their firing line. Stretcher-bearers exhausted.
Frantic appeals coming from the dying, but the bearers
have not one ounce of strength left. In firing line, most
are standing to – waiting for attack, tottering from utter
exhaustion and nerve-wracking experience.

Why don't they get relieved? Plenty of troops in 2nd line
fresh as paint. Those in firing line say pathetically when
Turks come, they cannot lift a bayonet or defend
themselves. The nearest Turks I have been to just retired
when I came, swarming over the parapet. Are we going to
be relieved or shall we go mad?

In morning as I was setting off, reinforcements of
RMLI came up road in close formation – of course
heavily shelled. I did what I could for wounded and went
for stretchers. My first experience of stretcher-bearing
under heavy shrapnel. Went to Field Dressing Station,
buried the dead and saw to wounded – but fascination
of trenches too much for me. Half the killed die from
exposure and exhaustion, loss of blood *and yet I found
7th Ambulance men playing cards and reading penny dreadfuls.*
Why don't they get more bearers? It would pay twice
over.

I wonder how many Staff Officers have been through the mill. Few know what modern trench warfare is like or they would not send men to certain death as they do. Then they court martial them if they use a little common sense and choose best time for taking trenches. My orderly comes back on horse, wounded. He is cursed for riding right up to HQs for fear Turks should see dust and shell Staff Captain, who lies secure in 10ft dugout.

Come back to Clapham Junction passing 4th E.Lancs on way – should have come via trench, but missed it and came across fields and ditches littered with corpses.

I hear sad tale of officer having to shoot friends down to save panic.

Monday June 7

Went up by Clapham Junction and Piccadilly Gully to see 9th Manchesters. Officers are scum of earth. Borrowed plumes, swelled heads – not sure of their position and by adopting airs make themselves absurd. It was disappointing. A comfortable communications trench usually 7ft both sides. Found there 5th and 9th Manchesters and 5th and 8th Fusiliers nearly dead with weariness.

Am in adjacent trench to Turks, hence sniping frequent and also bombs. Just sandbags between. Many little attacks and reverses going on. Jumpy work. Turks crawl up and shoot or drop bombs. Only a few yards separate Turkish trenches and our own. Our bivouac continually moving up. I came back via Shrapnel Valley in which I had held Whit Sunday Services. Heaps of Irish and Scottish troops going up. I hear Scots have only had 6 weeks training.

Some of HQ Staff make a pitiful spectacle. Meet them in dugout: you would fancy they were fire-eaters fearing nought. Walked with one – hardly any shrapnel, yet he would only walk near dugouts. At slightest noise he would bolt inside, whether our own guns or sound of a hammer. Ludicrous expression of agony and anxiety on his face. He sat down in hollow, presumably to light pipe, beads of perspiration on face. How hot he said – yet it was in cool of evening. Later I heard him court martial a poor boy of 15, whose nerve had gone after a week's murderous fighting. It makes one's blood boil.

Tuesday June 8

Walk up to bury dead at 5th E.Lancs. Walk near body of an 8th Lancashire Fusilier who is shot through clean as a whistle. Turks shooting from hip to catch those who approach within 5 feet of trench. Find owner of NT[1] recovered from Turks trench by Sikh. Sit in dugout while a shell about ¼ mile away skids off like a flat stone on a lake, lands just behind and gracefully hops over parapet without going off. Centre too far up hill we are yet told to advance. Why? All a jolly muddle. Men come up to relieve and cannot (or do not wish) to find trench.

Wednesday June 9

'Tis a vagabond life – always on the move. Trying to write a letter home. Shells smothering me in dirt & wind in fine dust. Hearing a 10th Manchester boy wishes to see me, I go to hospital. It is merely a case of nerves.

What ripping chaps the Scots laddies are. Beardmore tells me Kinloch[2] has gone off with a bad tummy. I never thought he would stick it. In such a hurry that he left his

1 New Testament.
2 Another regimental chaplain.

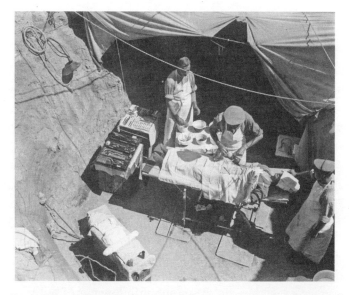

Removing a bullet from a man's arm in the operation dugout of one
of the Field Ambulances of the East Lancashire Division
© Imperial War Museum. Q13316

Communion Set, which I promptly borrowed. Coming
back I encountered some nasty black shells. On arrival
find my servant and various staff men laid out with
shrapnel. We are living in a regular death trap. Our
dugouts face road to Clapham Junction about 100 yards
off. Each vehicle or body of men who come along the
road is peppered with shrapnel as they pass us. A large
proportion are knocked out. It is more tantalising than
sitting in stalls and watching the grimmest tragedy.

*Ten weeks in the Dardanelles had had a considerable effect on
Best. In a letter dated 9 June he considers, with some amusement, how his behaviour on active service would appear in
the home environment:*

Someone will bang a door and you will see me dive headlong under the sofa or a pile of cushions as if they were sandbags. If the wind whistles in the trees I shall order the congregation to take cover while I bob down behind the pulpit ... It is extraordinary how soon one settles down to new surroundings – one gets used to anything in time. Even to dying ... The life is really great and amazingly satisfying. When (DV)[1] I pay my next visit to Sandon I shall have to hire snipers to pot at me all the way from Chelmsford to Sandon and see if I can prevail upon some Terriers to drop a few shells to beguile the monotony of the walk. I wonder if you will be able to spare me a little room in the kitchen garden in which to dig a hole. I shall return a perfect savage and shall have to be broken in gradually, otherwise I shall disgrace myself by dipping my knife into the jam pot and throwing what is left on my plate or in a cup on to the carpet. The sight of a bath or a pair of clean sheets would bowl me over.

Thursday June 10

Brigade reformed and mostly in trenches on right of Piccadilly Valley. Spend morning and afternoon in trenches trying to arrange for Holy Communion, but it proves impossible. Division now equal in number to Brigade. Hear that Manchester Brigade are embarking for Imbros. Go to ascertain its truth and then report to E.Lancs Brigade. It seems to be true. Wish it were Blighty, as the men call England.

It is said all letters and parcels have been left at Alex: Does this mean Division is going there? Typewritten note circulated to show 'Turks on last legs' – this is a childish

1 *Deo Volente* (God Willing).

and mistaken way of trying to keep men's spirits up.
Many men wish for Services to be held to boost their
morale.

Friday June 11

Feeling stupid all morning in trenches – the effect of
quinine. Back 2 p.m. to find my patch in flames –
practically all kit gone. Try to get it in part replaced, but
fail to sleep in fragments of blankets. 4th, 5th and 9th
now in firing line. Lot of firing and French guns busy.
Probably lucky, as if I had been in dug out I might have
suffered as well as my baggage. Look on bright side. Find
grave with Prayer Book marker at '*Lord how long?*' and
Easter Collect.

The Turks were pouring shrapnel over our trenches –
one shell landed in trench near us without going off.
Several covered us with dust. Men say they found
Turkish machine gunner tied to gun. Prisoners say several
German officers have been shot by own men. Find Kirby
at base. He spent 3 weeks with bullet in him, before he
found it coming out of his back.

Saturday June 12

Impossible to hold Services. Even a 5pm Service is
interrupted by urgent demand for fatigue party. Poor
fellows. They went through hideous time Friday and
Saturday last. Ever since our men have been standing by
in firing line with Turks 40 yards off – bomb throwers and
snipers trying to get at them or digging day and night.

No shelter from sun – trenches like cesspits, full of
flies and waste matter with dead bodies half-buried below
them. Unburied putrefying corpses all round, while
survivors are half dead with fatigue and unable to resist

disease. Lot of dysentery and cases of fever. Only pastime
is afforded by crack shots on each side trying to pot each
other and signalling misses with shovels. Needless to say,
neither side signals hits. Bathe in afternoon. Rather
stormy. To 4th E. Lancs HQ in evening to get batman.
Return with Drummer Craston. Very handy chap who had
been a boy scout at Preston. Some narrow escapes from
high explosives ...

Sunday June 13

Held a few short services in trenches with 5th E. Lancs.
My new batman Craston rigged up roof for dugout. He
promises very well. Manchester Brigade to embark, while
sea is calm. Shall we follow and if so, where to? Shall we
soon return and go to England? First quiet Sunday. Many
men want CEMS meetings. I find they mean Holy
Communion. They appreciate this above all other
services. Most of troops now seem to be provided with
respirators. We need rest. Roads and communication
trenches have to be made by all who are not actually in
the firing line.

In evening amongst 10th Manchesters. Had short
evening prayers in various parts of the trenches. Nearly
all knelt most reverently and added an Amen which
clearly came from their hearts. Some even in face of death
feel uncomfortable about professing themselves Christian
and said gruffly 'If you like'. But they all said thank you
and good night very warmly. One lad sat on a Turk's
corpse and deemed it a soft cushion.

Monday June 14

Up 6 a.m. Craston not told and worried he had not got me
tea. Get to Beach for 7.15 HC with Beardmore. Brekker

with 89th Field Ambulance. Very kindly lot. Complain of amount of sickness amongst E. Lancs on arrival. Explain it is due to lack of medical inspection on leaving England and on leaving Egypt. Mattins at 9. Evensong at 7 very nice but my criticism is that we are here to minister to our men, not to ourselves. Some of the regimental chaplains seem to lie in tents most of the day reading, and criticising those who go among troops. Attended a footling meeting.

Came back with RND chaplains and Clowes gives me bottle of port for HC. We pass fort guns which our naval guns knocked out. Lyddite accompanies our walk home. Signallers see me on way back and invite me to a birthday luncheon party. They are very refined, interesting lot. Return to find my dugout wrecked by shell. Water, fire and earthquake. I have been pretty fortunate. Ian Hamilton[1] is now on Peninsula. He is said to have sent one general home in disgrace because he criticised. Ian will have to look to his laurels methinks.

Tuesday June 15

Turks hurl round coalboxes[2] and shrapnel very generously. Go up to trenches with 10th Officers. Colonel Rye is depressed – feels responsible for the lives of his men. Bathe in afternoon with Craston – sea very rough. Coalboxes cast fragments several hundred yards and look like a mud fountain. Several lads, e.g. Driver Dean of 10th Manchesters, say how much they appreciate short family prayers in trenches. I wish I could get round to all. I can only take about 10 at a time and there are thousands

1 General Sir Ian Hamilton was Allied Commander-in-Chief of Mediterranean Expeditionary Force (MEF).
2 Shell bursts, usually from a heavy gun, emitting clouds of black smoke.

out there. They feel their leaders are lacking in sympathy. A lad is sent to do the impossible. He died in the heroic attempt *'Never mind,'* say red tabs,[1] *'we can get plenty more at 1/- a day.*[2] *But do look after the horses ...'*

Wednesday June 16

To Field Ambulance. Mostly sick cases now. Used to suspect Irishman's kind of stories, but believe the Sergeant-Major now. All the way down Gully shells followed me, but happily fell just short each time. Lunch – but the flies follow food into the mouth. No wonder Beelzebub was considered chief of devils. The refuse and corpses lying about increase the numbers.

Lieutenant Webster is sensitive and imaginative. Imagination is a curse out here. Luckily I am dense and unimaginative. What terrors men such as he go through. Tremble like a leaf when shells fall near. *'Mon Dieu – shall I ever come through alive?'* he writes.[3] Strange that such thoughts never occur to me. Yet it is not religion, I fear, which gives me such confidence, but inability to appreciate the danger.

Thursday June 17

Go to E.Lancs RE near French batteries. Lyddite falling like crash of falling warehouse. Arrange for Communion at 7 a.m. tomorrow in dugout. Call in to see Moreland established in comfort and luxury in our old Brigadier's apartment. He has a tale of some stupendous muddle on

1 Senior British officers.
2 The daily wages of a private soldier at this time amounted to one shilling or about 5p in today's decimal money, with present-day purchasing power of less than £1 ...
3 I.e. in a letter home.

the Canal and that honours are conferred not so much by
merit as by influence. Hence none in Army dare speak his
mind.

Going to bathe in the afternoon I am joined by Clauss
and other part of 5th Battery. Craston makes dugout
behind mine – much more convenient. Letters from
home and Joyce. Turks do a miniature bombardment
round Clapham Junction.

Friday June 18

The men are played out and need rest before another
such hideous attack. But where are reinforcements? We
hear of hosts of troops at Alex and Lemnos, but the
gallant little band here struggle on unsupported and
unrelieved – firing line or fatigue duties day and night.
Their numbers decreasing fast daily. The Turks are first
rate marksmen and so are German gunners. Put up a cap
with a mess tin inside. Directly it appears above the
parapet it is drilled through. Put up a periscope – it was
shattered. Their trenches are very ably designed and very
ably constructed with loopholes for firing – virtually safe
and impossible to locate. Only by bayonet can we drive
them back and prove ourselves superior and then our lads
suffer so terribly.

Go to left section of 5th Battery. Have tea with
condensed milk – glorious. Burial service over two of
their men. They are expected to have to run a gun up to
firing line in the dark before next bombardment. It will
be a very dangerous job. Go on to REs. Lyddite falling
with appalling crash and roar for they are in midst of
French batteries – which Asiatic-based guns are trying to
knock out. No service possible. Big fusillade in trenches.
Clapham Junction is hot with bullets – air sings with
them as I go back. Our cross-firing cover seems no use.

The Turks have rifles on tripods trained on the loopholes of each. When anything appears, they put a bullet through it at once.

Saturday June 19

Up early to trenches. Another terrible bungle. 9th Manchesters detailed to take trench just in front. They take it without much difficulty. They attempt another trench – find overwhelming numbers of Turks and retreat in confusion – not to trench just taken, but to old firing line and there spread panic of strong Turkish attack which was partially true. (Turks planned attack for the same time). They rushed down the communication trench, sending up the 4th and 5th E. Lancs.

Good old 4th E. Lancs go up and hold the line. '*Where are you going?*' I answer – '*To join my company.*' 4th and 5th go up and find Turks. With help of Worcesters they regain all, except about 30 yards. The 9th E. Lancs then complain that 4th have lost them trench. In reality they saved the situation. They were only meant to be in reserve. 9th Officers haggling as to who should lead. Major Cairns gets out and calls on men to follow. Only a few men support him. 9th throw down arms. Cairns gets hit. I spend day from 8 am to 8 pm without food, burying dead at side of trench or even in any dip where bullets were not very thick.

Sunday June 20

Most of E.Lancs Brigade in reserve. I wasted much time finding 88th Brigade HQ to tell them where the body of Staff Captain Ussher was and trying to identify whom I had buried. Chatted to men but could hold no proper service. In the evening went to try to find some more

Three Army chaplains (Church of England, Roman Catholic and
Presbyterian) attend the burial of four British soldiers
© Imperial War Museum. Q13390

bodies, but was lost and got into some very hot places. It
was a queer experience knowing that some Scots on
previous night had got lost in the same area. Some got
into Turks trench by mistake. Also I had been warned by
Scots Colonel not to go alone, but having been longer
than him on Peninsula, I scorned his advice. I arrived
back safe, with but one mishap, yet that a serious
calamity. I lost my best comrade – a good old Loewe pipe,
through a hole in my pocket.

More bigwig absurdities. Staff Officer sent to Alex, to
complain, because 'grub was not suitable for divisional
staff.' Better if he went into trenches and found out the
heroic self-sacrifice of the little Tommies. A Tommy must
have neither mind nor feeling – and be satisfied with 1/-
per diem.

OC 4th E.Lancs makes dog tired men dig trenches

deeper, instead of sleeping, so that he forsooth might not lose his precious life. Yet he never leaves dugout except in lull between fighting. He lies in bed – he was tired of sitting on his bum, while his men in firing line are in deadly combat with Turks. In his dugout right down Peninsula away from the action, he would not have 3 men stand up lest they should draw fire. He is sure to receive D.S.O. '*I must have my breakfast at 8 a.m. – shell or no shell.*' Brave fellow ...

Monday June 21

Aeroplane duel overhead. But the Taube[1] too quick for our machines. Later our planes got bombs and are supposed to have damaged Taube. Poor chap in 4th E. Lancs lost brother. Came broken hearted to ask me to bury him. On Saturday I asked the boy to identify the corpse being dragged down the trench on an oil sheet. He did not reply. I asked second time sharply. 'My brother', he managed to sob out. I felt a beast. Got back to outer dressing station – more wounded and dead.

The French seem to be having a terrific engagement and bullets are raining in the gully – hence casualties. Arranged for HC with 5th Battery section. Lunch with Major – he says French have captured 700 yards of 2 trenches. If they have captured left portions of trenches and been enfiladed out – now they are trying to get right hand portion. Later we hear they have taken three whole trenches. Turks casualties 8,000, 3,000 prisoners, French losses 3,000. Probably all exaggerated. Still they have no doubt made progress. Went off then to see 6th Battery

---

1 The Taube, a monoplane with a Mercedes-Benz engine and a top speed of 70 mph, was Germany's principal military aircraft at this time. It was used to bomb Paris and later was used widely for reconnaissance.

who are with Australian Battery. They have worn out
their old guns. They tell gruesome tales of French being
blown to pieces. Certainly Turks are putting horrid bits of
stuff among them on right ridge.

Australian cook offers to make me a new pipe. Gladly
accept. Back to 5th Battery. No service as had to send gun
up immediately to enfilade trench in front of Naval and
Indian Brigades. Men think that they become only an
isolated unit as guns almost done for and they are to be
sacrificed in a very hazardous experiment. Australians
love gamble – higher the stakes the better – even life
itself. Terriers more sober – only sense of duty will
motivate them and then they hesitate to put in bayonet.

Tuesday June 22

Off to bathe. Sea like mill pond. Back to bury three men
at RAMC – move headquarters back a bit. I find nice
place for self and servant in Intermediate Dressing
Station on other side of road. Gully heavily shelled.
Brigade brought down and Jocks go up to replace them in
daylight – more madness – lose a lot more men
unnecessarily. Play cricket of sorts in between attending
to wounded and burials. Callous? No! – only way to
prevent melancholia. Game abandoned – shrapnel
stopped play. Go up to Clapham Junction to bury a poor
fellow – by moonlight. Dead stillness on all sides.

Wednesday June 23

Write home and send letters re wounded and dead to
relatives. Visit from Canon Hitchens who relieved me at
Heliopolis, while I was at Suez. He has now replaced
Kinloch. Visit Senior Chaplain who came to Advanced
Base for a few hours. All chaplains are now independent.

No Senior Divisional Chaplains. Use own discretion. He approves of going into firing line when it seems advisable.

A 5th E. Lancs soldier is so fed up he deliberately stands up above parapet until hit. Others apathetic from utter weariness. Have a very nice service with 4th E. Lancs stores. Lt Bentz badly hit near my dugout. Grand mail – 12 letters, 4 newspapers, most of them very old. Before we light a match, we collect a number of smokers, to minimise risk of being spotted.

In trenches the Scotties kept me at the double, assuring me that snipers had so many places marked. It was a scouts double doubled up – '*keep your head down mon, there's a laddie just been hit here in the foot*'. Manchesters going up to the trenches again. Douglas[1] promises them good news in three days. They tell story of a major celebrating the return home of the survivors. '*Your fame has gone out into all the world and now let me in conclusion have the honour of shaking hands with both of you.*'

Thursday June 24

Poor old 4th. Dog tired, they are set to dig alternative route to Clapham Junction. They start and six are knocked out, including an Everton footballer killed. Go to 6th Battery. Australian artillery cook has failed to make pipe, wood is too green and cracks. Come back and bury soldiers from 4th E. Lancs. Go and see if I can arrange service for 10th Manchesters. As we walk, shrapnel whizzes by and bursts a few yards off.

Turks have seen Fusiliers going down to embark, and shelled them as they were picking up kit at stores which are in 10th Manchesters lines. One poor little fellow has

1 Major-General Douglas, divisional commander of the 42nd East Lancashire Division.

his back blown off. As he is being carried off he says '*see that Lt Stones gets his tea*'. He dies soon after in awful agony. Service impossible. Chat with 10th Machine Gunners in evening.

Friday June 25

See the E.Lancs in Australian trenches in morning. What a world of difference it would make if our Staff officers (as Aussie Generals do) would go into trenches. As it is, when Captain Ussher was killed, they said '*it serves the damned fool right.*'

Major Browning curses army methods. Red Tabs are sleeping partners. They cannot grasp situation from dugout maps. They must understand and study men more. They don't realise what modern warfare is like and what human nature can stand. Terriers are boys or married men and neither makes ideal soldier. New tactics: not to take Achi Baba direct, but work round left shoulder and join Australians. We shall have to be quick. In August sea is too rough to embark or disembark troops and in September the part of Peninsula we hold becomes a swamp.

If business was carried on like this war, it would go bust. Orders coming in in profusion and as often countermanded. Order, counter-order, disorder. There is no definite plan – no master mind, e.g. 5th Battery send up gun, lose 5 men and come back again having achieved nothing. So 5th E.Lancs were sent down out of the line to rest and ordered to return within a few hours. So it goes on – wasting energy and lives.

Saturday June 26

Pick up bomb-throwing apparatus in trenches. Went up to Australian lines. Men looking black. It is very hard to go

amongst them just now. A few are still cheery –
wonderful, unselfish fellows. Went to W Beach in
afternoon. Had tea and supper at Chaplains Mess. My!
they do have some comforts there. Have a bathe and
prepare an address for Sunday.

Going back met Moreland who tells me 9th and 10th
Manchesters are embarking. I rush back thinking
Brigade is off, but find only 10th Manchesters are going.
Call at 8th Fusiliers to make final arrangements for
service and find 7th and 8th are back in firing line. Poor
beggars. They were just ready to embark. A lieutenant
is full of the simple piety of the men. Nobody jeers
when fellows say their prayers in trenches. Is it '*when
the devil was sick, the devil a monk would be*?'[1] I hope and
believe not, but the men will be purified as through fire.
Meet Manchester Brigade coming out of the trenches,
but *very next morning* they go back. Usual mad waste
of energy.

Then there's the Staff officer who cuts all telephone
wires which hit his head saying he had given orders *they
should be 8 feet above ground*. The men have not sufficient
posts or stakes. Also how many lives might be lost by his
childish temper?

Sunday June 27

Go to 10th Manchesters for Holy Communion and find
them departed and 8th now in their place. They were just
going up again to firing line. Not keen but ready. One of
them had some letters for me – lucky find. Chat with men
from 4th E.Lancs. Most of the best have gone. Arrange to

---

1 The full version of this proverb, coined by Peter Motteux, is: When the Devil was
sick, the devil a monk would be. When the Devil got well, the devil a monk was
he.

have a service at 8.30 by moonlight. 5th Adjutant says
service impossible. Service is at Intermediate Dressing
Station 7.30 – light just lasted. Stretcher cases passing
through all the time. Unfortunately moon did not rise as it
should, so we had to [make] do with the two flickering
candles in ambulance dug out. About 30 present. Spoke
about Epistle for day. Men very anxious for another
service. Expecting bombardment on left to straighten up
line, where poor Indians got hung up on barbed wire and
cut to pieces by machine gun fire.

Monday June 28

Bombardment on left flank. Desultory fire by a few land
and ship guns gradually works up. As there is practically
no wind the smoke hangs about and soon nothing can be
seen of left shoulder of Achi Baba or Krithia. About noon
shell fire dies out and rattle of musketry announces
attack. After a while the guns resume. As our men seem
quiet, I go over to Pink Farm. The Scotch laddies very
depressed. Their battalion wiped out. By this time I am
used to reports of wounded and take them '*cum grana
salis*', – but it is quite probable they have lost about half.
Most of the casualties brought down today seem only
slightly wounded.

The Lowland Field Ambulance just arrived on shore as
bombardment started. Rather rough on them and yet they
have a very safe mule trench along which to work. I go up
this mule trench and now have completed the 5 different
routes to trenches. I gather that Indian Brigade took 6
trenches, but were driven back to 5th. Turks set fire to
gorse.

Scottish Rifles took 2 trenches – were driven out –
hence 2nd bombardment – then retook them – expecting
strong counter attack.

When I get back a sudden burst of rifle fire rings out, not counter attack. Scots Rifles casualties 2,000: 3 out of every 4 men and colonel and general killed.[1] Some say they were too keen – others that they fled in disorder. Turks and selves both pour shells on left flank and again everything is lost in smoke, white puffs of shrapnel and black columns of Lyddite can occasionally be distinguished.

Ghastly to think of the poor fellows I have just left being in midst of it. Men coming back from advance observation post say our troops are retiring in disorder (but we hear next day they held the 2 trenches successfully). Corporal Best comes to ask about Holy Communion. I go up and hold it at 8.30 – exciting walk there and back, though only a few hundred yards made worse by the fact that in the din one heard neither bullet nor shrapnel and only saw earth spluttering up at one's feet.

At 8.30 things were quietening down and about 30 came to service. Most of them officers except those on staff who have never been in danger. (Their nerves must be in a terrible state for they sit in secure places all day). I got through most of the service by heart, but after communicating, I had to hold candle in one hand and book in other. Used a dixie for altar. However unecclesiastical the surroundings, irreverence is absolutely unknown here. Even a hotly worded altercation between mule drivers did not disturb us though some of our men were kneeling right out across gully along which drivers passed. I had to cast about and managed to reach all. They were too packed to move.

---

1 On 29 June, the fighting strength of the 8th Scottish Rifles was down to 3 officers and 70 soldiers. This wholesale slaughter helps to keep modern-day casualties in perspective.

At 11 p.m. an aeroplane flies over, probably a Taube locating batteries and seeing effect of Asiatic shells. Another about 4 a.m, just before dawn. The full moon should help him observe, but not allow him to be observed. Beggar did his work well. One battery near Pink Farm had 3 guns knocked out. L Battery near Clapham Junction said to be wiped out ...

Tuesday June 29

Heat is terrific, but fortunately a breeze springs up about 10 am. But only by climbing into a tree can I get shade, breeze and escape flies. I simply had to risk shrapnel. Go to 4th E.Lancs stores. Taube (surely in form more like hawk than dove) circles overhead. She drops a bomb or two and hits one Scottie. Then she sails off and our own plane slowly and laboriously comes pip-pipping up. Only the French plane seems to approach anywhere near the Taube in speed and agility. They are supposed to have 3 aeroplanes now. Again I suppose we have to thank the Taube.

The Asiatic guns poured a quantity of lyddite into us. I used to think artillery had a soft job on and so they did until yesterday. A battery about 800 yards from us had J J[1] just in front and just behind. Must have done some damage and yet she continued to fire. You could just see the spurts of flame through heavy black smoke. Our guns have been busy since 5 p.m. while poor crows with doleful caws fly about – frogs and grasshoppers chirping merrily. At dusk I expected the guns to stop – but no, they still continue. There must be something important

1 A Jack Johnson was a type of German shell which burst, emitting black smoke. It was named after the champion boxer who was the first black winner of the World Heavyweight title in 1908.

doing, or our guns would never continue to give away the position with lyddite dropping all round.

I wonder – but perhaps I had better wonder inside my dugout. A big J J has just buzzed over my head and dropped a few yards beyond me making a hole big enough for my horse if only I had not lost it. It was a narrow escape. I wonder if a party is being landed between Indian Brigade and Gaba Tepe. I can see flashes of guns and no report – must be distant gunboats. Also cannot see where our battery shells are dropping – probably over left flank, for that was where several batteries have been recently registering target.

Now I can see no more. We are enveloped in lyddite smoke and so go to sleep.

4.30 am Awake and hear guns still busy, this time on extreme right. I hear French have advanced without difficulty to '5 Trees' on ridge. Our firing line could see Turks coming on in force and then were mowed down by shell and bolt for it. Many prisoners said to be taken. Welcome sound of ships guns again.

Wednesday June 30

The Turks yesterday dropped papers saying our Navy had deserted and left us to our fate – but that, if we would surrender, we should be fairly treated and that they had heaps of food. We had almost begun to think it true. We could see big shells, apparently naval, falling, but could not hear guns. Heavy bombardment by land guns in morning on right and by naval guns from mouth of straits in afternoon.

At 3 pm they are firing about once a second. I cannot see where they all are dropping, either Asiatic side or beyond ridge on right. Went to left section of 5th Battery.

They got gun up and back without loss and did good work infiltrating Turks trenches for Gurkhas. To left section in afternoon. They want a service. Then to 5th E. Lancs Parade of new draft. They look weak sickly lot – perhaps only when standing alongside our tanned old stagers. But doctor is fed up and says most of them are useless.

A Turk caught near our bivouac with Scottish rifle tunic and web equipment. How did he get those? He may have come through to Scots unnoticed. Have tea with Webster, 8th Manchesters, then on to 5th Manchesters in firing line on left of Nullah. Bad unsafe trench but 5th are improving it. Bombs thrown in by Turks while I am there. I have supper, soup, mutton and cocoa with Colonel and then at 9.30 have perilous walk home.

A Turkish sniper photographed immediately after capture, and while he was being brought in under guard. The Turk was ingeniously screened by a Jack-in-the-Green arrangement of foliage attached to his clothing
© Imperial War Museum. Q13392

It was one of the most weird and creepy experiences I have yet had. Pitch dark. I went through trench after trench feeling for someone to direct me. Then all at once halt! would ring out and I would pull up sharp with bayonet a few inches off. At intervals a flare would go up dazzling one's eyes which, with the guns, make a fair imitation of thunder and lightning.

Then, as if annoyed at this mimicry, nature produced a real thunderstorm. At last I got out of the trenches and could stand upright again – for bullets had been whistling over trenches and cracking into parapets. The Gully was not much better. It was alive with bullets. Here and there a dim light shone from a dugout, but I was the only traveller stumbling along, sometimes in stream, sometimes running into cliff or falling over boulders. Now and again waiting for flare or lightning flash to guide me. I wished I had not been such a fool as to stay so late in firing line.

At last I got to Clapham Junction and found ration carts going back. How delightful was company of Indian drivers. One cart stuck in ditch. I lent a hand and helped get it out. Got back and saw curious blue flares going up by W and X Beach. What did it mean? Hear that 3 tents of wounded at W were hit by lyddite. When will they knock out Asiatic guns? It is no use wasting shells on them – so well hidden and so easily repaired. Only demolition party can permanently wipe them out.

Thursday July 1

Though feeling a bit thick in head, like a fool I got a couple of No. 9 from M.O. with result that I hardly dare stir a foot. Tried to go to trenches, but got stuck in small ravine where I found a casualty – dead otter – beautiful animal. The 2nd Field Ambulance replaced by 1st. I miss

Humpey their pet monkey very much. Very affectionate and amusing.

Very quiet day. Just average toll of dead and wounded passing through. I hear Australian Light Horse took part in left flank advance. Our boys still think they are going home. Will they be relieved or reinforced till all the old originals have been knocked out? Had quite a dinner – steak and onions, tea with milk and jam pudding followed by rum liqueur. Hope I shall not be so bad as after mulberry dish. I have my eye on some vineyards – grapes should be ripe in 6 weeks or so.

9th Manchester men say they see nothing of Padre W and that he ignores wounded without saying word of cheer. Felt up to now an intruder, but will see more of men in future. Hear at night they are off to the trenches.

In 1914, First Lord of the Admiralty Winston Churchill formed the Royal Naval Division from naval personnel who were not required on warships. At the end of August, when the crisis of the war of movement was at its height, the BEF was fully extended and the desperate shortfall of trained officers and men in the Regular Army became all too clear. The first assignment of the Royal Naval Division – sometimes known as Winston's Little Army – was to be sent to bolster the defence of Antwerp, which they were unable to save.

The Royal Naval Division (RND) was sent to Gallipoli in 1915 and suffered massive casualties in May and June. Several of the battalions in the RND were named after distinguished admirals such as Anson, Collingwood, Drake, Hawke and Hood, in order to maintain their naval origins while they were serving alongside the Army. Those battalions made up from the Royal Marines carried the names of their home depot, such as Chatham, Deal, Plymouth, etc.

Best's close friend, Tucker, was in Collingwood Battalion, which suffered so severely at the hands of the Turks that it was broken up and the survivors distributed to the other bat-talions. The heroic exploits of the RND are legion: the records show that, between 1914 and 1918, 10,200 of these gallant naval soldiers were killed in action.

Friday July 2

Write home comparing my present existence with that of a rabbit, and thinking of my shooting rabbits with Louis Tucker,[1] when letter reaches me from home saying that he had fallen on June 4 with the Collingwood Battalion. Spent afternoon making enquiries for details. Find Dundas[2] and Watts, the only two officers left, but fail to find 4 Platoon Company which was Tucker's Company. They were split up among Anson, Hood and Howe. His familiar friends called him Tommy. How dense I am getting. It was only four hours later I recalled the nursery rhyme. He was a 'good boy'. Lt. Dundas specially selected him and Lt Watts[3] said he was quiet with quaint humour but very friendly. He fell when main body retired, after failing to hold trench. He was with digging party behind and hit in the head while retiring with them.

---

1 Sub-Lt. Louis Tucker was a popular and very capable young officer who had received his commission in the Royal Naval Division just four months previously. He was killed during the 3rd Battle of Krithia along with 24 other Collingwood officers.

2 Lt. Kenneth Dundas, RNVR, survived the first wave of landings on Gallipoli – and was transferred to Anson Battalion when Collingwood was broken up. Anson was the only RND Battalion to take part in the second wave of landings at Suvla Bay in August – and Dundas was killed there by a shell, when landing with his men on 7 August.

3 Sub-Lt. Arthur Watts was wounded on 4 June, carrying ammunition to men at the Front. Three men were assisting him. Of these, two were killed outright and the third died of his wounds a few days later. His brother, Sub-Lt. John Watts, was the senior surviving officer in Collingwood in the carnage on 4 June and he was then transferred to Hood Battalion. This was the battalion in which Rupert Brooke served before dying from septicaemia on a hospital ship, near the island of Skyros.

RND say the French are very plucky and cool. Instead of going to reserve via common trench, they get out and stroll quietly across open ground. Retirement their method of fighting. Poor Watts just heard that brother had lost a leg. He therefore was more or less sole support and is trying to get transfer to ASC, but OC won't forward application. Watts is the only old Collingwood officer left. To Moreland for supper. Grand feed, and what is better – borrowed a little literature.

Saturday July 3

Went to visit our Brigade in Eski, Australian and Redoubt lines. Then to RND firing line to find remainder of Tucker's command. No luck, but explored Oxford Street, Regent Street and Piccadilly Circus. They are wonderful mule trenches. The men always ragging me about optimism. *'Got yer ship painted yet? A rowing boat? It'll take all that's left of us home.'* New Brigade of Jocks arriving – most in kilts. They look a sturdy, cheerful lot and religious too. It troubled them much that the Sabbath was not observed here. Last batch said they never came to fight – but to dig and to guard communication lines. We have not got any – a few strides and you are in the firing line, if Mr Turk does not get you first. This last lot is ready to fight. *'Only take yon wee hillock – we'll soon do that'*. I hope so.

Sunday July 4

Wet night. For some time tried to keep out rain, but saw I should be kept awake at night if I tried – so gave up – rolled myself in blanket to keep warm and slept quite well. Only real services I could hold were at 2nd Field Dressing Stations. Ambulance men and Headquarters Staff at Intermediate, 4 E/Lancs and Field Ambulance at

Clapham Junction. Transport sunk. Big explosion on right flank – probably a French magazine blown up. I spoke of brotherhood in times of hardship and danger. Saw General Prendergast[1] about getting bodies buried during service – not just thrown into a hole. He was very sympathetic. It means much to those at home.

Monday July 5

At 3 a.m. Turks counter-attacked on left and at 5 a.m. on right. Dublin Fusiliers wounded said they let them advance in close order within a few yards and then fairly wiped them out with shrapnel, machine gun and rifle fire. On right I hear Turks broke through two lines but very few got back alive. Note from Major Browning[2] to say Lt Bury had been killed by shrapnel in mule trench. Only a boy, very good keen officer. Major badly cut up about it. Turks are giving it to us hot with shrapnel and lyddite. Also Taube drops a bomb near dressing station.

Visit 5th E.Lancs Regiment. Major as usual pessimistic, but more sympathetic with infantry. General Douglas has been grossly slighted, he says, and in turn will courtmartial the next officer who makes a mistake. Scowcroft to go back to Egypt. Lord Rochdale has gone home on leave (sic).[3] Make arrangements for burial at

---

1 Brigadier-General D.G. Prendergast (1861–1938). At the outset of the campaign, he commanded the East Lancashire Brigade (Gibbon, p.18), then later 126th Infantry Brigade. Previously he had been attached to the Egyptian Army and served in the South African War.

2 Major John Browning, DSO, commanded the 5th Lancashire Battery, Royal Field Artillery.

3 Lt.-Col. Lord Rochdale, had served in the South African War before becoming MP for the Heywood Division in Lancashire from 1895 to 1906. At Gallipoli, he commanded the 6th Battalion Lancashire Fusiliers and, as temporary brigadier, the 126th and 127th Brigades of the 42nd Division. Best is clearly unimpressed that Rochdale should choose to go on leave at such a critical time in the campaign.

8 p.m. Major dubious that men are fundamentally good. Hypocrisy, not religion, is what we see here. Men live for ease and pleasure – not work and duty. No high ideals. Spoilt by weak masters – they are apt to spend last 1/- at footer match while family starve. Don't value money because it is so easily come by.

Ride to beach and return Beardmore's stole. Borrow purple stole from Kirby and race over to 5th in quarter of an hour. Most of Battalion men and officers at the service. Discuss afterwards treatment of our division. Col Birtwistle very jealous for honour of E. Lancs. I feel that, if E.Lancs fail, it is due to lack of medical examination – e.g. in the new draft of 50 for 5th E. Lancs, only 3 passed as fit. Cut out boys and medically unfit and there is hardly any division left. If boys could see home again, they would fight with new heart. Egypt training no use for this kind of warfare – also leaves them neither developed nor fit, but crocked and played out. Found a few letters at Cox's Brigade Headquarters. Also hear some are at Base Brigade HQ. Get lost in Clapham Gully on the way back.

Tuesday July 6

Wish we had French artillery and their amount of ammunition. Wonderful support to infantry – we use rifles ... For French it is costly in shells, for us in men. Our fellows giving life blood for 1/1 a day – living in mud on bully beef etc. At home we hear of men with £4 – £7 a week (which these men used to earn and have sacrificed) haggling for more – yet they have home comforts. It makes one's blood boil – they are brutal murderers – should be hung on same rope as Hun. If ammunition were plentiful and reinforcements too – we should get Turks on the run and finish off this business in no time. As it is, we have to stop. Men and ammunition are exhausted when Turks driven out of last trench and then given time to dig new trenches. I feel horribly rheumaticky, could not sleep for dull ache. Go for swim and feel much better. The only way to keep fit seems to be to drink freely and sweat freely. We are all becoming lousy – write home for underclothing and Keating's.[1]

Wednesday July 7

The 6th E. Lancs arrive. I meet Sgt Major Ferguson, brother of SM of the 4th & 5th. Down to beach to get communion wine and stole. Turks keep up a continuous series of shells on beach and sea and clearing station. The bathers soon hopped it.

Irish priest down there who has just come over for the Munsters. How good to be RC. They have only to speak the word and it is done. He took me back in his 'jolting' car as he called it. Passing a broken bag of potatoes the boy got out and helped himself – '*don't forget the best for padre, laddie, or you don't get absolution*' – half comic, half serious. He is the typical Irish priest – sleek, flabby, corpulent with face piggy in features and absolutely characterless. Yet far nicer than the gaunt, long-faced wolfish one in our Division who rules his flock by fear. One lad very fed up. '*Well, what's your job?*' '*Dunno – on guard over stream – to see it don't run back'ards, I suppose.*'

Buried Baylis whose body was found near latrine sap he was making.

Thursday July 8

In trenches, 4th E. Lancs in firing line, 5th in support. Word passed that Brigadier is coming along. Men fuss

1 Keating's Insecticide Powder.

about and pretend to be busy – but general evidently got stuck somewhere. The man with periscope arm begins to ache. *'Tell your general to buck up. I can't wait dinner for 'im no longer.'* Eventually he comes and lo! and behold he is preceded by O.C. We try to stand up and look smart, but this is too much. We collapse in mock amazement. This is the first time I have seen him out of his dugout.

Down to beach to try to discover parcels, etc. No luck. Frightfully dirty. Go to 4th E.Lancs stores to take a service 7.30. A Welsh laddie from 29th Div Ammunition Column comes over, an interesting, clever lad. So different from the hopelessly stolid, illiterate, unimaginative Lancashires. He thought it would have been better to have landed other side of Achi Baba and driven Turks into sea – and so cut off their provisions. Promise to get him a New Testament. Tells of Turks being sent out of trenches line after line of them tied together with ropes – then dragged back together.

Lancs Fusilier sentry nearly put me out on way back. I dare say I did look a bit like a Turk in dark woolley and handkerchief for head gear, collarless, dishevelled, dirty and very brown.

Friday July 9

Over to 5th Battery to meet Col. Birtwistle. He has used up nearly all his Brigade guns and hears that his Battalion will shortly be relieved.

We got to Observation Station. Things very quiet. A lot of white flag work – armistice in progress, approved to bury Turkish dead, but it is rumoured that 2,000 Turks who are more or less cornered and yet an awful nuisance to us, desire to give themselves up.

Men of the 1st Australian Division in charge of a working
party of Turkish prisoners at Anzac
© Imperial War Museum. Q13829

The Gully is full of Kitchener's Army. At King's Own[1]
HQ, I find a boy from Seymour Meads. He tells me that
there are lots of Lytham lads. We then took a so-called
short cut to forward gun position. 6th E. Lancs were
coming the other way. A strong wind was blowing – sun
blazing down in full strength – so we were choked with
dust, it was a most unpleasant cut. By going down into
Park Farm Valley and up a mule trench, we eventually
arrive.

Chat to Lt Cairns and Williams, an Australian
attached to 5th Battalion, then slope off to King's Own.
Find boy from Lytham with Collinson. Like the rest he
is a fine promising soldier. As we chat, an old RF[1]
comes along and tells us of a white flag man just going

1 King's Own Royal Lancaster Regiment. The 6th (Service) Battalion was one of
the first Kitchener units to arrive at Gallipoli.

out to meet Turks Crescent flag. Firing ceases, but not by the Turks. A shell burst right over parapet and yet not a man hit. They treated it as a joke. Some of them, I hear, went out sniping the first night they were in the firing line.

Later I met Challenor who used to be plague of my life – reporter to *Lytham Standard*. He used to be a ghastly individual – lank and pasty – now he is fit for anything. His crowd seem right sort – bigger and stronger than Terriers and more refined. I wish I were with them. Still I don't wish to desert the poor little Terriers.

Went with Col Birtwistle to find position for naval 3 pounder gun which is to knock out enemy's machine guns. Found a rattling good place in a disused trench. Smell of corpses lying around is nauseating – feet, trouser legs with bones and tendons showing at end – a ghastly grinning face with teeth showing and most murderous expression – green mud and clothes and equipment (Turkish) made a perfect nightmare picture. Parapet mostly broken down and snipers busy on it. Also only about 40 yards from Turks. When put in order Williams should do deadly work from it. We could see our own and Turks trenches. Returned and had supper with Colonel Birtwistle. Got back home and found my bed riddled with shrapnel ... Providence is very good to me. This is the 3rd time ...

Saturday July 10

Up Clapham Nullah to arrange places for Sunday services. Major Browning tells me in confidence that 42nd Division are to be given a job on their own – a rather dangerous and difficult one, I gathered. I had hoped we should get home without any further big losses. If we are to escape winter campaign, for which troops from Egypt seem unfitted, we shall have to leave in about 7 or 8 weeks. Perhaps this will be last show. May it bring honour and not disgrace to us. Yet I fear – the men are spent – their courage is at low ebb and nearly all the trusted officers gone. Why have 7th and 8th Lancashire Fusiliers and 5th E.Lancs left?

Afternoon went up Little Nullah running left of Clapham Valley at top of ridge to Eski line. Found a soldier drawing water at White House, who was hit in knee by shrapnel or sniper. Leg broken. They were trying to drag him along. I got stretcher from Clapham Junction. Turks chuck some shrapnel about. General Prendergast goes to Little W and they have high words. E. Lancs Brigade not given fair chance – given dirty job when exhausted: all censure, no praise. Gained no kudos for work done in conjunction with Regulars there. As good as other Brigades. Little W said they were useless – so General P. has been gazetted out. Note from HQ saying only 5th E Lancs were off. But movements of troops makes all arrangements for Sunday out of gear. Go over to 5th Battery to get corkscrew and inform about early service.

Sunday July 11

7 a.m. Holy Communion. Well attended by RAMC in their dressing station dugout. Then I went to 4th E. Lancs in Australian lines. Arrange for Evening Service 9 p.m. in a little hollow at side of Nullah. Went through 9th firing line and met men from 10 Manchesters coming into reserve lines on my way back.

Afternoon down to 4th E. Lancs stores. Held the Service and had a grumble about their language. I talked very straight saying that I do not object to barrack-room language in itself, but to the mental cesspit it implied and in part produced. Instead of being offended, they asked me to come again as soon as possible.

Met Dr Henry just back and highly delighted to be in it again. He fears poor Hornby has gone under. Troops moving and therefore shrapnel all over Peninsula. Met General Prendergast with new brigadier – an inoffensive sort of individual (I heard later that he received orders to return to Mudros and a real live Lord is to take his place). General P speaks of my ingenious Sunday arrangements and wishes he could attend, but cannot leave 'phone.

No service possible owing to troop movements – something big is impending. Staff men galloping about, ammunition wagons going up all night. Got back not having had meat since brekker, to find some silly ass has kicked my mess tin over with stew in it. Bread and cheese.

Monday July 12

Bombing starts 4 a.m. I watch it for a bit and then sleep till 7. Brekker and then off to the trenches. Hail of bullets over Gully – nobody about. 8 a.m. French advance gallantly. They then retire and go up again though shells falling thick amongst them. Reinforcements doubling up a few at a time. Each man could be seen clearly from firing line – a grand sight. Noon fairly quiet – intermittent rifle and gun fire. Machine gun bowled over in our firing line trench and gunner hit in chest by bullet which ricochets. Several hit and killed by bullets. I wonder there are not more as they are firing over the parapet all along the line. I take some snaps and have a good look over parapet into Turks trenches – only a few yards off.

Bury Percy Clegg in Gully. Story of chat between Ian Hamilton and Kitchener of Khartoum in years to come, about different regiments '*By George yes, there was a 42nd Division: they must be there still*'. At 4 p.m. another huge bombardment. Jocks with tin plates on back can be seen swarming all over hillside up to Badger Wood. Glorious sight. All our pessimistic thoughts vanished. The 5th Manchesters cannot keep still for excitement. Hugely elated and their progress seems too good.

Then faces fall. Is Achi Baba going to be taken without them? Eventually they retired from two most forward trenches and consolidated in the two first taken. Probably enfiladed and also desperately short of ammunition. At night they evacuate one of these trenches at the command of a German officer in disguise, but soon retake it. I go over on left wing in afternoon and find Dubsters failed to take redoubt and got cut up.[1] Then up to firing line for HC service. Unfortunately everyone was standing to, awaiting Turkish counter attack.

Thinking things would be interesting and expecting our lads would have to advance on the following day, I spend night in the trenches. Unfortunately I accept an RSM's offer of his seat with result I was constantly being woken up by mistake. The last officer I saw that night was killed shortly after by shrapnel. Poor boys are not allowed even to lean on rifle or they would fall asleep. Made even more uneasy by strict orders to have respirators handy. I had not got one. Got a bit of fever I fancy.

Went to 10th Manchester stores and got respirator and sun cover. Had lunch there with officer, who had just

1 The Royal Dublin and Royal Munster Fusiliers were known as the 'Dubsters' for a few weeks after 25 April, when the remnants of the Dubs and Munsters were merged into a single battalion.

been to Lemnos, and QM. QM says the NZ have approached General Douglas with view to utilising his dugout as a base for reinforcements. NCO says there are only two ways of General D getting killed – by lyddite on top of direct hit, or by bullet from his own men.

We are told 100 officers assigned to lines of communication live in luxury on *Aragon* – enjoying fresh fruit, wines etc. life on deck and stroll in Lemnos between times. So they earn their DSO[1] while officers are being killed by the score in the trenches unrecognised. A battalion is led by 5 officers instead of 30. '*What an unpleasant thing war is, but I suppose we must be prepared to rough it*', said an officer when he was called away from his coffee to answer telephone. '*Isn't it damnable? Can't we even have lunch in comfort now?*'

Bombardment continues in afternoon and another glorious charge by Jocks. Their kilts looked glorious and by George, they are a tough lot. From support lines, by looking over parapet we did not see so many fall, yet ever thinner grew the line until apparently only a dozen or so men dropped into last trench. It was a glorious yet terrible sight, for one realised they could hardly hope to hold on, but must retire when the Turks counterattack. 2nd Battalion got lost but succeeded in getting back with losses not unduly high in view of circumstances.

I really think the Turk soldier is finest in world. Fancy fighting and accounting for 2,000 Scots after that hellish bombardment. Will affairs have come to an impasse? Arrange to bury Lt. Dixon in Gully. Buried Bombardier Woods RC after waiting an hour for Furlong. Had supper with ASC Officer at 5th Battery. Huntley and Palmer biscuit. Lobster and chips.

1 Distinguished Service Order.

Wednesday July 14

In the morning found the Wesley Padre[1] (cackling body-snatcher) had taken funeral. Feeling rotten. Go to Clapham M.O. in afternoon to get tablets. Still rotten stomach and head, so go to Lt Woodward. Shrapnel Valley, for exercise. Men of 6th Battery welcome me warmly. Come back in dark – no easy job. Things quiet – too windy for bombardment they say – probably no shells.

Thursday July 15

Feel even more rotten. Try M.O. after M.O. and a walk to W Beach, where I see V8 aeroplane[2] in water. Engine trouble. Foster, RND chaplain, is going home: nerves shattered. At length Blandy M.O. of RHA, thinks to take my temperature and finds it's 102°. I walk to Forward Base Field Ambulance on cliffs and get a fairly comfortable night. Feverish dreams of wounded men howling out commands and asking for water. As my mind was running on trenches and corpses, this assisted its wanderings.

Friday July 16

Fragments of shell fell on roof. Wrote home and sent off official notes. Feeling better, but also weak. Temperature 100. Find myself lying next to Lt. Edge of 7th Lancs Fusiliers. Never came across such a snappy, whining customer before, pretty sure he is swinging the lead.[3]

---

1 The Methodist Padre. Charles and John Wesley led the Methodist movement, which was a reaction to the Anglican Church in the early 18th century.
2 Probably a seaplane, lowered from the naval seaplane carrier, *Ark Royal*, a converted merchant ship.
3 Malingering.

He is not ill, so has to act as if he were, whereas a real case rarely complains. He pleaded dysentery. No signs or symptoms – temperature normal – said he has pains in tummy and head – which nobody can deny.

See Kirby about doing my work. My headache started at 2 p.m. to make itself objectionable – by 7 p.m. it was unendurable. Lt M. came down and said I had better go to Mudros. They had no treatment here. We were in cutting in a steep ravine running down to beach and over us are the rigged up roofs of two marquees.

Saturday July 17

Canon H came down and intoned a few obvious commonplaces about the war. Said also not one word of sympathy, though I had a bumper head. Edge and his groans having been taken away, I turned to my left neighbour. What of him? I said. He smiled, and then we got on to cases of sham – from generals to privates – and yet they will be carried shoulder high – centres of admiring crowds – hold audiences spellbound, while they rehearse their glorious achievements. Yet they were working by QM stores until time came for the trenches and then they went sick.

The Captain, who is Ammunition Officer, rather than staying with his Company tried to get taken on as assistant to a subaltern who is marking out latrines on Imbros. Another fellow, who is attached to 8th Lancs Fusiliers sat with head in hands, complaining of headache. After doing nothing for seven days he went home to pose as hero of the Dardanelles. Afternoon headache once more – my fate sealed. After nightfall, a shell set on fire a stock of ammunition collected from dead and wounded and picked up on W Beach.

Best struggled to keep going despite his illness. But he is now a victim of enteritis, aggravated by close contact with the many corpses he has buried. He hints darkly at the insanitary conditions and infected drinking water at the dressing station. He continues to deplore those officers who seem to be 'swinging the lead', whose illness is feigned and who volunteer for anodyne tasks, behind the line, such as helping the Quartermaster.

The decision had been taken to evacuate Best to Alexandria. He describes the buffeting he receives on his stretcher as he is carried down to the waiting lighter. He cannot immediately go on board, but has to lie on the quayside while hay and other stores are unloaded to make room for the outgoing wounded. Once on board, he is totally ignored, and left out in the open without any protection from

Loading up a lighter with sick men for conveyance to a hospital ship at Mudros. Kenneth Best experienced this when he was invalided out at the end of July. So few suitable hospital ships were available that some of the same vessels used for bringing out horses had to be used for transporting patients

© Imperial War Museum. Q13508

the powerful rays of the sun in the heat of the day. He is given
nothing to eat all day.
  If this is how officers were treated, what about the men?

On 22 July Best is sufficiently well to rise from his sick
bed for the first time – though there is still confusion about
his condition. The Soudan *(hospital ship) arrives at*
Alexandria. He wishes he was back in the front line at
Gallipoli and is irritated to find the city is full of 'pampered
loafers'.

Sunday July 18

7am HC in tent. Then I pack up my traps and depart on
stretcher in pyjamas with rug over top and clothes for
pillow. So I started on an interesting day's journey – made
all the more interesting by the fact that I was feverish and
saw things in unreal proportions. As I left, Col Parker
beamed on me and shook hands most warmly – always
found him hard and cold before. Wondered if he fears I
shall lay charge of enteric to insanitary state of
Intermediate Dressing Station and of their water?

My stretcher is slipped into motor ambulance van like
berths in a cabin. Off we go to clearing station –
somebody pummels me a bit and sends me to officers'
ward where I find Lt Col of 29th Field Ambulance and Lt
Col Isherwood both working a rest. Not only that – they
admitted they were after Alexandria. The boat was full of
old soldiers. They say *We've done our bit.* Yes, but think of
the poor devils left behind who are doing their extra bit
and yours as well . . . Lay there for some time talking, till
my head grew too bad.

At length about 12.30 I was borne off and placed again
in a wagon. Drove down to pierhead and then was carried
by smelly Greek natives and laid on one side of small

constructed pier. While Greeks, Indians and Gyppies and our own men carried stores etc. on land – depositing samples on me as they passed. Next I was dumped into a lighter from which hay was still being unloaded, and there I rocked about till all hay was off and all sick men on. We were towed to the *Newmarket*. I was first to be put on, so last to be taken off. Got off and was laid in blazing sun with men constantly passing over me – no food or drink.

Later I was pulled into shade and given a little barley water. That was all that I had all day and yet the non-stretcher cases were having glorious feeds. Got under awning in bows of boat on main deck, where Colonel Isherwood finds me and has a few words. My valise never put on lighter. My ticket is marked W.S. – Wound Serious or Slight?

We come up to HMHS *Soudan* (Hospital Ship No.1). All serious calls to go aboard, the rest ashore. What a farce. Lots of fellows fed up with roughing it, but with no real ailment, sneak aboard. Wonder what those were like who went ashore. I was laid on a sort of tray stretcher, hauled up and twisted round by a crane – two men with ropes controlling movement of tray. I was rolled down into officers' ward and rolled off onto a real bed – sheets and pillow – still nursing a nasty head. Nothing all day by way of nourishment.

Monday July 19

Found Lt Hunt, 4th E.Lancs, next to me and Edge who is still without temperature and still with a weak whine. Wrote home. Had bath in the morning, but did not get back owing to faintness and everything going black. Now feeling much better. The usual evening pain has almost disappeared. Chaplain came round to know if we had enough to read.

Tuesday July 20

We set sail 10 a.m. Where for? Alex or Malta? Leaving *Mauretania* in Mudros harbour – plenty of troops around. Ships about full up. Hear there is to be a very big engagement shortly.

I am in a long room which looks like several cabins knocked into one – ceilings and walls painted white – electric light and fan and metal spotless. Even painted iron beds with tables which will fold either across or along side of bed. In shape like a child's cot and in size too. I have to tuck myself away carefully. Supports hanging from ceiling. Yesterday's experience with just a tablespoonful of barley water was the limit. Despite temperature, I have a good appetite.

Sailing for Alex, Doc has put me on soup and fish – wish they were more generous with helpings. Find Hunt in next bed is Old Rossallian. Padre came in and lent me V. Staley on Natural Religion. Latter afforded me a little gentle mental exercise. I felt I was wholly dissociated from realities of life. It took me back to quiet scholastic days when I felt I was on the brink of discovering universal truth. The problem is that there is now a ghastly encounter going on. I wish I were back at the Front in Gallipoli and fit again. Shaved by an Indian barber. Wrote to Robin.

Wednesday July 21

How I do like middle-aged Scotsmen. They gave this fellow porridge with SUGAR – fancy for a Jock. On full rations again and yet temperature not yet down, still 99.4. Told I could get up, but too weak to do so.

Find Edge is also an O.R.[1] We gas on about stories of German who walked in trench, asked for Essex O.C.[2] and deliberately shot him dead. Also the Artillery officer on our side who, when range was 2,700 yards, fired deliberately at 1000 into our trenches. Officer led out men by night. One of their own rockets went up and showed them they were being led into Turks line. They shot officer. Apparently Turks let bodies get inflated – and then fire into them.

Naval muddles: a 15cm gun was carefully stowed away with ammunition. It had come in May – but stayed at Lemnos, because no crane to lift her out. Only solution – run her ashore and blow up boat. 4 lighters of ammunition were brought ashore, but were delivered to no one and left – result – drifted down to Turkish lines. Lighter full of lyddite – naval fellow to save trouble threw on match. It was the last straw. She overturned.

Thursday July 22

Got up for the first time. Horrors of getting back into filthy old clothes worn for weeks. Sat on deck with Col. Isherwood (the only original Colonel left in the Division). Amused myself at piano. Given my medical ticket: 'diarrhoea' – rather funny diagnosis after 3 weeks constipation! Morley said 'enteritis with pyrexia' – sounds more suitable. Wrote a letter or two. Got into Alex about 4 p.m., having taken pilot on board at 3.30. Returned books to Chaplain. Strange to be back in Alexandria ...

Chaplain of the 39th Division who had been a day or two on Gully Beach, was also on boat and very fed up

1 Alumnus of Rossall School.
2 Officer Commanding the Essex Regiment.

with frauds – who play about all day and eat four course meals. Driven to No.15 General Hospital (Abbasich Schools) – shown to room which I share with Scots Officer. Grand airy place. In fact so windy, we had to close one window. Went down to supper – soup, fish, chicken, cutlets, sweets, fruit and coffee. Drinks available whisky, hock, lime juice, beer and all free.

No wonder place is full of pampered loafers who come fearing typhoid. They ought to be dug out and sent to the trenches. Excellent selection of books in hospital library. By Jove, it is a paradise. We landed by Seamen's Home at almost same place we left 11 weeks ago. Handkerchiefs with eau de Cologne and cigarettes doled out to stretcher cases.

Saturday July 24

Pack box. Go and see my horse, which I find is swollen with cold and moth-eaten. On to Moustapha and then to see Hordern – still very unfit – result of dysentery at Ladysmith. Officers going to races! Contrast scenes across water. Back and do some shopping. Meet Darke of CEMS. Cairo Boy scout and blind Arab very useful in hospital.

Doctor tells me I must go to Cyprus. I say that it is absurd and argue that I only want a day or two's rest and then shall be fit again for Gallipoli. I am told not to argue, but to do what I am told. '*What I have written I have written*' and your name is on the Cyprus list. As I was free for the day I went into Alex and did some shopping, armed with English silver, whereas when I went to Gallipoli I had only Gyppy money.

Perversity of things. Spent all my money and still short of a lot. In afternoon went to Moustapha Barracks and got chaplain's box and saw other kit bag still with 5th

Manchesters. How strange it seems not to have to beware shells. I find I cannot listen to people or concentrate mind. I suppose it is because I am listening for shells, watching whether bullets are strays or a sniper on your track and so am paying but superficial attention to matter in hand.

Sunday July 25

Not knowing time of service, I go in good time to St Mark's. A service is on. Several men from my old Brigade, the 1st RFA were present. How nice to see old faces, but how different they look from their confrères at the Front. How much childish conceit is absorbed into their natures from spit and polish. It rather disappointed me. Yet the men were very pleased to see me.

I go to 11 a.m. service and with what a thrill I entered. Over 12 months and then the last 3 months how often have I longed for the peace and quiet of Church and its beautiful inspiring services. I am grievously disappointed. A fair congregation, partly military – all very finely dressed. The services intoned by one who could not intone. The congregation for most part did not sing – those who did were girls evidently thinking mostly about their dress and the impression their singing was making. The sermon had a pseudo historical and apologetic theme, based on the continuity of the Church.

How different from our little services in the trenches. God seemed to have nothing to do with this morning's service.

Had a talk with Archdeacon Ward and met High Commissioner afterwards in vestry, stupidly forgetting to apologise for not having called after dining there. The evening Service was far more encouraging and full to overflowing with soldiers. Archdeacon gave a sound practical address on manliness of Christianity, adding that prayer is source of life of soul and of extreme courage. Curious! He repeated ideas and very nearly the words of one of Bishop of London's sermons on Joshua. I recognised it and I have so often used it myself.

Monday July 26

Baker, the Wesleyan chaplain who loafs around in bedroom slippers, has been sent out to convalesce – another comes in. Two chaplains had to be sent straight back. Why do they send out such crocks? I am fed up with Alex and its toy soldiers. As for these Colonials. They think they run the show. We thought England was doing her all. We lent a helping hand – sacrifice home and anything from £1000 to £5000 a year. Then, when shunned and slighted, must be prepared for sacrifice. I have been put in tent, Bruce at one end, I at the other because we would talk so. Got my khaki drill out. Drew £5 from Anglo-Egyptian Bank.

Tuesday July 27

Had a glorious ride in Rolls Royce down along Cairo Road by side of canal – under shade of trees most of way. Some boats scudding down, full sail billowing out, others dragged by men. Oxen and boys bathing. On our side up to date houses and on other side native huts. All much more moist – grass in parts seems actually to grow naturally. Went into Mongha Gardens – glorious growth much more luxuriant than at home, palms and fern trees. Horses everywhere. Got back at noon. General King came to see me, but I was out.

Ramadan. Little kiddies fairly scoot home when gun

goes at sundown and the fast is broken.[1] Further
shopping. Concert for men in evening. Simple – but how
exquisite to hear music. A French boy played violin with
taste, verve and fine execution.

Wednesday July 28

Get suit altered. Called and left note for General King.
Last of Worcesters' officers promoted from ranks says
Krithia was first objective, then Achi Baba, all on 25 April.
Some hope. Red tabs want honour and glory, but whole
operation is disorganised. Brigade staff were killed but
top brass could not replace them, not knowing what was
happening. Said ships' guns did very little damage. I
could verify that – Turks' trenches were hardly damaged.

Saturday July 31

Driven down in hospital motor van. We are driven all over
docks and eventually put on board SS *Surada B15N* en
route for Cyprus. 16 officers and 13 cabin rooms. Weigh
anchor 4 p.m. Have a smoke and a liqueur with skipper.
He seems to think that it is only on stormy days we could
not land in Morto Bay.

Sunday August 1

Sore throat better – first day of rest for a long time.
Arrange with one McCrae to have service at 4 p.m. Sat in
deck chair as we smoothly slipped through the wonderful
deep blue Mediterranean.
   At 4 p.m. I had short evening service and spoke on
picture '*The Great Sacrifice*'. By practising self sacrifice in

1 Practising Muslims do not eat between dawn and sunset during Ramadan.

everyday life – self denial, including wine and women – I said that there lies our crusade to destroy selfishness. Our comrades died for it – to crush German love of power and attempt to capture world market. The thought of our friends being cold and stiff should inspire us not to leave their work unfinished. Nearly all men and officers attended in the aft well.

Went up on deck and saw Cyprus just visible about 50 miles away. Talked with Welsh Border officer on comparative beauty of language. I held modern Greek was decadent, basing my contention on lack of conjugations and use of auxiliaries. This he held added to languages' powers of expressive thoughts and even mood underlying thoughts. He gave first place to English.

Indian sailor brings up rats in trap. Captain tries to get his dog to catch them with unnecessary cruelty. Have chat with 1st ship's officer, R.C. and gentleman out of common run. Midshipman Dilley of RNAS[1] wishes for HC Service. Have arranged it for 6.a.m. Monday.

Monday August 2

I get a man to fetch my bed on deck and I sleep there. Rats swarming everywhere, running along rails, up rigging and on deck. Ship's officers have never seen them so bad.

Tuesday August 3

Feeling very limp. Find I am panting for breath even when sitting doing nothing and feel as though something

---

1 The Royal Naval Air Service provided Sir Ian Hamilton with his only means of aerial reconnaissance, as no aircraft from the Royal Flying Corps had been released from the Western Front. In 1918 the RNAS and RFC amalgamated to form the Royal Air Force.

wrong with heart. In afternoon go for a short walk and watch tennis tournament among civilians. Many of the men might be in the trenches. Old Syrian gentleman gives me tea. He had shot in Sussex, Scotland, France, Germany and was now practically laid up.

Wednesday August 4

Anniversary of Declaration of War – the war which '*would be all over by Christmas.*' We tramp up to summit of Mt. Olympus feeling better for it.[1] Grand view from just beyond top of whole island – much of it waste land. The Surada Lake is like a speck on the blue – reflecting like glass on the Olympic hotel Troodos. Go for glorious walk by myself in cool of evening along a lone path through pines on edge of ravine.

Sunday August 8

Walked to Government House for Holy Communion at 8 a.m. Sir John and Lady Clauson, 2 Tommies, Chaplain, and self were present.[2] Lady Clauson offered me milk afterwards – she evidently thought I was an invalid. At Mattins Lady C kept changing key in hymns. We sang one hymn unaccompanied. While waiting for his Excellency, I was turned out and put in front row. Chaplain fussed about much too much. This takes away from dignity and reverence of service. He read from a little manual and interpolated gags, before moving on to special prayers after the service.

Richmond came to lunch and talked about spiritual

1 At 1952 metres, Mount Olympus is the highest point in the Troodos Mountains, Cyprus.
2 Sir John Clauson was the High Commissioner for Cyprus. He died in 1918.

healing and anointing with oil. In afternoon he talked mysticism till my head reeled. He is a good fellow.

Monday August 9

Tennis – rode mule to Platus. Lunch with Lewis. They ask after padres Hitchens & Creighton. They give me apples grown from grafts of imported trees. Ride mule to Troodatissa Monastery. The Abbot had died a few days before – black flag flying half-mast. Deacons may marry, but not after being priested. They should live fairly comfortably with poaching, gratuities and gardening.

I came to last part of the bridle path in dark, let mule have her head and got back safely. Monks give me preserved cherries. We take a spoonful out of jar and a drink of water. Their chapel is dark and musty, but pulpit is effectively in roof. Readings from Books of Saints on lecterns. Deacon wears green and gold surplice – priest a sort of smock with spotted red and blue stole.

Tuesday August 10

Inspection of Guard and convalescents, by Sir John Clauson who then gave us a talk.

He is insignificant in person and not an eloquent speaker. He gave an outline history of Cyprus. Afterwards I took Bruce his pony back, but first went for a ride down the valley. Met man and woman on mules, who seemed pleased to have photos taken. Saw a dozen vultures and was only a few yards off them when they flew away. A mule can apparently hear footsteps ¼ mile or more off – he stops and wags his ears – despite noise of his own feet and of stream tumbling down over rocks.

Wednesday August 11

Sign in at Government House. Cricket match: '*Yeomanry v Convalescents*'. Same officer who captained team against us on Avon. Convalescents hardly batted as such – made 229 and got 3 Yeomanry wickets for very few runs. Talked to Stewart of 10th Gurkhas. He spoke of the dog-like fidelity of men, even to harshest of masters. Yet they are always able to discern a gentleman.

Iniquities of RAMC M.O. hoping to acquire a C.M.G.[1] by keeping hospital empty. Men sent to a Gyppy hospital – doubtful if native doctors would give best attention, as feeling in Egypt is by no means friendly to Australians and British. '*Hope you'll soon be well*' they say to British patients, *and would you like fruit, books etc.* to an Australian.

Convalescent officers play the deuce. When in private houses they order servants about, finish whisky and fetch new bottles from cellar in absence of host! They come stumbling in at 2 a.m. while their comrades in trenches are doing 2 or 3 men's work. Red Tabs treat men and officers in trenches like dirt, says Gurkha. Hospital ship suddenly sent back here with lots of officers and men – so though I was to stay over until next boat, I have to go and am glad, too.

Thursday August 12

I heard two officers come in. They had great difficulty in finding latch of door in early hours of morning, yet too ill to go back to front. Are you fit to go back? Yes or no – that is the medical examination. At Platus we had wine and a Frenchman at our request played piano. He knew most of

---

1 Companion of the Order of St Michael and St George.

the popular classical pieces by heart. This was the first time I have encountered decent piano playing on the island.

Friday August 13

Waited for horses till noon, then went off on foot for Troodos Monastery by high bridle track. Soon got above monastery, but had to scramble down. Steep rock, thick undergrowth, and trees masked the monastery. Lunch consisted of stringy vegetables, goat cheese and communion wine with water. Came back by ever diminishing stages – finished up with a stagger.

Wednesday August 18

In evening went to 15th General Hospital, where Captain Cameron repaired two teeth. Saw good many of the old Field Ambulance team who came away with me.

Thursday August 19

Had teeth finished. Afternoon shopping, tea with Colonel Walker, Ward and Geoff Bolton. In evening, went to Moustapha – could not find trace of my valise. Had tremendous job to find ghazi to get back to hotel. Dinner with Ward at Khedival Club. Men singing hymns in train coming back, while natives looked in at window begging. Received note that I was to embark on Quay 45 at 10 a.m. tomorrow.

In hospital the wounded were under the impression this last feint attack was worse than June 4. I saw long list of casualties at 42nd Divisional Headquarters, Moustapha.

Friday August 20

Drove with luggage to 45th Dock, pack luggage on board and then went back. The ship was due to leave at 10 am, which I knew meant in the evening, at the earliest. Did some shopping and got on to the boat 4p.m.

Found a lot of familiar faces, including some who were at Cyprus. *SS Huntsgreen* is the name of the boat. I remarked how like it is to *Derfflinger* – the boat on which I first sailed for Dardanelles.[1] It turned out to be the same men doing life saving drill.

1 It was the same vessel – a captured German transport – with a new name. See footnote to diary entry for May 2.

Suvla Bay – A Bungled Opportunity

There is no one in command at Suvla or Anzac – except Kemal[1]

Earlier in August, while Kenneth Best had been convalescing on Cyprus and awaiting re-embarkation, the Allies had taken action to break the deadlock. The second great wave of landings had taken place on 6 and 7 August – principally at Suvla Bay. Unfortunately this campaign was doomed from the start by ill-prepared and dilatory leadership. Sir Ian Hamilton had asked for Byng and Rawlinson to be his corps commanders. Unfortunately he got neither. At the age of 61, Sir Frederick Stopford, a retired lieutenant-general – or 'retread' in today's parlance – had been appointed to command the IXth Corps. He had seen active service, but had no battle experience as a commander. He seems to have been too paternal by half and had difficulty in gainsaying his own chief of staff, the domineering Brigadier-General Reed, VC. Apparently no thrusting generals could be spared from the Western Front.

---

1 John Hargrave – *The Suvla Bay Landing*, Macmillan, 1964 p. 181.

A field kitchen at Suvla Bay, where, on 7 and 8 August, there
was an unwarranted delay in confronting relatively light Turkish
opposition and a great opportunity was missed
© Imperial War Museum. Q13612

Major-General Sir Alexander Godley commanded the
Australian and New Zealand Division, who were deputed to
advance from Anzac Cove. Their target was the capture of
the Sari Bair ridge. A British Army officer on detachment
with Anzac troops did not always make an effective mix and
Godley was not a popular figure. The difficult terrain over
which his men advanced had not been reconnoitred and
many of the soldiers were replacements for earlier battle
casualties and therefore inexperienced. They were handi-
capped by having to carry all their supplies on their backs for
the first 48 hours as no wheeled transport or mules were
available. The supply of water was strictly limited. One
column got within a quarter of a mile of Sari Bair after a
night attack with only a handful of Turks ahead of them –
but then stopped.

Chunuk Bair, the easternmost point reached by the New Zealanders on 8 August 1915. This photo shows the bodies of the dead soldiers laid out for burial on the site of the future cemetery where the New Zealand Memorial now stands. The Narrows are visible in the distance
© Imperial War Museum. Q14338

Suvla Bay – nowadays a wide, attractive seascape with a gentle slope behind – opens out on to the Gulf of Saros. It was here that the main thrust of the invasion was to be made. Twenty thousand men of Kitchener's New Army were put ashore before dawn from 'beetles' (flat-bottomed barges), whose light armour protected the men far more than the open boats that had been used on 25 April. Only about 1,000 Turks barred their way. The 11th Division Commander, Major-General Hammersley, whose health was suspect, was entirely out of touch with his troops. The GOC did not come ashore, but was nursing a sprained knee on board a sloop, the *Jonquil*. No action was taken to establish contact with the shore, nor was any report sent to GHQ.

At this stage, there was a startling opportunity to catch the Turks unawares, before they had brought up reserves. But the opportunity was lost. At dawn, Suvla Bay was crammed with men, the way up Kiretch Tepe lay invitingly open – but chaos reigned and they awaited orders to move on. But orders came there none. At noon, Hill 10 – the first objective – had still not been taken – yet even then, Sir Ian Hamilton did not order Stopford to take any positive action. By that time, the day was hot and water was in desperately short supply. Michael Hickey writes that not only were men sometimes fighting each other for water – but were reduced to drinking their own urine by the end of the day.[1]

Thus, the Turks had been given the respite they needed to bring up reinforcements – and when, at last, on 8 August, the order to advance was given, it was too late. By then two Turkish divisions had been moved from Bulair to Suvla. The old pattern of trenches and dug-in enclaves began to take shape and the Turks had taken over the initiative. It is revealing to read what Germany's Admiral Tirpitz wrote on the morning after the Suvla Landing, 7 August:

'Heavy Fighting has been going since yesterday at the Dardanelles ... The situation is obviously very critical. Should the Dardanelles fall, the World War has been decided against us.'

One week later, Private Harold Thomas, who was attached to the Royal Army Medical Corps, landed at Suvla Bay. Thomas had been ordained before the war and had been a curate at Alsager in Cheshire – so he could have served as a chaplain had he chosen to do so. But, driven by his conscience, he rejected the life of an officer and decided the best way for him to come into close contact with all sorts and conditions of men was to serve among other ranks, at first doing menial tasks as a batman. Thomas volunteered later for the RAMC and was employed as a stretcher-bearer at Suvla. He kept a diary of his experiences, and it is thanks to this that we have an unvarnished and eyewitness account

1 Michael Hickey, *Gallipoli*, John Murray, 1995, p. 273.

of the shambolic scenes prevalent when he landed on 15 August. He starts with a vivid description of the situation as they disembark from the destroyer:

> ... We rushed swiftly on towards a bay shaped like a horseshoe glaring yellow in the sun, with low hills rising behind it. At first it seemed entirely bare of life and it was only when we came close in that we could see that it was really swarming with men and mules and carts and stores. Our destroyer cast anchor and horse barges came alongside, into which we were packed, and motor lighters towed us ashore.

Horses landed at Suvla Bay, following the second wave of landings in August 1915. As on the Western Front, huge numbers of horses were required by the Mediterranean Expeditionary Force. Kiretch Tepe in background
© Imperial War Museum. Q13452

I carried with me, besides the thin khaki uniform I had on, a rolled overcoat, water bottles, mess tin, haversack

(containing two shirts, eight pairs of socks, six hand ker-
chiefs, one pair of pyjamas, two towels, soap, shaving
tackle, notebook and pencil, and prayer book), 'iron
rations' my cigarette case (full), pipe and pouch, and two
boxes of matches.

We struggled on to the beach and at once were set to
work unloading officers' baggage and medical chests. I
had just hoisted an officer's valise when a sudden tremendous crash behind me made me drop it. I thought a shell
must have exploded but on looking round discovered it
was only the firing of a six-inch gun on a cruiser in the bay.
That was the first of a long series of noises which were to
continue day and night for four months ...

The scene was a beautiful one, the sun shining bril-
liantly on Suvla Bay and Imbros, whose blue bulk
confronted us across the water. Suddenly the heavy roll
and crackle of rifle-fire, swelling louder over the saucer-
like rim of hill behind us, reminded us of the grim
business for which we had come. We fell in – most of us
with a feeling of shakiness – but there was no getting out
of the boat now, we were fairly launched and committed
to the Adventure.

Slowly we moved off in the gathering dusk, through
clouds of dust raised by the swarming mule trains and
light Indian carts driven by mysterious and much be-
draped Sikhs, and began to climb the ridge[1] behind
Suvla, using a dry 'nullah'. Then suddenly came the first
bullet with a 'fizz' like a monster mosquito and then
'thump' into the side of the gully. More and more flew
over as we neared the fighting.

It was very dark now. Suddenly a halt was called and
half of our men were led off into the darkness while the

1 The Kiretch Tepe Ridge.

other half were ordered to remain where we were. Two sergeants and an officer were busy over an indistinct blurr under the gully bank, a 'hand' was needed and I ran up to find that it consisted of three Turks, one dead and two badly wounded. Our first sight of blood and the meaning of War.

After this a connected account of that first night becomes impossible – it is merely the recollection of a dis-ordered nightmare. I remember the tremendous crash of rifle and machine gun fire close to and the 'thump' 'thump' of bullets and sparks flying from the stones while an officer and six of us pushed through the scrub towards the curve of a hill which showed darkly against the night sky. Between the bursts of fire the silence was broken by agonising cries which will always haunt me. From all around that hill there were voices crying 'Ambulance', 'Stretcher-bearers', 'Oh damn you my leg's broken' and then again 'Stretcher-bearers'.

It was horrible, we would start for a voice and it would cease and another far away would begin. That hillside was a shambles. Evidently there had been fierce hand-to-hand fighting there a few hours ago, rifles, kits, water-bottles, khaki, Turkish tunics and headgear were strewn every-where among the scrub. While we were following a phantom-like voice, we came suddenly on a half dug trench which an RAMC officer had made into a combined mortuary and first aid station. As we set furiously to work sorting the dead from the living, there reeled among us out of the darkness an officer raving 'My men have taken that bloody hill but they're dying of thirst.' He passed on and we continued our ghastly work.

I found myself one of the party of six told off to carry to the base a man shot through the breast. We linked hands and shuffled off with no idea of our whereabouts, the poor fellow we were bearing moaning piteously at

every stumble. The hot night was thick with the whirr of
bullets, the sharp metallic cry of crickets, the ghastly calls
of undiscovered wounded and the sickly smell of Gallipoli
thyme. We blundered on, trying to find the rough path by
which we had come but getting more lost at each step.
Now and then we would catch a glimpse of Suvla Bay
with the hospital ship aglow with the lamps of fairyland,
but try as we would, we did not seem to get near to
them ...

It is clear from the above eyewitness account that the medical services were overwhelmed by the casualties incurred on
15 and 16 August during the fierce fighting for command of
the heights above Suvla Bay, and were totally inadequate to
deal with the rising toll of casualties.

Kenneth Best had embarked on 20 August for Alexandria –
ironically on the same vessel on which he had first arrived on
the Peninsula on 6 May. Fortunate still to be convalescing on
Cyprus when the landings at Suvla Bay took place, Best had
so far been shielded from the carnage there. But not for long.
Once in Alexandria he enjoys an unexpected reunion for one
evening with an old friend – a fellow chaplain – but then it
is back to the reality of war.

In a letter home he writes that he is due to embark for the
Dardanelles immediately. He knows about the heavy casualties at Suvla and wonders grimly whether he will find any
chaplains still alive on Gallipoli. And is there a chance that
the 'gallant little remnant' of the 42nd East Lancashire
Division will be allowed home soon?

The Only English Hotel in Alexandria
Facing the Sea
Friday August 20, 1915

My dear Family,

I had a few more days in Cyprus, after I last wrote to you. This glorious slack period came to an end far too soon. Things had become active once again on the Peninsula and all possible accommodation was needed for a tremendously long casualty list. Therefore everyone who could be removed was removed. I found myself once more in Alex. I proceeded to report myself at Headquarters to receive orders. They did not know anything about me or my condition.

I had to go to the proper medical authorities and receive my discharge as fit. They put a tent at my disposal but that was not much use as I had a second time lost all my kit and I did not relish sleeping on the cold ground (or rather hot sand) without even a blanket. I therefore thought I would do the thing properly and get a good breath of civilisation.

Therefore I got a ghazi and drove off to the best hotel I could find. I had just got into the hall and was signing my name in the book when a silly ass thumped me on the back and called out '*Hello Beast*'. Turning round, there was old Waffle Andrews in the uniform of the Australian AMC. He had left the Peninsula with dysentery and was convalescing at this very hotel into which I had strolled.

I cannot tell you what a real evening we had. He did not know I was in the MEF and I never thought he would come back from Anzac alive. He has had countless narrow escapes – been slightly hit 2 or 3 times and all the rest of his stretcher squad have been killed. For 3 days we have done nothing but feed, sit about and talk. He has been doing chaplains' work as well as stretcher bearing and the Australians were so pleased with him that they offered him a chaplaincy.

However they have muddled things up and so he is trying to get a post among British troops. If this fails he will go back to England where he has been asked to chaplain some Brigade of London Scottish in France.

My marching orders have come. I embark for the Dardanelles today. The last transport was sunk by a submarine, so I shall be canny and sleep on deck with a life belt. Handy in case the Germans give us a free bathe. I have not of course received any letters from home since leaving the Peninsula a month or so ago. They are chasing me round I suppose and will perhaps catch me up when I settle down once more on Gallipoli.

I fancy the show here is nearly over. It is time too. I don't suppose that the rate of casualties per unit area has been so heavy in any other field of operations as it has been here. I wonder whether there will be any Chaplains left on the Peninsula. Alex is full of them – fit, wounded and sick. A few necessaries have yet to be purchased so I must say farewell. Hope you are all going strong.

PERHAPS our gallant little remnant of a division may be sent home soon. *They would not require much deck space.*

Heaps of love to all.

Yours affectionately

Kenneth.

Saturday August 21

Parade for boat drill – nobody comes to instruct my boat astern and cabin for'ard. I could not get near to my allotted boat. Men would all be running in the opposite direction.

Sunday August 22

Holy Communion 8.30, Church Parade in life belts. A Wesleyan Chaplain takes Church Parade on port side and I do same starboard. During afternoon we reach Mudros Harbour off the island of Lemnos. Evening Service informal and was taken by YMCA worker, Wesleyan Chaplain and self. Talked to YMCA man about supplying literature and writing paper to men on Gallipoli.

Wednesday August 25

After being moored at Mudros for two days, this evening we transferred to the *Ermina*, a beautiful little boat built last August for ferry service between Ireland and Scotland.

Thursday August 26

Arrived Lancashire Landing[1] at 10 p.m.

Friday August 27

At 5 a.m, disembarked on pier formed by a number of ships sunk end to end. Senior CF away – so took possession of his home and made myself breakfast. Then went to Gully Beach and discovered my Brigadier. Back on Gallipoli at last – but with mixed feelings.

Saturday August 28

Found Church tent just vacated by sick CF and installed myself. A stray stretcher has wandered into my tent, so I

1 W Beach. See footnote to diary entry for May 6.

shall use it as bed. My new orderly – another little drummer-boy – has made me a table and stool, out of boxes.

Sunday August 29

7 aeroplanes, 1 Taube. Quiet day but they can do nothing as none are far enough back. Chat with 4th E.Lancs. Troops moving about all over peninsula – surely Turks will shell? They open up about 6 p.m. – shrapnel and small lyddite all over place. I go up Gully but 5th cannot have service. 7.30 RAMC Service and 8.30 4th East Lancs. Thought moon would be up, but it comes too late – so we manage with flickering candles, shielded from view of enemy.

Tuesday August 31

Wrote letters in morning, when I was not on the run. Tried to reach trenches in afternoon, but only got about half way. Came back to Morland's dug-out and he took me to Cumberland Howitzer Brigade for tea. The Doc there, like Smith and myself, could not wear leggings – they are too big.

They tell there how a battalion got a bit hot at Suvla digging trenches. They looked at it with legitimate pride – it was a grand trench. So leaving a few men to hold it they went down to bathe. Our friend Johnny Turk thought it was a grand trench – he has good taste in such matters, so he took it. Polished off small guard and proceeded to pick off bathers until all were gone.

Shells which should have gone to Anzac arrived at Suvla and *vice versa*. 4th E. Lancs of no use to anyone at present, so they are left in rest camp while rest of Brigade are in firing line. They don't much mind – too weary to worry about honour or disgrace. Their consciences can be quietened by realising they were asked to do the impossible. They were so exhausted they fell asleep as they fired.

Wednesday September 1

Tried again to reach the firing-line and again failed. It was very windy and gully was a foot deep in dust and I met an unending line of horses. I went to Pip Point; met Jerry Garnett, a naval observation officer and the artillery officer. The two latter had just returned fit and so we got on to usual topics – the disgusting blatant scrimshanking among officers serving in Cyprus, Alex and Cairo because of cold feet and nerves. Artillery officer very harsh in criticism of infantry – showing his rank ignorance of real conditions.

Still on low diet and feeling very weak. In afternoon try to find a way along cliffs above Gully. Find no path is very exposed to enemy. Instead I find only unburied men, rifles and ammunition. These are relics of the first advance of the Lancashire Fusiliers.

Saturday September 4

A day of funerals. I started with a 10th Manchester – a grand little lad of 18, sniped while out digging – buried him on Gully Beach. Went up to get second inoculation against cholera. Then hearing that the Bird Cage had been blown up by Turks, I went up Gully. One 9th Manchester was being brought down. He had been buried from noon to following morning, yet still alive and cheery. Three Engineers were brought down dead. Buried another 9th Manchester behind trenches. Still at least two missing.

One other dead soldier we could see just over parapet by means of periscope, but could not of course fetch him in. A whole traverse by No. 2 Listening Station was filled in. A pity we did not tell our men first. We had heard the pick-pick of the Turks mining for some time, but left it too late. Curiously I was in the Bird Cage the day before – at the time of the explosion too. We are now very short of men, so that means nearly every man is a prisoner, tied to his post. Hence those a few yards away hardly knew what had happened, though of course they had heard the explosion. Some men here and there had limbs broken by falling debris.

Met Hassall of Moravian College against whom I played footer – now officer in the 10th Manchesters. Got back to bury another man from the 9th. Had lunch at Battalion HQ. Steak, rabbit and pineapple macaroni. Excellent repast.

Sunday September 5

Early service 6.45. 11 present, mainly brought by Cpl Best from his company. 10 a.m. service near top of the Gully and in a bivouac another good church attendance. All officers including C.O. present and nearly all stayed to Holy Communion. 26 communicants.

On to head of the Gully where I arranged as far as possible for those who desired to communicate to attend at 3 p.m. Cpl Wilde and men present. Again all 10th Manchester officers except one attend, including Hassall. I could get no change out of Col Whitehead (5th East Lancs) who said that with his thin firing line and scanty support, it would be too risky to spare men. Yet many from 10th and 9th Manchesters came – in all 30. Holy Communion not 50 yards from Turkish trenches. Yet so used to that it did not distract our attention from Service.

Evening Service at 4th East Lancs on cliffs about Gully Beach – not so well attended by only some 30 men. Spoke from Malachi 3. Are we doing God's service in the war, i.e. do we come prepared to make the supreme sacrifice or to get honour and glory and feel we are doing our duty at the least possible expense of ease and peril? *'Take my yoke upon you and learn of me.'* He set his face steadfastly to go to certain death. *'Take my yoke'* involves Christianity and self: the Christian bears the load. If object is to do duty as cheaply as possible, we have to bear the burden ourselves and it soon becomes intolerable.

Supper as usual at stores. Just finished when shrapnel from Achi Baba comes crackling and spurting round followed by whoof whoof of Anne of Asia and her cubs as they belch forth H.E. The lamp goes out. We find we have had enough supper and retire gracefully to dug-out.

Monday September 6

Have a bathe at 7 p.m. – seem to be clear of stiffness from inoculation. Gas drill and gongs all over Peninsula. New kind of respirator helmeting now in fashion – a sort of diver's helmet. One man absent when new issue was made and had only old respirator for nose and mouth. Yesterday at parade order to fix respirators, a man gazed at his little pad, bewildered, glanced wildly round, but got no tips on how to cope. All he had was stupid little pad. Eventually in desperation he put pad on top of his head and tied string under his chin like a bonnet.

Wednesday September 8

Bury 9th Manchester, shot by his own men – did not realise challenge was meant for him.

Thursday September 9

The collectors of curios have got going. When last I was
here you could not walk without treading on shells etc.
Now when I want to send one home, there are none to be
found. Eventually found one poor specimen. Some
bombardment starts. Visit 26th Battery, 4th Gun at
Clapham Junction. Of men being examined, 75% of the
original 42nd Division are certified medically unfit.

Also my indent for materials for winter quarters has
been returned. Kirby comes in. He is of the opinion we
shall go home, be amalgamated with 3rd line and then
drafted out, say to France, after a short rest and training.
Already many men who have recovered have joined 3rd
Battalion, instead of returning to our Division.

Friday September 10

New draft of officers look very ill at ease and green. The
cynosure of wandering eyes, as they sit bunched together
waiting for orders. They look like new boys at school
going through ordeal of examination by old scholars. A
tornado strikes as I struggle down to beach with
toothache, motor goggles on and my cap drawn over my
eyes. But I feel very bucked – having made a discovery of
importance to me personally.

I had done for fun a few gymnastic and Swedish drill
exercises of an elementary type such as we endured at
prep. school. I found to my joy that the appalling dull
heavy sickly feeling, which I have experienced almost
continually since even before leaving England
disappeared. Physical weakness, malaise and mental
torpor obsessed me to such an extent that I was getting to
the very nadir of depression.

I could not preach or carry on a sensible conversation.

Yet perhaps it served a purpose for so dull was my mind that I could not apprehend or realise danger, however imminent or near.

Saturday September 11

Another chaplain, Furlong, comes to see if he can have my hut for 7 a.m. service and seems consumed with idea of his own importance. Threatens to go home if more pains are not taken to get him a congregation! He fairly let drive on authorities. It seems to have had its effect. I have profited by it and escaped the unpleasant experience of a row. OCs are now ready to take more trouble to enable men to attend.

Towards evening is the best light for artillery work and wind has gone down. The Turk sends a few shrapnel just over my tent into the bluff just beyond. Don't know what woke him up. I fancy that he is putting odd shots haphazardly all over the Peninsula to give the impression they have many guns and a plentiful supply of ammunition.

Sunday September 12

The morning service mainly consists of RAMC and RE. The 10th Manchesters were quite ready to come when ordered to do a fatigue which ultimately was cancelled. Major General Douglas and Staff came and sat in front row. About 30 strong for Holy Communion including whole of Divisional Staff. General Douglas stayed behind and invited me to lunch. But before that I went up to Eske Line and held service for 5th E.Lancs. I have never had such a large turnout, quite remarkable as they were not led by officers. Again a good number stayed for Holy Communion.

Got back and found General Douglas waiting for me for lunch. I was given honour of his right hand place. He seemed annoyed at GOC's management of things in general, for instance the delay in forming a canteen. The red yellow green double series of signals was jeered at as an amusement for a lot of out of work subalterns, who wanted something to play with. Large congregation for evensong on Gully Beach. Singing was fine. Received some letters from Winnie, home and Jen Marriott.

Monday September 13

A story doing the rounds ...
<u>Naval Officer:</u> *Well, what do you think of the work of the naval guns?*
<u>Military Officer:</u> *Damned fine, damned fine, Sir! and so impartial. What do you think of Ian Hamilton?*
<u>French Officer:</u> *Fine man, fine man – he write English so beautiful ...*

Help to arrange a sing-song. Got some men together and had a bit of a concert. Brig. General and a good many officers present. Stage was a semi-circular ledge on side of cliff between Y and Gully Beach. We sat on boxes covered with blankets and men squatted up and down the cliff side. We were overlooking the Aegean Sea. A few minesweepers and destroyers were moving about, the *Scorpion*[1] letting off shells now and again. She is a regular little spitfire.

I am afraid I did not listen much to the concert. The sun was sinking behind Imbros with the most gloriously brilliant colours and further away I could see marvellously delicate tints. The sea turned from clear-blue to slate grey

1 A 'Beagle'-class destroyer.

and then to dark and murky, for thick rain clouds were appearing. The ships now became vague dark forms moving on the face of the water. Here and there a bright star shone through clouds throwing a ray on water.

Then I was brought back to earth by discordant laughter produced by a Lancashire dialect recitation.

Tuesday September 14

Dearsley still away and my tooth getting more impertinent each day. I got some talc powder and bottle from SCF Beardmore has gone to Imbros and the padre who took his place is in hospital. Medics say a 'big and final effort' is to be made on September 22nd to avoid a winter campaign.

A group of chaplains on Anzac in September 1915. From left to right: Chaplains Merrington, AIF; King, NZEF; Dale, Royal Irish Rifles; McMenamin, NZEF; O'Connor and Crozier, both of the Royal Irish Fusiliers
© Imperial War Museum. HU57401

Meeting held to decide how best dugouts can be heated. No plans for winter quarters yet and indents for materials cancelled. '*Get your raisins before you set about making a plum pudding*'. That's the Army all over.

Wednesday September 15

Rien à remarquer except that it rained heavily in the night – harbinger of winter? The boy forgot to loosen guys with the result that we narrowly escaped having tent down on top of us. This tent is a great boon – must stick to it at all costs. Most of the men looked a bit bedraggled, but seemed all the cheerier for a bit of rain. We have had only a few showers the whole year. Had the usual morning dip off end of pier.

Thursday September 16

They say some medic of the rank of General came over to enquire into health of troops. The result of the enquiry was that it was pronounced appalling and that the only solution of the difficulty was to send the Division away. Yet last week our sick and wounded were only 250, whereas Lowland Division has 350 and RND over 600. Can all be relieved at once? Possibly if it is found impossible to force way across Peninsula at Suvla. Troops can be spared from there as there are more than enough to hold the line.

OC 10th Manchesters complains that junior staff officers live in luxury, while senior officers of infantry battalion are shown a filthy dust heap and told that is their quarters. They have all the strain and hardship and yet nothing is done for them when in bivouac. NCOs in Gunners or Sappers live more comfortably, while Field Ambulance men with medical comforts and all sorts of presents from home can cultivate friends by means of the mammon of unrighteousness and so get material and, having nothing to do, build themselves a row of villas. The cooler weather is a relief.

Friday September 17

Fletcher pays us a visit. I go to spy out land for the Sunday services. Y Beach, Trolley Ravine and Fusilier Bluff seem 3 possible places. Down to the Beach and get £5 from paymaster at X Beach. Get 2 letters from home.

Saturday September 18

4th E. Lancs moving draw fire just over my tent. Sgt. Major in hurry to get cover breaks his ankle. Taube flies over quite low – puffs of smoke all round her, but she sails back safely. Probably trying to find the 6" guns which have been brought up on cliff south of us.

Go with Steinthal[1] to Y Ravine – leave him at bottom and tramp around finding spots hidden from Turks and accessible to different units for services. Go back to find a batch of letters from Cyprus awaiting me – 19 in all. Work out address for tomorrow and got to dump for evening meal.

Coming back from arranging Services, I suddenly run into Ian Hamilton. I wondered why everyone had been looking so stiff and expectant. Not being trained in ways military, I could not salute instinctively, but instead I waved my pipe which I was holding in an inane fashion. He did not appear displeased. But it is said that the only thing he had to report after his last visit was '*three men failed to salute me*'. However today he called out very cheerily '*good afternoon*'.

---

1 Lt.-Col. W.M. Steinthal commanded the 3rd East Lancashire Field Ambulance.

Sunday September 19

Started with threatening signs of diarrhoea. Tramped along shore from Gully to Y Beach. Smell of dead horse very strong in places. Some confusion about Field Ambulance time and so breakfast which should have been over was still going on when I arrived. I could not postpone as I had to get to Border Ravine by 10 a.m, for service by the side of the coast road at which seven soldiers were present. Wind very trying. Altar cloth difficult to fix and dust covers everything.

Eat one of my bully beef sandwiches. I told orderly to drown the bully in mustard and without a doubt he did. I wept copiously, but 'twas that or nothing. So I persevered.

10 a.m. Trolley Ravine. Glorious service – practically a parade. Men only require the initial impetus to be given to them and then they enjoy the service well enough. In Essex Ravine a service is impossible. Afternoon service at Fusilier Bluff – just behind firing line, which is only about 20 or 30 yards from Turks. It is cancelled owing to a 'stand to'. Came back and had a hearty evening service on Y Beach.

Monday September 20

Take a coat and lie down by latrines on top of cliff. Rush off to 3rd Field Ambulance and get castor oil and brandy. Colonel Steinthal was composing a satire on L of C.[1] Why should a Field Ambulance ridicule them for luxury, while they exist in their own cosy houses? I return to haunt the latrines for rest of day. The nights are the worst. Constant griping so that I cannot sleep. Frantic rushes to water's edge and so cold. Ugh!

1 Lines of Communication. Officers working on these were said to live in comparative luxury. See diary entry for July 12.

Tuesday September 21

Am living on a little badly made corn flour 3 times a day.
In afternoon bury one of 5th East Lancs. Why send a
burial party down fully equipped tramping several miles
when they are already dropping with fatigue? They are
falling out like as flies when Field Ambulance, with
exception of about 1 day a month, are kicking their heels
eating medical comforts. Smoking ditto and basking in
sunshine listening to the '*Song of the Sea*'.[1]

Just finished burial when I am rung up by Staff Captain
asking me to bury another 5th East Lancs in Fusilier
Bluff. A Turk had been seen and this poor chap in his
excitement put his head above parapet and had top of it
blown off.

I borrow 4 legs from the dump as my 2 legs won't carry
me. Ride up to Geogheghans Bluff – pass above
communication trench and visit 5th East Lancs. HQ,
feeling ready to drop. I fortunately meet Baird who gives
me a stiff brandy and chlorodyne.

Glorious ride back and impressive funeral – only I was
just about played out. Eleven times during the night did I
have to bolt for it. Curiously enough I would wake up
regularly at twenty past hour. This was too much – pain
and sickness intolerable.

Wednesday September 22

See Steinthal again. Have had 4 days passing blood and
mucus and nothing to eat except milk. He tells me to be
ready for 7.30 ambulance. Stancliffe gets my things
packed. I am not going to let them out of my sight this

---

1 Sung by Moses and the children of Israel, after the pursuing Egyptians with their
horsemen had been drowned in the Red Sea. See Exodus, chapter 15.

time. Captain Williamson and I have whole motor to ourselves. Our luggage we send ahead on an AT[1] cart. There is quite a rattle of musketry and lot of gun firing.

I wonder what it can mean. No attack likely to be made – it is a case of mining and countermining. Our Sappers are first going to mine for defence and then for attack. After all that labour they will surely not take up new firing line. Get to clearing station at 4 p.m. and sit about waiting.

See Dearsley who like a silly ass has lost my Maori songs. We are not going on 5 pm boat – so go to bed. Have a 12 hours night disturbed considerably by having to get up frequently. All of the officers are sick cases. I had an injection which seemed to relieve the griping considerably.

Thursday September 23

At 10 a.m. we get on to lighter and to little tug boat which draws lighter to mine sweeper. Minesweeper takes us from within the Lancashire Landing Harbour to Hospital Ship No. 10, Union Castle Line – the *Gascon*.

It is pretty stormy and first time we come up alongside we miss and have to make another circuit. Succeed second time round. Stretcher cases and baggage are hauled up by crane and we get up ladder by jumping on to it as boat swings near. I am put in dysentery ward and am given soup, fish and custard for lunch. How unspeakably delicious it tasted. I fear what the result will be, but doctor should know best.

Padre on board living on the fat of the land. They feed like fighting cocks at best hotel. He keeps walking past door, but does not come in. He has better fish to fry and

---

1 Army Transport.

spends his time in close converse with one sister or another. I want not to see him, but to get him to have my letter home posted. At 5 p.m. lots of returned fit men shipped off to Peninsula. I sent some notes.

Doctor comes round and inspects visits. Padre comes round for a chat. He is a young burly curate – no very striking qualities. They should put older men in hospital ships. About half an hour after injection have a little griping and 2 visits, then at 3 am have about as bad an hour as I have yet experienced.

Hospital Ship Gascon No. 10
Thursday September 23

Dear Family,
Don't be alarmed, they say a tiger once having tasted blood is forever a man eater. When once after hardships of trench warfare a man tastes the joys and peace of hospital ships, he frequents them, of course if given a suitable ailment. Having tried enteric I am giving dysentery a trial. A good excuse for you not to write letters as we are moored up and no trench address will catch me. However letters to Brigade, 126th B, MEF will reach me in time. My internal economy is not able to stand Gallipoli's climate, therefore, I may be sent home, but don't build on it.

If I do get home I shall try to go to France. There may be snow and mud but not micro-bearing dust. I am full of dead germs and so immune to most diseases, vaccinated for small pox, inoculated against typhoid and cholera, injected for dysentery. The War Office will acquaint you of my second downfall, but I hope you will first get this. Probably you will, as official notice is sent from a land hospital. But as our ship has got its full complement of

sick and wounded we should probably sail tonight. If I
get a chance I will cable too. Wonder what Chaplain
General will tell you this time. He can't kill me twice. I
will get this off by mine sweeper at 5 p.m. I don't think I
should cope with a job on one of these floating palaces,
but I should soon get sluggish liver and bad temper from
too much eating and sleep and too little work. Already,
after a day's treatment on hospital ship, I feel much
better, in fact hardly an invalid.

There's a delightful and fascinating uncertainty about
active service. You can't take thought for morrow, because
not known, where you may be or be doing – you can't lay
plans. I shall cut down forethought to a minimum, if I get
through this. It saves so much mental energy. Colonel
Indian Medical Services has been and booked me for
Ausonia which is bound for home. I told him my inside
and sense of fitness did not warrant my going home, so I
don't know what will happen. I gather I am now for
home, but whether just a sea voyage there and back with
a few days in hospital or convalescence ward or really
'<u>home</u>' I can't say. *Nous verrons tout à l'heure.*[1]

No chance of letting you know where or when we
arrive or how I should get to Chelmsford. I should be run
in as a vagrant – boots worn – clothes filthy, dirty old
jacket of a Tommy which doesn't fit. Must sneak in in the
dark. I shall have to report first to Chaplain General. If I
wire you, you might meet me in London, show me the
way and take me home – assuming I do get home. Why
not enjoy fancies when one can?

All the best

Ken

1 We shall see later.

Friday September 24

10 a.m. set sail for Mudros. PM – another injection – read and write letters. Here I suppose we shall stay till the overworked base wallahs, weary with hardships of 7 course meals and soft feather beds, can turn from wine and women to decide where the wounded and sick are to go. It is an Indian Medical Services boat and the Colonel, an awfully nice fellow, is himself IMS – perhaps that accounts for treatment. As a rule padres come after the rest have been attended to. Within the Indian Army, padres are treated with deference. You never can tell from a wound a man's chance of life. How many of those suffering from trivial wounds, I find, have died, yet how many serious cases have pulled through? French Junior Subalterns have quarters which a Brigadier would jump at in British Army. They know the value of a little comfort and luxury in prolonging the duration of a man's usefulness in the trenches.

Wave theory does not work in attack. First wave of men goes waving on till it dwindles to nothing and then has to return. Succeeding waves never materialise.

Saturday September 25

How fertile is the imagination on a sunny fresh blue morning in the Mediterranean ... For months, nay years I fancy, my *regiones internae*[1] have been seriously disordered. Dysentery or the treatment of it seems at all events to have temporarily remedied this. My mind torpid, my tongue tied, my body without energy. Perhaps I was better fitted for vegetable than human world.

I was almost convinced I could be a poet in these early

1 Internal workings.

hours of the morning while the mind is still fancy-free.
Sweet flowing phrases come easily to the lips. Rich
metaphors crowd the brain, noble ideals and hope fill the
breast. Then dawns the dull prosaic day. Reason fetters
the language of the muse, the delicate metaphor, in the
wake of inexorable logic. The little drab words of
business form the confines beyond which we may not
pass. No thoughts imagining beyond the sphere of desk
and £sd are permitted. The child's dreams which people
the earth with lovely lovable beings and furnish it with all
that ministered to true joy is now restricted to those few
brief moments 'twixt sleeping and waking. Since the
cheerless laughter, deep lines and furrows on the brow
have appeared, enthusiasm is dead and life but bravely
endurable.

How I waste good paper.

The five of us in our ward brightened up yesterday and
talk flowed merrily. Two are MOs and they pulled my leg
because I am given medicine shortly before meals. They
say my hearty feeding was causing a shortage of ship's
food and they were choking me off! Of course I had a
meal, but only the milk diet (soup, fish, jelly), with no ill
result in ¾ hour. I hear of another Division of boys (a
Welsh Division, probably 11th) who were totally useless.
200 held up their hands. The Turks took their rifles and
ammunition and sent them back (sic).

Major Lawford and I recall Canal days. How the Turks
were repulsed and were allowed to retire unmolested.
Our men ordered not to leave the trenches. A six inch
gun brought up and taken away unmolested. The Cavalry
itching to be at them, were kept for 2 days flicking flies
off their noses and then told to go and find the enemy
they could. One man so weary he forgets which is his
right hand and which his left, and goes wandering like a

sleep walker towards a Turkish trench gathering sticks. Fortunately Turks are not awake. Colonel comes to give me final injection and tells me we leave on the *Ausonia* tomorrow, while *Gascon* goes back to Gallipoli. Probably something is going to happen again and I shall be out of it, unfortunately.

Feel great – night was undisturbed. 7 a.m. we are alongside *Ausonia* – Cunard Line. Temp 97°. It is the ideal, I fancy, for me. Have never felt better or more cheerful in my life – or perhaps it is the sea doing it. I don't want to go back to the old profitless woolgathering days. But I wish to be able to think logically, to express myself clearly and readily and able to form well defined mental pictures. The Scots clipped form of speech and stolid prosaic literalness rather tries one's patience. A little is a tonic, a lot is a drug.

8.30 a.m. Colonel Hugo has just been in and put me down for the *Ausonia* which is bound for home. Feeling rather better, my conscience made me blurt out I am not bad enough for that. So I know not what will happen. 300 to go on *Ausonia*, the rest on shore. You are bound for home, the sister says. Orderly says *Ausonia* is due for Plymouth. The *Mauretania* has run ashore to avoid sinking.

If K of K[1] came out and saw how things were organised (or rather were not organised) out here, he would have a fit. Saturday night on the *Ausonia* is a striking example of the law of associations. I had been trying to recollect tune of a Maori song which an officer had sung to me as I lay in the bunk on *Huntsgreen*. Once back in my bunk in *Ausonia*, within a few seconds it came back to me in a flash.

1 Lord Kitchener of Khartoum.

Set sail at 6 p.m. Again quite a sporting chance of getting torpedoed. I notice half-a-dozen very plucky sisters on board. They keep very quiet – nothing frivolous about them.

Sunday September 26

Glorious evening service. Most of walking wounded and some officers came. England had turned to her idols – gold and pleasure. Will England turn to her old ideals? Thus Tennyson – following the king. Keep trotting to piano and having a tune. How refreshing it is. Talk to Major Lawford after supper. HQ a mass of meanness and spite. '*Where is my pack animal?*' says peevish Staff Officer, '*but I don't want it there*'. Two big leather cases – a few sandwiches and one soda water. Then he collars the headlights from a man, so that motorcyclists risk their neck. ¾ of medical comforts go to Officers Mess. An order for medical comfort is sent in, in triplicate, to Society of Friends Ambulance aristocracy – clerks in Government Office who are lazy easygoing beggars – marquises doing office work.

We are waiting for orders. Some say we are all to go to England – others say that boat is to be cleared. It is a pathetic sight to see sorting out process – so near and yet so far. Sheep and goats – the casting of the die. In many cases it means life or death.

Cottonera, a barracks turned into a military hospital, is several miles from the harbour where we landed on Malta.[1] When we got there, we saw the harbour from the window, looking but a few yards off. Major Lawford

1 While in Malta Harbour on the outward voyage, one of the men in 42nd East Lancashire Division was overheard saying to a friend 'Well, mate, I suppose this is this 'ere b_____ Empire we have heard about!' *Letters from Helles* – Sir Henry Darlington, London, 1936, p. 16.

and I have been put into a large bare dreary room with
two beds. It seemed cheerless to me after seeing nothing
but a tent dug-out cabin for a year. The wind outside
howled over the cold bleak prospect.

We felt rather miserable at being turned out of the
Ausonia homeward bound and the surroundings
intensified our depression. We got into bed after a little
soup and milk pudding – a meagre diet for convalescents
suffering from debility with temperature below normal.
All they ask is *age, rank, religion, unit* – and then, looking
wise, prescribe for you same treatment as all the rest,
whatever the complaint.

Looking out at dusk, I detect the sun sunk behind
ridge opposite, lighting up some buildings on the edge
like phantom castles. It is a noisy place and every footstep
echoes. The sentry outside and the orderly inside are
always on the tramp. Outside the bugle blows, inside the
bell, i.e. a brush handle and dust pan. Most harsh,
discordant and unpleasant. Sister says we took a zig-zag
course coming out here and that we were disembarked
because of submarine danger. Or else a yellow flag was
flown when we left because of an infection case and we
were put in quarantine.

Almost clear of dysentery, I think, but very weak. At noon
guns fire, buzzers ring, bells toll there. Seems to be an
endless number of clocks and church bells and much
tolling for the dead. Strange treatment by the RAMC –
milk and bed so a change from the *Ausonia*. I get up and
go on full diet. Cottonera bed and milk diet again.

Thursday September 30

Finished jigsaw puzzle which I started yesterday. 200
pieces. Must be getting stronger. Maltese chicken for

lunch. Hymns being played on harmonium in a ward. How like home here in this cold dreary hospital 13 months away from home. With all clocks striking 6 p.m. and many bells ringing for service and harmonium playing, it feels like Sunday evening in Manchester or perhaps Chester. The Sirocco is getting up.

Friday October 1

My medical history has been taken – this presupposes sitting in front of a board, I suppose. Then home. Bought Maltese lace. Expecting a visit from matron in charge of all hospitals, so we got things tidy and put on our most wan invalid's expression. Instead, in marches Lord Methuen, the Governor of Malta.[1] Chatted with us and finds I come from Lytham. He relates how he was at school with old Harry Clifton who used to walk in his sleep. Such delinquency meant a severe swishing because Head said it was a good cure. He saved Harry often and knew Rosebery,[2] Charles Beresford[3] and Lord George Hamilton.[4] He and Beresford were the bad boys.

Saturday October 2

Same as yesterday. Read, wrote postcards and played chess. Was visited by Surgeon-General. Some rain last night.

---

1 Field-Marshal Lord Methuen, 1845–1932, was Governor and Commander-in-Chief, Malta, from 1915 to 1919.
2 Lord Rosebery left Oxford without a degree, but still achieved his three stated ambitions – to marry an heiress, win the Derby and become Prime Minister (1894–5).
3 Admiral Lord Beresford unusually combined his career in the Navy with being a Conservative MP.
4 Lord George Hamilton served in the Cabinet as Secretary of State for India, 1900–3.

Sunday October 3

More bells than usual which says a lot. This eastern smell is sometimes foul, sometimes aromatic. A glorious Sunday morning. WHY AM I A PRISONER? How I would love to answer the call of those bells. But I think I am only allowed to go up to the 5.30 p.m. service somewhere upstairs.

Chaplain Glew of Birmingham tried to get me to take the service – but I found the previous Sunday on the *Ausonia* was too much for me. So I just played organ for him. He seemed to think himself overworked – having been out here 3 weeks. Had a clerical voice and delivery – and got me to finish the service.

Monday October 4

Waited on bed as usual for MO's visit – then got up for lunch. Internal workings rather disturbed. MO gave a pleased smile, but it did not cure me. Why cannot War Office appoint respectable ladies as sisters, instead of these impertinent women with red noses? They either look like a stuffed pig, or a vicious one, or else they attempt sarcasm and descend to poor and vulgar wit. Perhaps they are afraid some officers will try to proposition them.

Drove to ferry. Went by dower to opposite side and then by steam ferry to Valetta. Hired a carrozza for 2 hours. Saw Chapel of Bones, Military Hospital, St John's Church and armoury. Remarkable coincidence that I should meet Waggle Andrews in St John's. He had been appointed to be in charge of the Australian Recreation Camp at Lemnos in conjunction with Creighton.[1] The

---

1 Revd Oswin Creighton had served with the 89th Field Ambulance, 29th Division, until he was shipped home with dysentery.

cabby would not take legal fare and tried to use physical
force. As I was weak as a kitten, I had to call native
policeman. Cabby did not seem to care much for bobby,
but Major Lawford came up and I managed to get off.

Glew came along. In course of conversation I said, '*You
are evidently a sticker*'.

'*Yes, I don't think anyone can accuse me of shirking*'.

'*Why, old boy, do you then ask me, an invalid, to do your
work?*' thought I.

I think he is a stick-in-the-mud and still quite a boy. He
complained of G.G's incapacity as an organiser. We
baffled him over a chess problem. I weakly promised to
take service for him on Sunday.

Tuesday October 5

Morning in bed as usual. In afternoon go to Valetta, drive
to Strada Reale, walk to top and then along rampart,
commanding good views of Upper Barakka Gardens
where I met the ubiquitous Waggle Andrews again. He
was just going back to Lemnos, came down lift and then
tobogganed down steps to landing stage but even that
quick descent did not enable us to catch the boat. So late
again for tea. Gramophone, piano, organ, band all could
be dimly heard. Very annoying trying to separate and
identify tunes.

Wednesday October 6

Hear Bulgaria has not replied to Russia's ultimatum.[1]
Interesting afternoon – went to National Museum.

---

1 Bulgaria joined the Central Powers on 11 October 1915. Britain responded by
declaring war four days later.

Excellent collection of coins, all found in Malta through various stages of her history. Phoenician Scarab, flints and many other curious items. At 3pm it closed. So I went out to take photos.

Immediately a Maltese Sergeant pounced and marched me to police station. The police explain they are sorry, but law must be complied with. They develop my roll of film and confiscate it. Get to hospital 5.30. Go to concert – a Private in RAMC is one of the Follies – he is a great asset. One VAD[1] sings sweetly and daughter of Admiral Limpus plays violin delightfully and performs Schumann's *Reverie*. Spotted a chaplain in the room and find he is a Dominican. Strange to see him in uniform and still more strange to hear him join in ragtime.

Did not sleep well, mosquito ping pings round my face and the sand flies bite abominably. For several hours I listened to the innumerable clocks striking each quarter. They only strike the hours up to six and then start again. I hear that bells used to be much worse. Three hours a day and night, a chorus of full-throated bells were clanging – till Lord Methuen forbade them as injurious to health of sick and wounded! Also one could hear the loud tones of Maltese soldiers turning out the guard or performing some manoeuvre every quarter.

Thursday October 7

Went before medical board. They did not publish their verdict. Took train to Museum Station Notabile. The carriages were in form of tramcar at home – tickets were issued and collected. The whole country looks like a huge jigsaw puzzle – a maze of small terraces here and there, villages of white square-built houses dominated by

1 Voluntary Aid Detachment i.e. Red Cross Nurse.

a church. Also I saw a number of wells and occasionally round domes e.g. Mustapha Church. In between wall and terraces lies a little stony ground on which a few vegetables grow sparsely. At Museum Station I get carozza carriage to drive to catacombs, St Paul's Tomb and St John's Cathedral.

In the Cathedral, there was a service going on. Some very solemn festival for the Archbishop. Consequently I could not see the whole of it. The service was very theatrical with only half dozen old men and children present. All the rest were monks, men's choir and priests. Boys walking about everywhere with candles. The Archbishop was on his throne, 2 boys holding a huge book in front of him.

Most hideous noise and nearly all the service was sung. The principal treble sounded as though he was shouting '*Evening Paper see latest war news*!' – in loud harsh piercing nasal tones, and then the rest would join in with roar like spectators at a football match. To my thinking it was most unbecoming. Then the Archbishop kept dressing and undressing and so did the rest, only they were more modest and did it in the background.

Friday October 8

I go to Casal Paula by train and visit hypogeum.[1] It was discovered accidentally by table falling through floor or man falling down well which was being sunk – a most interesting place. A sacrificial altar shows it was once a temple. Many bones (of which I collared one) show it to have been an ossuary. Also used probably as a place of refuge and for storing dried fruit. Get back but cannot learn my destination. Wife of Admiral Limpus pays us a visit.

1 The underground chamber.

Saturday October 9

After writing home and many postcards I learn at
10.26 a.m. that I am to be *invalided home*. Sounds rather
strange coming in midst of this sightseeing and
gallivanting about. Much cheering in barracks hard by.
The German prisoners are greeting the Bulgarians who
are being confined. The Governor is really waking up and
at last taking measures promptly.

In the afternoon, after transacting some business, I get
carozza at 3 p.m. to go up to Hagar Qim[1] Neolithic
temple. Do a little haggling, till I find one to take me for
5/-. Get clearer view of country. In many places these
relics were by the wayside quarries which showed what a
thin layer of deep red brown earth there was, sometimes a
foot or so, sometimes only a few inches. Mules used for
ploughing. Houses built of squared stone, greyish white
or light buff – one or two stones with steps outside. Road
narrow with rough stone wall on either side – often only
carozza could squeeze through.

Only here and there is it possible for carriages to pass
each other. In villages we passed through somehow,
turning and twisting very sharply between two high sided
walls like those of a mediaeval castle. Here we got held
up several times – beautiful arches in one place led only
into a field. I saw no gates as at home. None of the dirty
timber and mud hovels, as in Egypt. Mainly because
there is nothing much but stone as building material.
People not very good looking – local boys very rude and
impertinent – cheek develops into cowardice.

KOMRM[2] sent to garrison Cyprus, but cried so much

1 Described as the least understood of all temples in Malta. The most significant
relic found there was the 'fat lady' figure of a naked woman whom archaeologists
dubbed the Venus of Malta.
2 King's Own Malta Regiment of Militia.

they were sent back to their mammies. Caught sight of an occasional spinning wheel. Returning I felt rather tired. The carozza is not built with a view to comfort of the traveller. Yet passing through these mediaeval villages they appeared to my mind dreamy with sleepiness.

Then suddenly blazed forth the sunset and we just happened to pass a line of palm trees. My heart leaped – a touch of Egypt and at once I understand the call of the East. I wonder if I shall be able to stay away. The stars came out, and nearing Cottonera I was recalled to realities by passing a dozen motor ambulances bearing men to hospital ship.

Sunday October 10

Went to Holy Communion 7 a.m. – feeling rather washed out and headachy. At 10 a.m. had foot dressed. In afternoon I dozed in sun on the veranda gazing at the blue Mediterranean. Foot dressing again at 5 p.m. and temperature above normal. I talk to men and play organ at evening service. They were very attentive. I talked too long and was rather done up – had to get sister to give me aspirin (called by new name now). My text was *'Hereby we know that we know God if we keep his commandments'*.

Talked about Bahars whose tenets were Christian before it became respectable, meaningless and without savour. I quoted a paragraph about the proof of Christ being power of faith he left behind. Has our religion for us as much power to bear sorrow as Mohammed's? i.e. note the resignation of Turk Kismet – *it is the will of Allah* – so no grumbling or cursing his fate. God is real to them. Hear them chant their evening hymn to Allah – worship and supplication. Notice that their code is not very high or exacting, but in fear they obey the Koran.

The muezzin calls from his minaret – men prostrate themselves. During their long fast, they keep commandments, so they know God. God is a real help to them – not like us. We suppose there is a God – but really don't *KNOW*. Their childlike joy, twinkle in eye, untroubled calm shines through as with the Bahar Allah.

Trouble may disturb the surface of the water, but beneath is a deep untroubled calm and joy – *the peace of God, which passeth all understanding.*

Hear three ships have been sunk off Valletta.

Monday October 11

Got choked off with the Colonel's compliments etc. (for playing the piano in the morning). In the afternoon I tried many of the Upchen songs. Shopped in Valletta, and met chaplains going to serve somewhere on the Med. who looked *morituri*.[1] Have not yet had the self important and mysterious air rubbed off them. I was itching to tell them the Turks would soon put them out of their misery. '*Cheer up, you'll soon be dead.*'

In afternoon and early evening had tea and music at Admiral Limpus's house.[2] Miss Limpus played some delightful outré violin pieces mainly by Dvorak, and Upchen sang all very modern songs. It was better than a tonic. So far did I forget myself that I had to brave a cold supper. The cook, being contrary, was punctual for the first time.

Thursday October 14

Went to Valetta in afternoon and bought photos of Hagar Qim. Then several games of chess with the Major. More

1 About to die.
2 Admiral Sir Arthur Limpus, 1863–1931, had been Naval Adviser to the Turkish Government from 1912 to 1914. When Best met him socially, he was Admiral Superintendent and Senior Naval Officer, Malta.

argument with police over my camera, which they had confiscated.

Friday October 15

Rest most of morning – a little chess and music in the afternoon. Go down to Admiralty at 5 p.m. and try some songs for Upchen. Mrs Limpus arrives as we were having tea. Upchen quite controls things – does himself well and greets Mrs L with 'Hello, old dear' – they embrace. I was embarrassed at seeing a Private and Admiral's wife so comport themselves and yet it seemed quite natural and rather pleasing, for she is an old dear and U is a man of much feeling and unEnglish in his demonstrativeness.

Then Miss L arrives – much fluster. The music is sorted out and off we go to perform at a concert at St Ignatius Hospital. We go in naval boat pulled by two sailors of Custom House – drive to Sliema Harbour, passing a dimly lighted entrance which led to a sort of subterranean underground town, a modern hypogeum where the criminals and scum of Valetta live. Only in the company of a priest or police officer is a visitor safe. Cross by ferry boat and then drive up to hospital. Carozza goes at sedate walk uphill and downhill, and even on level because of pedestrians. We arrive with concert in full swing. It was in the big ward. The atmosphere was decidedly apathetic. Some broad comic turns were missing and so little enthusiasm had been worked up.

Miss Limpus's refined harmony was not appreciated and she sang Mendelssohn's '*I would that my love*'. Her violin was suffering and Upchen's voice was not enhanced by breathing ether in operation room all day. A new batch of wounded from Suvla Bay. Perhaps men felt they were not expected to appear hearty, but play part of invalids.

Came back by same route, except that we drove from harbour to harbour via Floriana.

Got back to Admiralty 9 p.m. Found dinner in progress. We therefore chipped in. Had much too good a meal for an invalid, but enjoyed it immensely after hospital diet. Asked for whisky and soda, perhaps a rather bourgeois drink. To keep up appearances they mixed it in a glass jug and poured it for me to drink into a champagne glass. Apparently I should have been teetotal. The Admiral drank barley water.

Argued with Mrs Limpus about matron. She was highly offended, because I suggested that most of her cases appeared to be light. Trod on her pet corn. Apparently each boasts that she has the worst and most cases of the sun. Mrs Limpus contended that they like to feel they are doing good work and are finding scope for their skills. I said they seemed to desire brutal scraps which cause men to get badly wounded and so afford them a chance to parade their skill – therefore callous. We just get in by 11 p.m. Night sister meets me and says I am to be packed and ready to leave for England by 10 AM NEXT DAY. I find my cablegram in answer to family enquiring *'How are you?'* has not gone off as it was not filled in on right form ... Therefore I alter it to *'Progressing famously. Embarking for England today!'*

Saturday October 16

Having no money I gulp down brekker, dash off to Anglo-Egypt Bank to cash cheque, but not being introduced by a resident fail to get any. Left Cottonera in motor ambulance at 10.15 a.m. At Somerset Wharf 10.30. There we sat about and waited till hospital boat was brought alongside. 12.30 – delay due to French hospital ship. Where she should have made way for our ship, they began to pull her engine to pieces, so our hospital ship had to moor up on next wharf.

12.45 – Lord Methuen comes to say goodbye. He singled me out and chatted, then, wishing me good luck, he shakes hands all along the line. 3.40 we leave. If we are not out by 6 p.m, we have to stay overnight. On Somerset Wharf were 17 guns c.18 inch and the submarine which went up Narrows, also in dry dock.

1 p.m. 1st class lunch. I get corner berth with 2 portholes on promenade deck (single berth). Gozo's 3 big churches are silhouetted against glorious sunset. How do the natives find money? Each does his bit. I see from my couch search lights blazing all over the ship, instead of gutting candle and all cracks carefully covered up. *The Carisbrooke Castle* is very fast, but somewhat unsteady – needs a lot of ballast. She was used as a staff ship. Malta looking very grey and miserable as we left her in a misty drizzle.

Sunday October 17

7.30 – 8 a.m. Have a bath, passing Carthage. 11 a.m – Held a good service on aft troop deck. Told men not to damp martial ardour at home, but by words and examples point to duty – duty to God and Country. Officers, sisters and men attend in good numbers. 12 noon – We pass Galeta Islands on right, while keeping Africa in a view on left. Glorious sunset again.

Monday October 18

Found my old 'bob' issue razor and had first good shave since I lost it months ago. Clocks back half an hour. Hugging African coast – slipping smoothly through blue lagoon of the Mediterranean. Sun shining warmly. M.O.'s find it hot – I find it a trifle chilly out of sun and fear what England, where they have already had snow, will be like.

Play chess, read *East and West* by D.T. Wilson and work gramophone – Tannhäuser Scharwenka[1] and Gilbert and Sullivan – really enjoyable selection of music. So we float in luxurious idleness, broken at intervals by rich feasts. Occasionally boat slips by or appears for a few minutes on horizon. Muggy, misty night and we fear we may not see Gibraltar.

Tuesday October 19

By 10.30 when we arrive at Gib. sun is shining though a sea mist hovers round Gibraltar Rock. Shall we be pitched off or shall we have long to wait? *Gloucester Castle* already in harbour so I take photo of it with *El Desire* behind. *Royal George*, sister to *Royal Edward*, passes us outward bound. Natives as usual come with fruit, sweets, scent and baccy. Fruit not allowed, as nearly all of us on board are cases of enteric and dysentery.

11.55 *The Gascon* rolls up. It started from Malta 24 hours ahead of us.
12.35 Launch comes out. '*You are to proceed to Southampton*' bawls officer through megaphone. '*Cheerio!*' Engines start as if by magic.
1.30 Off goes the *Gascon*
1.45 We are homeward bound. Seagulls flying round. Our robin disappears – he had accompanied us from Malta.
4 p.m. Overhauled the *Gascon*, though she was taking inside course – as she was passing Parifa.
5 p.m. Land disappearing, cling to Spain up to here. Some beautiful ships pass by in full sail and then, in the dark, a fairylike hospital ship.

1 Xavier Scharwenka (1850–1924) was a Polish-German pianist and composer.

Singsong below decks. Ship's butcher was one of the most naturally gifted humorists I have seen. His expressions were quite original, and good '*My Old Dutch*'. Also ship's carpenter who had been a Music Hall stage performer sang with great panache – the rest were poor.

9.30 Chess.

10 p.m. My turn for evening treatment. Wafting across the sea is the spicy smell of Spain. It reminds me of Cairo.

Wednesday October 20

Really lazy day at sea. No land in sight – we all swarm round stern of boat making most of last bit of warm sun. Most of us sleep in our deck chairs. Porpoises playing round ship. Captain prophesies fog – but it's still calm and bright.

1.45 off Belen Roche, near Lisbon.

Thursday October 21

Must be getting better. I have left both the Gallipoli gallop and the Turkey trot behind.

5 am On deck I saw a light in the bay which must have been Cape Finistère. All morning we rocked in the cradle of the deep under the grateful warmth, but not scorching heat, of southern sun and sleep most of the morning.

1 pm Porpoises are still playing round the ship and we have just passed through the scene of Trafalgar.[1]

1.30 Whale slips by and blows a bit. We are doing jolly well, but almost need fiddles at dinner-table, and cloths are damped to prevent glasses and plates slipping off.

1 Furthermore, Best was there on the anniversary of Nelson's great victory.

Friday October 22

6.45 Off Ushant – black point of land jutting out from
French coast with lighthouse. Most brilliant sun rise –
blazing red with streaks of gold. We seem to have just
missed a storm – a fair sea on. I expect the ship to turn a
somersault, if she gets into a real heavy sea, judging by
her antics.
8 p.m. St Catherine's Light. We run into St Helen's Bay.
Move about a bit and hover in obedience to signals.
9 p.m. Pilot and examining officers come aboard. Pilot
takes us into Netley. I find that the stoppage and signals
were because a German submarine had just blown up two
ships with loss of 19 lives. The submarine is said to be
caught in nets.
10.30 Moved into Southampton Water.

Saturday October 23

Morning – find we are off to Netley Hospital.

9.40 Pilot comes aboard and we move off towards
Southampton. 12.15 MO comes aboard – booked us
all for London. At 12.45 we are told to leave the boat.
Just missed lunch. Train leaves Southampton 1.20. We
get a little to eat at 2 pm. See a few aeroplanes on the
way.

    Arrived at station near St Mark's, Chelsea at 5 p.m.
Stewart and I have been sent to St Mark's College
Hospital. I sent a wire home. Band in grounds playing
very indifferently popular martial airs. Why can't we get
away from war? Boy Scout comes back with change for
telegram – decent, smart little fellow. Everywhere the
scout is proving his worth.

    We meet members of the Expeditionary Force to

France in train. They seem depressed compared with our lively contingent.

Having survived the hazard of being torpedoed during the eight-day voyage from Malta, Kenneth Best arrived safely back in England, having convalesced to some extent on board the Carisbrooke Castle. He was an in-patient at St Mark's College Hospital for only two days. Discharged on 25 October, he returned to Sandon Rectory near Chelmsford, where his father had the living, to be reunited with his parents.

Much as he would have liked to go once more to Gallipoli, he was not yet fit enough to serve abroad. He spent much of the next six months on chaplaincy duties, first at Weymouth and then with the 3/6th Battalion, South Staffordshire Regiment, at Catterick. He was posted to the Western Front on 21 June 1916.

Meanwhile, high-level changes had been made to the command structure on Gallipoli. Sir Ian Hamilton had been replaced and the new C.-in-C. was Sir Charles Monro. As will be seen in the following commentary, the decision was made by the end of October 1915 to evacuate the Peninsula – despite the strong opposition of Lord Kitchener, who had not yet been out there to see the situation for himself.

Evacuation

By the autumn it was clear that the Suvla Bay offensive had ground to a halt. It was true that a base for supplies had been established, and the Turks had not succeeded in driving the invaders back into the sea. Equally, the Allied campaign had not succeeded in winning Sari Bair or any of the vital high ground which might have enabled the Royal Navy to make a fresh bid to open up the Narrows. The inability of Stopford to strike while the iron was hot on 8 August, before the Turks had time to bring up reinforcements, had cost the Allies dear.

As a result, Sir Ian Hamilton was now requesting three more divisions. Even as Kitchener was mulling over this request, he was under pressure from the French to support Joffre in his plans for an autumn offensive, in what would become the costly Battle of Loos. The Salonika Expedition, aimed at bolstering the hard-pressed Serbs, had been launched at the end of September, for which the 10th Irish Division had been taken from Hamilton's forces on Gallipoli. Given the superior status of the French Army – who held so much more of the front line on the Western Front than did the British[1] – Kitchener was obliged to turn down Hamilton's request for more troops.

---

1 Because the French Army had so much more manpower available. The British Expeditionary Force (BEF) had arrived in France in August 1914 with four infantry divisions and one cavalry division. The French had seventy-two divisions.

Changes at the top had come. Following a disagreement with Hamilton over the timing of an attack in August, the hapless but genial Stopford had been removed from his command of IX Corps on 15 August, being replaced by General de Lisle. As Michael Hickey writes, '*His (Stopford's) appointment in the first place was a sorry reflection on the rigidly hierarchical system which made appointments to key posts on the basis of Buggins' turn.*'[1]

De Lisle was not in command for long. Hamilton's request earlier for Lieutenant-General Byng to take overall command of the Suvla Bay landings had been turned down by Kitchener – but now, too late, it was granted. Byng had proved himself a highly effective commander of the 3rd Cavalry Division in the testing and close-run circumstances of the First Battle of Ypres.

In the words of H.G. Wells,[2] '*Here is a man who is nothing if not a soldier . . . He knows Clausewitz by heart, he is a master of tactics, he has studied every battlefield in the world. He has the physique of a machine and the brains of twenty men, which fits him eminently to be a cavalry leader.*'

Yet Stopford had been selected over him. Ironically, with Stopford back in England, Byng was now appointed to be the commander of IX Corps. He arrived at Suvla Cove on 24 August and was shocked by the conditions on the beach in front of his eyes and the ramshackle nature of the shelters in the hillside – so different to what he had been used to in France. In his well-researched biography of Byng, Jeffery Williams describes the scene as being '*more typical of a Middle Eastern bazaar than an army base*'. But Byng had taken over too late to resurrect any chance of the Suvla landings being a success. Within a week he was instructing his staff to draw up a secret plan for evacuating Suvla –

1 Gallipoli, p. 304.
2 See his article in *Town and Country*, 17 October 1914.

even though it would be months before the final decision was taken.

There had been mutterings about Hamilton's leadership for some time. On 14 October, the Dardanelles Committee decided to recall both Hamilton and his senior staff officer, General Sir Walter Braithwaite. General Sir Charles Monro, who had been commanding the Third Army in France, was appointed in his place. He was a Westerner who had never been in favour of the Dardanelles Campaign. He arrived at Gallipoli on 28 October with a remit from Kitchener to report back to the Government on how best to lift the stalemate on Gallipoli; and to decide whether evacuation of the Peninsula would be a feasible alternative. Monro did not mince matters. He made a rapid evaluation from the three invasion bridgeheads and deduced that further attacks would be fruitless, since the Turks still held all the high ground. He recommended evacuation. He warned the Dardanelles Committee that casualties would be heavy.

General Sir Ian Hamilton with some of his staff and
French liaison officers at Kephalos, on the morning of
his departure for England, 17 October 1915
© Imperial War Museum. Q13557

This was not the recommendation that the Committee wanted to hear. There were conflicting views in the Cabinet and it was impossible to predict the scale of casualties if it was decided to evacuate. Kitchener strongly opposed evacuation, which in his view 'would be the most disastrous event in the history of the British Empire'.[1] He at last went out to make his own evaluation on the ground in early November – and took over a week to reach a decision, even pondering a fresh invasion at Alexandretta.

In the end, Monro stood firm, and he was supported by his corps commanders. He did not believe that a fresh influx of troops would make any substantial difference, and declined the offer of four fresh divisions. De Robeck would not contemplate a fresh naval attack. There were reports of German artillery reinforcements. Winter was on the way and the sectors held by the Allies would become overcrowded by the arrival of so many new troops, as well as even more insanitary than they were already. Even Kitchener, after his visit, now saw that evacuation was inevitable.

By the late autumn, morale among the troops was at a low ebb. Few escaped the scourge of dysentery – nicknamed the Gallipoli Gallop – and it was this, as we have seen, which had caused Kenneth Best to be shipped home earlier. Dysentery, combined with the heat and flies, sapped all the energy of its victims, rendering them listless and unfit for combat. In October, 300 men a day were being evacuated sick and artillery ammunition was tightly rationed.

Morale was further lowered by the devastating weather which had struck the Peninsula at the end of November. The troops in the Suvla area, especially those on the Kiretch Tepe Ridge, were the most exposed to the continuous downpour and gale conditions which were more reminiscent of a monsoon. Men of the 1st Royal Munster Fusiliers were

1 Dardanelles Committee Minutes, 11 October 1915.

An ambulance wagon from the 42nd East Lancashire Division
ploughs through the mud in Gully Ravine after the
torrential rains of November 1915
© Imperial War Museum. Q13642

drowned in their trenches, having no time to escape. The
cascading rain was then followed by snow and biting cold, so
that many more died of exposure.

The remnants of the battalion were pulled back. Men
streamed back to the beaches exhausted, and many were
frozen to death on the way. The Turks suffered casualties
from the same freak weather and there was an unexpected
truce. On the beaches, the medical facilities were overwhelmed, the hospitals were crammed to overflowing with
casualties, and no relief was available from outside until the
storm was over. This emergency must have been reported
back to London and on 8 December the decision was taken
by the Cabinet to evacuate Gallipoli.

In the Second World War, the evacuation of Dunkirk at the
end of May 1940, was deemed by the British to be a remarkable success. Similarly, the evacuation from first Anzac and

Suvla, then later from Helles, was the most successful part of the whole Gallipoli campaign. This was largely due to brilliant planning, and the wholehearted support of the troops for whom the carrot of returning home must have been a strong incentive. How was it contrived that the Turks seemed to have no inkling of what was happening? Deception was the order of the day – and various strategies were employed.

Soon after Byng had arrived in August he devised an uncomplicated scheme for the withdrawal. The front line troops would gradually be pulled back to two defensive lines located near to the embarkation beaches. By setting to work on constructing these lines in the autumn, it would be possible to prepare for a fighting withdrawal, should the Turks discover what was happening. The Navy would take men off only at night – and those troops, animals, supplies and equipment not required for defending the beaches would be taken off first.

By the middle of December, the loading of freighters and lighters under cover of darkness was well under way, and the massive task of taking off about 80,000 men, 2,000 horse-drawn vehicles, 5,000 horses and mules and huge stocks of ordnance, had started. At Suvla, the chief naval beach master, Captain Staveley, controlled the sequence of loading immaculately. By this stage, Byng's headquarters were on a sloop off-shore, but he was present on the beaches until 3.30 a.m. every morning.

Meanwhile, everything was done to give the Turks the impression that nothing had changed. Guns continued to be fired and snipers operated as before. Machine-gun fire continued sporadically to give the impression that all was normal. There was even a delayed-action rifle produced by the Australians, which sustained firing from a trench long after its occupants had left. The tents of the medical personnel assigned to the field ambulances and casualty clearing stations were purposely left in place, even though they were unoccupied. The Turks still had no idea of what was happening – and by the night of 18/19 December, the original figure of 80,000 men had been reduced to 5,000.

At Anzac Cove, the final withdrawal began at 1.30 a.m. and Michael Hickey describes the emotional departure of the last Australians and New Zealanders:

*'At 4 a.m. there were no living defenders ashore at Anzac. The last men off had been profoundly moved at the thought of leaving their dead comrades whose simple graves they had done their best to maintain. As one Australian soldier said to General Birdwood, "I hope **they** won't hear us marching off . . ."'*

By dawn on 20 December, nobody was left and the Turks had been successfully bluffed. The evacuation from Suvla and Anzac, despite some shelling on the last morning, had passed off without a serious hitch and was undetected by the enemy. There was not a single casualty, and the only contact with the enemy was the arrival of two Turkish deserters.[1] Even the Germans were full of praise for the textbook manner in which the difficult exercise of evacuation in the face of the enemy had been conducted. The *Vossische Zeitung* reported on 21 January 1916, '*As long as wars exist, the British evacuation of the Ari Burnu (Anzac) and Anafarta (Suvla) Fronts will stand before the eyes of all strategists of retreat as a hitherto unattained masterpiece*'.

And the reputation of Byng, who had believed all along that the evacuation could be accomplished without heavy casualties, was enhanced.

History will never be able to relate the possible sequence of events if Byng had been appointed corps commander from the start. Later, in March 1916, he received the KCB[2]

---

1 *Byng of Vimy, General and Governor General* – Jeffery Williams, Leo Cooper, London, 1992, p. 107.
2 Knight Commander Order of the Bath.

for his leadership at Gallipoli. In a typically self-deprecating way, he commented, 'My great-great-uncle was shot for running away from Minorca. I was given a decoration for running away from Gallipoli. Now which is right, because surely they cannot both be'.[1]

Lieutenant-General Sir Julian Byng is welcomed aboard
HMS *Cornwallis*, the last ship to leave Suvla Bay. Behind him
is his ADC, Captain Sir Basil Brooke, who remained
with Byng for the remainder of the war
© Imperial War Museum. Q13687

The successful withdrawal from Suvla and Anzac encouraged those who were now planning the evacuation of Helles to sustain the blockade of the Dardanelles. Meanwhile the French had begun to make their final departure in mid-December, leaving only a single colonial regiment in place by Christmas.

1 *Army Quarterly*, September 1935.

Helles presented a stiffer task, in that the Turks would now be expecting the Allied troops to leave. Also, the troops had far further to march from their trenches – about 6,000 yards – to reach the beaches than they had had either at Anzac or at Suvla. Thus General Davies, the corps commander, had a tougher nut to crack. Aware that an attack by the Turks might still be possible, he decided to minimise the risk of detection by reducing the number of nights when the troops would actually withdraw.

In the event, the same deception strategies were employed as for the Anzac and Suvla operations. The cover of darkness was used every night as before, and by 7 January the remaining number of troops at Helles was down to 17,000. There was a scare when the Turks produced a two-hour bombardment – and threatened to make a frontal assault. However, the would-be attack fizzled out, and it is unclear why the Turks did not leave their trenches at this vulnerable moment for the Allies. There was a rough sea running when the last contingent was taken off, and when daylight appeared on 9 January, not a single British soldier was to be seen.

One difference from the evacuations further north was the destruction of many animals and stores. Robin Prior reports in his recent study[1] that 500 mules were shot, as many as 15,000 vehicles of all kinds were rendered unusable, and hundreds of tons of stores were torched or set alight by naval gunfire. This was deemed a small cost to pay in the light of the projected casualties.

But there was a more bitter pill to swallow: it was all over.

Heroic it certainly was, but the Gallipoli venture was a costly and unmitigated failure, redeemed only – as Kenneth Best so poignantly reveals – by the stoic resistance and courage of the men who fought and died in this ill-fated campaign.

1 *Gallipoli – The End of the Myth*, Yale University Press, 2009, p. 235.

British Army Chaplains
in the Great War

The role of chaplains in wartime has always been peculiarly difficult to define. This was never more so than in the Great War, when Army chaplains were said to come into their own. The number serving with the British Army rose from 117 in 1914 to 3,745 in 1918; about a quarter were Roman Catholic padres (649 by the end of the war).[1] One hundred and seventy-two were killed, and three were awarded the Victoria Cross. In 1919 King George V officially recognised and honoured the work of the Army Chaplains' Department by giving it the royal accolade.

The duty of the fighting soldier was clear – he was trained to kill the enemy by bayonet, rifle, grenade, or whatever means he had available. Not so the chaplains, who, like the medical officers, were not combatants. Inevitably their consciences were racked by the Christian doctrine of 'love your enemy' and turning the other cheek. How could this Christian ideology fit into a pre-battle talk to the troops, when any such suggestion of treating the enemy mercifully might become infectious, perhaps causing the men to fight in half-hearted fashion or even to desert? Was it certain that

1 Michael Moynihan, *God on Our Side – the British Padre in World War I*, Leo Cooper, London, 1983, p. 12.

God was 'on our side'? Any talk along these reflective lines might infuriate senior officers, whose clear-cut orders were to win the next battle, and ultimately the war, by inflicting the maximum number of casualties on the enemy with no awkward questions being asked. Many chaplains felt their duty was 'not to oil the wheels of war, but to support those caught up in it'.

In reality, of course, chaplains were able to still their consciences to some extent by sheltering behind the concept of the just war. In order to maintain peace and the liberty of the individual, one must work for justice and be prepared to fight for it. This line of argument presupposes that, in pursuit of global freedom from oppression and the upholding of human rights, it is justifiable to kill your enemy (even in large numbers) in order to destroy the powers of evil and to overthrow tyranny. This argument was used to justify the use of the atom bomb at the end of World War II. However much the ensuing horrific number of deaths was deplored, the use of the bomb did bring about the end of the war within a few days.

The attitudes of commanding officers to chaplains in the Great War varied. Many chaplains were not permitted to go near the Front – others insisted on doing so, like Kenneth Best in the Gallipoli Campaign. Best had had no military training prior to the war, but his diaries reveal his conviction that he could fulfil his pastoral role by going up close to the front line. There he could encourage frightened men before they went over the top, comfort the wounded and, when the fighting stopped, bury the dead. He is scornful of some of his fellow chaplains who, he felt, hung around further back and viewed the fighting from afar.

Ten days before Best arrived at Gallipoli, **Father William Finn**, a Roman Catholic padre, blazed an inspirational trail for front-line chaplaincy. On 25 April, undeterred by the hail of Turkish bullets on V Beach, Finn led from the front of his

battalion, 1st Royal Dublin Fusiliers, and died on the beach
below Sedd-el-Bahr fort. Finn had been ordered by his C.O.,
Lt.-Col. Richard Rooth, to stay in the boats, but disobeyed.
They lie side by side in the V Beach cemetery, still at the
head of the battalion. Finn exemplified the courage of many
Catholic chaplains and was the first Chaplain to the Forces
to be killed in the Great War.

The most effective chaplains were all of the ilk of
Kenneth Best. He was attached to the 42nd East Lancashire Division – the first TF (Territorial Forces) division to
serve overseas in this conflict, so arguably the least experienced in the ways of war. The reader will soon have
discovered how wholehearted and thoroughly committed
Best was to the welfare and solace of the men in his division.
There were other chaplains of the same calibre as Best and
I wish I could pay tribute to all of them – but few of them
left diaries! My prime motivation in editing Best's letters and
diaries is to illustrate the major contribution he made to the
morale of the troops in Gallipoli. But also to enable a wider
audience to appreciate the dire conditions which he experienced and some of the reasons why this ambitious project
failed.

The Reverend **A.W. Horden**, Principal Chaplain in the
Middle East, was responsible for the care and transfers of
chaplains of all denominations. He made a visit to the
Gallipoli GHQ on 21 June 1915, and soon realised the
conditions under which chaplains tried to operate – which
differed from those on the Western Front. He came away
convinced that chaplains' postings should be regularly
changed. In his *War Diary of the Principal Chaplain* he wrote:
'*The difficulties are very great as no part of the Peninsula is free
from shell-fire.*'[1] These were the difficulties – along with
the heat, the flies and the scarcity of fresh water – which

1 Linda Parker, *The Whole Armour of God*, Helion and Co., Solihull, 2009, p. 33.

contributed to the high rate of sickness among chaplains, and to which Kenneth Best gives chapter and verse in his diary. He laboured on until he was struck down by dysentery himself and shipped home, reluctant to leave his men and protesting that he was not ill enough to return to England.

However, this short piece also looks at the wider picture and enables me to sketch the achievements of chaplains in other theatres of the war. My intention is also to pay tribute to the heroic contributions to the morale of the troops made by other chaplains, for instance **Geoffrey Studdert-Kennedy** – known to the men as Woodbine Willie – **Philip (Tubby) Clayton** of Toc H and Poperinghe fame, **Edward Noel Mellish, VC** and **Theodore Bayley Hardy, VC**.

Studdert-Kennedy died on 8 March 1929 at the age of 45. His early death was ascribed to asthma, inevitably aggravated by his chain-smoking. He gained his nickname through his well-known practice of dispensing cigarettes along with spiritual aid to the troops. An indication of the deep veneration in which he is still held was the exhibition – 'Woodbine Willie: the Worcester Years' – organised by Canon Paul Tongue in Worcester Cathedral in March 2009, to mark the eightieth anniversary of his death. This culminated in a special service of commemoration in the cathedral. Earlier in the day there had been an ecumenical service of Holy Communion in the Royal Garrison Church of All Saints in Aldershot, arranged by the Assistant Chaplain General, at which the Bishop to HM Forces presided.

Born in Leeds in 1883, Studdert-Kennedy was the twelfth of fourteen children in a large clergy family. The family had Irish roots, as was betrayed by the intonation of his voice. From Leeds Grammar School he won a scholarship to Trinity College, Dublin, where he was described as clever rather than academic. After a nine-month course at Ripon Clergy College, he was ordained in Worcester Cathedral during the summer of 1908, and it followed that Worcester became his family and spiritual home. However, it was at Rugby, where he had his first curacy, that Studdert-Kennedy first felt the call to minister to the poorest in society and where, according to Jonathan Gurling,[1] his eccentricities and complete lack of self-awareness or self-importance first became evident. A short period as curate to his ailing father in Leeds followed in 1912. After the death of his father he agreed to take on the slum parish of St Paul's in the Blockhouse, Worcester, and arrived in Worcester in June 1914 – the same month as the assassination of Archduke Franz Ferdinand at Sarajevo, which was to unleash the First World War.

Initially he strongly supported the war and worked hard to encourage men to join up. He wrote in the parish magazine, '*There ought to be no shirking of that duty.*' In 1915 Studdert-Kennedy left his parish, was appointed as an Army chaplain on 21 December, and four days later was leading a Christmas Service in a French village square. He won the Military Cross for acts of conspicuous gallantry during the attack on Messines Ridge. Later, after experiencing the carnage and waste of human life which the Great War brought in its wake, his views – like those of Siegfried Sassoon – changed radically to a rejection of war. Like Sassoon, Studdert-Kennedy was a poet as well as a serving officer. He turned to poetry in his endeavour to come to terms with the problem of faith in a God who seemed to stand by and watch his world destroying itself, apparently indifferent to the endless suffering of humanity. His volume of poems, *Rough Rhymes*, was published in 1919, and republished in a special memorial edition after his death in 1929.

This collection includes a searing indictment of war in a poem with the simple title 'Waste'. It was read by the Mayor

1 *Church Times*, 6 March 2009.

of Worcester during the service in Worcester Cathedral on
the eightieth anniversary of Studdert-Kennedy's death:

WASTE[1]

Waste of Muscle, waste of Brain
Waste of Patience, waste of Pain,
Waste of Manhood, waste of Health,
Waste of Beauty, waste of Wealth,
Waste of Blood and waste of Tears,
Waste of Youth's most precious years,
Waste of ways the Saints have trod,
Waste of Glory, Waste of God –
WAR!

Described in David Raw's excellent biography[2] as a diffi-
dent schoolmaster and an unassuming country vicar, the
Revd **Theodore Bailey Hardy** VC, DSO, MC (1863–1918)
sounds an unlikely candidate to play a heroic role in the
Great War. He taught for many years, and among his pupils
at Nottingham High School was the controversial novelist
D.H. Lawrence. Hardy was not ordained until the age of 35.
In 1907 he was appointed headmaster of Bentham Grammar
School, but resigned from this position because of the illness
of his wife, Florence, in 1913. She died the following June,
and thus Hardy was a widower when the fateful shot at
Sarajevo rang round the world.

At the age of 51, his decision to volunteer for the forces
was astonishing. He was turned down more than once by the
Chaplaincy Department on grounds of age. But he would
not be put off and was determined to help the war effort. At
last he was called for interview in the summer of 1916 and

1 This appeared in Studdert-Kennedy's second book of poems, *More Rough Rhymes of a Padre*.
2 David Raw, *It's Only Me, A life of Theodore Hardy* – Gatebeck, 1988.

was accepted – the Somme had produced a shortage of chaplains. Hardy joined up with a large intake of raw recruits and an equivalent army rank of captain. As a chaplain, he was deemed to be Temporary Captain – Fourth Class! But there was nothing fourth class about the exceptional two-year stretch of service which followed. From December 1916, after four months at Etaples, he was attached to the 8th Battalion, Lincolnshire Regiment. His arrival coincided with the hardest winter on record since 1880–1. Before long he also had the 8th Battalion of the Somerset Light Infantry in his pastoral care.

At the end of June 1917 Hardy moved north of Ypres, then in March 1918 to Gommecourt, north of Albert, where he served until August 1918. During Passchendaele, or Third Ypres, when the reward for three months of fighting in gruesome conditions was about seven miles of Flemish mud, gained at appalling cost, he insisted on going up to the front line – often at night, despite heavy shelling. There he would tend the wounded, and carry them to the dressing station, which was also subject to heavy shelling, and try to bolster the morale of the men whose nerves were all but shattered. Then he would never withdraw or take rest until he had buried the dead – so frequently that it was reckoned he knew the burial service by heart. His opening gambit when visiting troops in front-line positions was generally '*It's only me!*' (Later, these self-demeaning words were chosen by David Raw as the title of his biography of Hardy.)

Death came to Hardy three weeks before the Armistice. In August 1918, he took part in the final Allied offensive. All efforts to persuade him to come home were unavailing. The Bishop of Carlisle had offered him the vacant living of Caldbeck, but Hardy would not leave the line. He was totally committed to the men in his two battalions and deflected any attempts to make him change his mind. Very early in the morning of 11 October 1918, he was wounded east of Cambrai and said to those helping him, '*I've been hit. I'm sorry to be a nuisance*'. He was taken to the British Military Hospital in Rouen, where he died one week later.

Hardy – the humblest of men – would have denied that he had done anything special. David Raw describes his devoted service to his men and his unselfishness as 'one man's Christian witness which the most determined atheist must respect'. It is appropriate that, to this day in Carlisle Cathedral, a brass plaque commemorates the distinguished war record of the most decorated non-combatant of the First World War.

Tubby Clayton was another of the Great War chaplains who became a legend and whose name will always be associated with Talbot House at Poperinghe, Toc H.[1] Tubby Clayton (1885–1972) was born in Queensland – though the Australian in him was largely uprooted as his parents brought him back to England at the age of two and sent him to St Paul's School, London. From there he went on to Exeter College, Oxford, where he gained a first in Theology. While studying for ordination, he became involved with the boys' club activities of the Oxford Medical Mission in Bermondsey, where he worked one night a week, joining up there with, amongst others, Barclay 'Barkis' Baron, who was later to join the central staff of Toc H.

From his early curacy at St Mary's Portsea, Clayton went to France as an Army chaplain in 1915, and it was in December of that year that he opened the soldiers' leave centre behind the lines at Poperinghe, a few miles west of Ypres, and turned it into a club for troops. Clayton was assisted by his great friend Neville Talbot and the house was named after Neville's brother Gilbert, who was killed

1 Toc H was the code name used by the signallers, Toc being part of the prevailing phonetic alphabet used by the British Army.

on 30 July 1915, while leading a counter-attack[1] near Zouave Wood. Both Talbots were sons of the Bishop of Winchester.

To this day, Talbot House, with its small but evocative garden, retains its informal atmosphere. Clayton insisted on the suspension of rank in Talbot House so that all sorts and conditions of servicemen were treated alike and pomposity was unknown. A notice greeted new arrivals which read *Abandon rank, ye who enter here*. The chapel in the hop loft on the top floor – known as the Upper Room – served as a sanctuary for men of all denominations. Here, many of them gleaned a sense of spiritual reality for the first time, before returning to the Front. By his welcoming open-door policy, Clayton overcame seamlessly any latent hostility between differing Christian traditions. At the same time the morale of the soldiers was subtly boosted by the watchwords which Clayton put in conspicuous positions in the house, such as 'Pessimists This Way Out!' or 'Don't Lose your Temper – Nobody else wants it!'

Like Woodbine Willie, Clayton had an exceptional gift for communicating with the soldiers, and at Talbot House he succeeded in lifting the hearts of the men who came there seeking respite from the horrors of the trenches.

The spirit of Toc H lived on after the war, and survives to this day. The first Toc H House to open after the war was in Kensington and within a year there were other houses in London, Manchester and Southampton. Philip Clayton had the self-imposed task of bringing about the rebirth of Toc H, not merely as an ex-servicemen's club but as an organisation with a broader base, aimed at building up fellowship within the framework of an inclusive Christianity for future generations. The movement lives on – today there are still 150

1 Lt. Gilbert Talbot (of the Rifle Brigade) is buried in Sanctuary Wood Cemetery. At Oxford he was President of the Union and a brilliant debater.

Toc H groups and 55 projects. The original Talbot House is open, and welcomes thousands of visitors every year who wish to experience the unique atmosphere of the Upper Room. The building is in frequent demand as a residential and conference centre.

The Reverend **Ernest Courtenay Crosse** was ordained in 1912 at the age of 25 and appointed Assistant Chaplain at Marlborough College. From here he volunteered to join up as a padre and found himself posted to France in mid-1915. After some early frustrations he found his métier with the men of the 8th (Service) Battalion, the Devonshire Regiment, whom he joined in early October 1915 and served with unremitting commitment and courage throughout the war. The Regimental History reports: '*It was at this time that the 8th had the good fortune to have the Reverend E.C. Crosse attached to it as Chaplain ... he was always up in the front line with the stretcher-bearers, helping the wounded.*' The same report emphasises the large congregations which attended his voluntary services – a clear indication of the high regard in which he was held.

Crosse survived the war and in later years became headmaster of Ardingly College. He wrote a book based on the work of the Chaplaincy Department during the Great War. Sadly, it was never published, but his wartime diary survived and the Crosse papers are held by the Imperial War Museum. A section of Crosse's book was reprinted in the Toc H *Journal* of May 1946, in which he writes movingly of a fellow padre – the Reverend the **Hon. Maurice Peel**. Here was another chaplain with a total disregard for his own safety. Peel seemed fearless, and never accepted that the place of the chaplain could be behind the lines:

'*Just before an attack was due to start he would walk along the assembly trenches with some appropriate text on his lips; or, if he couldn't get along, he would pass the word down the line and hard-bitten soldiers, whose language sometimes knew little restraint,*

would pass the sacred words along with obvious satisfaction ...'[1]
Clearly, Peel could inspire the men just when they most
needed help and before being exposed to the machine guns
of the enemy.

He continued to support the front-line troops, albeit con-
troversially, but with the permission of General Sir Hubert
Gough, by accompanying his battalion over the top at the
Battle of Festubert, walking stick in his hand. Inevitably he
was hit and was sent home, severely wounded. Later, Peel
insisted on returning to his old battalion, the 1st Royal Welch
Fusiliers, and carried on as before. This time there was no
querying the padre's right to be in the front line. Shortly
before Ascension Day, in May 1917, Peel was involved in the
fierce hand-to-hand fighting against the Prussian Guard at
Bullecourt. While moving forward to tend a wounded soldier, he was shot in the stomach and died where he fell, near
the ruins of the church.

The Reverend **Noel Mellish** VC, MC, who was vicar of
the parish of Great Dunmow in Essex from 1928 to 1948,
was the first chaplain to be awarded the Victoria Cross in the
Great War. Previously, he had served in the South African
War as a trooper under Baden-Powell and had received the
Queen's Medal with two clasps. On the outbreak of war he
had hoped to enlist as a soldier-priest, but his bishop would
not release him from parish duties. In 1915 he re-applied,
and this time was more successful. He gained a commission
as Chaplain to the Forces, 4th Class, and left for France on
5 May 1915. From the start, he showed tremendous commitment and devotion to the men in his pastoral care. After
a spell with the Northumberland Fusiliers, then with a field
ambulance, he was attached to the 4th Battalion, the Royal
Fusiliers.

Here indeed was another chaplain who, like Kenneth

1 Toc H *Journal*, Vol. xxiv, May 1946, No. 5, pp. 83–4.

Best, insisted on serving in the front line and doing work which far exceeded his normal sphere of duty, as this extract from his citation shows:

> From 27th – 29th March, 1916, during the heavy fighting at St Eloi, Belgium, he [Mellish] went to and fro continuously between the original trenches and the captured enemy trenches, attending to and rescuing wounded men. On the first day, from an area swept by machine fire, he rescued ten severely wounded men. On the second day he returned and rescued twelve more. Taking charge of a group of volunteers on the third day, he again returned to the trenches in order to rescue the remaining wounded.

In a letter to Mellish's mother, the chaplain's commanding officer, Lt.-Colonel Glendower Ottley, wrote that Mellish's place should have been at the rear with the ambulance and fairly safe. However, he chose to remain with his battalion up at the Front and 'treated most murderous and incessant machine-gun fire and shell-fire simply as if it was not happening and, regardless of danger, rescued any number of my poor wounded men'. His C.O. went on to say that there was one person Mellish never spared, or thought of, and that was himself.[1]

During the last two years of the war, Mellish returned no fewer than three times to the Front, despite being invalided home twice. He spent the final months of the war with the Royal Fusiliers. As vicar of Great Dunmow in 1928, he especially concerned himself with pastoral work on behalf of the returned servicemen and served the parish there for twenty years. He was appointed Deputy-Lieutenant of the County of Essex in 1946. He died at home at the age of 82 in 1962.

1 Karen Dennis, *Journal of the Western Front Association*, *Bulletin 82* October/November, 2008.

In subsequent years the people of Great Dunmow felt that they should honour their most distinguished son, the only man connected with the town to be awarded the Victoria Cross. Accordingly, on 19 June 2008 – the year which saw the ninetieth anniversary of the Armistice and the sixtieth anniversary of the year in which Mellish retired from his living at Great Dunmow – a bronze plaque in his honour was unveiled in the presence of the Chaplain-General to the Forces, the Venerable Stephen Robbins, and members of the Mellish family including Claire, Mellish's daughter.

Another padre who throws much light on the conditions under which the soldiers fought in Gallipoli was the Revd **Oswin Creighton**. His diaries were published in February 1916, only one month after the evacuation from Gallipoli, under the title *With the 29th Division in Gallipoli*. His book provided the public readership with one of the earliest eyewitness accounts of the ill-fated campaign. It is significant that he had received orders from the Chaplain-General never to go in front of the advanced dressing station – a dictum that Woodbine Willie would never accept. After being appointed to the 86th Brigade, 29th Division, Creighton was attached to the 89th Field Ambulance and arrived in Alexandria in March 1915. Soon after the initial landings, he arrived at Gallipoli, witnessed the gallant but unsuccessful attempts to capture Krithia, and the Battle of Gully Ravine at the end of June, but then was shipped home with dysentery in early August, before the Suvla Bay landings. He did not survive the war, but was killed on the Western Front in April 1918.

Shortly before Creighton was shipped home, the Revd **Ernest Raymond** was travelling out to Gallipoli on board the troopship *Scotian*, along with seven other young chaplains. Like Kenneth Best, Raymond was a chaplain attached to the 42nd East Lancashire Division. Also like Best, Raymond kept a diary, on which he later based his extraordinarily successful novel *Tell England*. Published in 1922, it was reprinted fourteen times that year, six times in 1923, once every year until 1931, and intermittently thereafter. Nobody was more surprised than the author himself. The book has been dismissed in modern times as being sentimental and dated. But that is to look at it through today's eyes and to ignore the tremendous wave of idealistic fervour which swept through the country in response to Kitchener's brilliant recruitment campaign. This mood was reflected in the poems of Rupert Brooke and the early poems of Siegfried Sassoon.

As Michael Moynihan has written,[1] no campaign in the First World War had a more potent religious appeal[2] – or a more romantic background, set as it was in territory close to where Agamemnon had waged war on Troy. The Dardanelles, formerly known as the Hellespont, over which Xerxes had built two bridges in 482 BC, were redolent of Greek legend. Raymond looked on the war as a crusade. In his novel, his leading padre character, Monty, convinces the young officers Ray and Doe that to participate in such a war was ennobling, even unto death.

In a recently published and thought-provoking article, Hugh Cecil[3] draws an effective comparison between *Tell England* and *The Path of Glory* by George Blake, who 'reiterates throughout the book the utter irrelevance of the war to the lives of ordinary Scotsmen'. It is significant that the latter work, with its black, pessimistic view of war, is relatively unknown – while even in the more cynical times of today, *Tell England* – partly, perhaps, because of its inspired title – continues to attract attention.

---

1 Op. cit., p. 80.
2 With the possible exception of the campaign in Palestine, leading up to the capture of Jerusalem, in December 1917.
3 In the *Gallipolian*, Autumn 2007 edition, under the title *British Fiction of the First World War*, p. 16.

Raymond's experience as an Army chaplain did not end at Gallipoli. He also served in the Middle East, at Ypres during Passchendaele and, after the Armistice, in Russia. It is perhaps surprising that such an ardent Christian should later stand down from being a priest, having apparently lost his faith. In this respect, too, there is a parallel with Kenneth Best, though there is no hint of this – far from it – in the pages of Best's diaries. Not only does Best make it clear that he feels – like Studdert-Kennedy and Hardy – his rightful place is up in the front line – but also he was immensely concerned, as the reader will have discovered, with the spiritual welfare of the soldiers in his pastoral care.

Kenneth Best arriving at Buckingham Palace with his parents
for the award of his MC, which was announced in the
London Gazette on 1 January 1918
© the estate of Kenneth Best. Imperial War Museum. BestJK_010297_1
© Imperial War Museum. Q13340

Gavin Roynon

Epilogue

The 1967 Pilgrimage to Gallipoli and the Reverend J.K. Best, MC

The 1967 Pilgrimage to Gallipoli was organised by a Mr Rex Palmer who had served in Gallipoli with my father, then Captain, later Major, C.F.F. Fagan. They were both in 85th Field Company Royal Engineers Special Reserve in 10th Irish Division. It was an aspiration of Rex Palmer's to get up a pilgrimage to go to the battlefields in 1965, the fiftieth anniversary of the Campaign. He enlisted the help of Mr Pop Lyster, an old friend living in Turkey who ran the British Legion branch in Istanbul. I had met him in Cyprus in the late 1950s when he came there to interpret between ourselves and the Turkish Cypriots during the EOKA troubles. He was an impressive man with a neck like a bull!

Getting to Turkey, and particularly to the Gallipoli battlefields, was not simple at that time. Air transport was nothing like as easy then as it is now, and diplomatically there were difficulties. It was hoped that there would be official help from London in making arrangements for a pilgrimage. The British Legion in England had told the Ministry of Defence that they were not prepared to undertake the organisation of a British veteran contingent, but suggested that the Istanbul branch should do so. There would be no financial assistance.

However, the Istanbul branch could not act because no foreign association was allowed in Turkey. On the other hand, both the civil and military authorities had promised their full support. In particular there was a Turkish general, General Aran, who was liaising with the Australians. Eventually the proposed pilgrimage did not take place, although a British group of veterans did go there in 1965.

Arrangements for a subsequent pilgrimage became more difficult officially. Pop Lyster reported from Turkey that Commander Longsdon, the Naval Liaison officer at the British Consulate, was obliged to leave because the Turkish Government had banned foreign diplomats in Istanbul after September 1966. However, Rex Palmer had not given up, and around July 1966 he wrote to the *Daily Telegraph* and started planning for a pilgrimage in May 1967. Some 48 people signed up for this, and great arrangements were made for their reception in Istanbul. It was tragic that only a few days before we were due to depart, Rex Palmer became unfit to travel and he asked me to take over the duties of tour leader. This was a fast ball for a 31-year-old in a party of veterans of the campaign, all of whom would have exceeded their three score years and ten!

Forty-three years later, two of those veterans remain clearly in my mind. One was Mr L.F. Lunnon, who had served in the Royal Bucks Hussars and been wounded in both arms at Suvla on 17 August 1915. The other was, of course, Kenneth Best. He was a great character, full of interest and enthusiasm, and a wonderful addition to the party. He wore a smart white jacket and I remember him as tall and impressive. I could quite imagine that he would have been an outstanding military padre and I have little doubt that he would have gained the respect and even love of the soldiers with whom he came into contact.

The importance of the role and presence of a padre in such awful circumstances cannot be over-estimated. Best landed on V Beach with 6th Manchester Regiment on 6 May 1915, and was often up in the front line doing what he could. The fact that he was awarded the Military Cross later confirms his outstanding courage. It says a great deal about Kenneth Best that I retain such a clear picture of him and was able to surprise Gavin Roynon with the information that I had actually met the man whose diaries he had been invited to edit by the Imperial War Museum.

On our arrival in Istanbul the Consul General, Mr R.A. Burrows, arranged a cocktail party for us in the embassy ballroom to meet local British and Turkish ex-servicemen. We also met General Aran, who was to be our charming guide and mentor for the whole tour. We were treated magnificently by our Turkish hosts, and gathered for a special parade in front of a war memorial in Istanbul arranged in our honour. There was a march-past of Turkish troops led by a military band. It so happened that my father was the senior officer in the party and so took the salute.

We moved down to Cannakale by boat from Istanbul, and many ceremonies were arranged for us on the Peninsula, notably at the Turkish Memorial, and the British Memorial at Cape Helles, where Kenneth Best held a moving service. Over a period of days we went more or less everywhere, and I had the remarkable experience of climbing up Kiretch Tepe, with my 78-year-old father, to Jephson's Post, where he had had the task of commanding a party to throw grenades which they had made themselves from jam tins and chopped up barbed wire. My father told me they were very careful to get the timing of the slow fuses right! He also showed me the approximate spot on the branch of a tree at Chocolate Hill where he had hung his binoculars. Split seconds later the branch was shot off. These were the same binoculars that we were carrying with us 52 years later.

There was an incident during the tour when we lost two of the veterans. When we returned to the hotel they were not with us and so I formed a search party and went out to find them. They had been determined to find a particular beach which had featured in their part in the campaign. As luck would have it we did eventually find them, on the beach that they had been so keen to find. They were totally exhausted and very lightheaded, behaving rather as though they had had all the rum ration! Luckily, it became very amusing and no lasting harm was done. I cannot remember if Kenneth Best was one of them, but they displayed the same spirit.

My overall impression was that these veterans were made of very stern stuff and they kept the individual thoughts and emotions that they must have been experiencing much to themselves. They were thrilled to return to the places that they remembered, places where all hell had been let loose 52 years before, and to see it again now in complete peace and with the freedom to wander around and identify particular locations. They were very glad to see the numerous beautifully kept and moving cemeteries, identify graves, and remember some of the comrades they had known. However, there was no bitterness against their erstwhile foe.

One thing was very striking: the friendship that was extended to us by General Aran and all the Turkish people we met. Fifty-two years earlier, from their point of view we had invaded their country and they had suffered some 300,000 casualties. Therefore, they might have been less than welcoming. It was quite the opposite, and all the British veterans that I have met have confirmed that there was a healthy respect between the two sides when fighting each other. Atatürk's famous message to widows and other Allied pilgrims in 1934, reflects the attitude of reconciliation and friendship that I have experienced from my meetings with many Turkish people.

These include a number of Turkish ambassadors to the United Kingdom who have come every year on 25 April to lay a wreath at the Gallipoli Memorial. All this is a superb example, possibly the best, of a firm friendship being formed between two countries and their people, not long after a bloody conflict in which they were deadly enemies. There is Turkish representation now at many of the Gallipoli-based ceremonies that take place annually throughout the United Kingdom.

Two years after the 1967 pilgrimage, the Gallipoli Association was formed at a time when most WWI associations were closing down. Originally it was for veterans only, but later it opened its doors to anybody with an interest in the campaign, especially those with a family connection. Once most of the veterans had faded away, the aims and objectives of the Association were redefined. They are now to keep alive the memory of those who fought and died there, and to encourage and facilitate the study of the campaign so that lasting benefit can be gained from its valuable lessons.

In 1995 the Association, recognising that there was no national memorial to the casualties of the Gallipoli Campaign, organised an appeal to raise funds to place a memorial in the Crypt of St Paul's Cathedral. This was unveiled by His Royal Highness, the Prince Philip, Duke of Edinburgh, and was the last official occasion at which Gallipoli veterans were on parade. There were eight of them, mostly over 100 years old. The appeal was sufficiently successful to raise a surplus amount, and this is being used annually to grant bursaries to students to go to Gallipoli, study an aspect of the campaign of their choice and give a presentation to their peers on their return.

I am quite sure that the memorial and the existence of these bursaries would have been particularly gratifying to a man of God like Kenneth Best. I am so glad that I had the privilege of meeting him.

Christopher Fagan
Chairman of the Gallipoli Association

Acknowledgements

There are two people without whom this book would never have seen the light of day. The first is Peter Arnold of Alderney, who had the foresight to deposit at the Imperial War Museum all the diaries, letters and memorabilia bequeathed to him by his uncle, the Reverend Kenneth Best, who died in 1981. He, along with Richard and John Arnold, have contributed some photographs and much useful background information about the family. The Best papers then came under the aegis of Roderick Suddaby, under whose leadership the Department of Documents at the Imperial War Museum has thrived for so long. Roderick is the other key person in this enterprise and I am most grateful to him for entrusting me with the fascinating task of editing these diaries.

Michael Hickey probably knows more about Gallipoli than anyone else alive. He led no fewer than 26 expeditions to the Peninsula and I was fortunate to be a member of his last one in 2007 and to benefit from his wide experience. His book *Gallipoli* remains the authoritative history of the whole campaign and contains some excellent maps, two of which, 'The Theatre of Operations' and 'Operations at Helles', he has permitted me to reprint. He was also kind enough to cast his eagle eye over the diaries and detected a number of textual niggles (his phrase!) which enabled me to sharpen up the accuracy of the military and historical detail. Of course, the responsibility for any remaining errors is solely mine. I am also grateful to him for agreeing to write the foreword.

There have been other generous contributors. Despite his onerous responsibilities, Lieutenant-General Andrew Graham, the director of the Defence Academy at Shrivenham, takes a special interest in the role of army chaplains and kindly wrote the wide-ranging preface to this book. I am also grateful to Anne Brooks, who catalogued the Best papers on behalf of the Imperial War Museum and produced a detailed summary of Kenneth Best's military career.

The Reverend Paul Tongue, Canon Emeritus of Worcester Cathedral, showed me a number of original documents relating to the heroic wartime service of the Reverend Geoffrey Studdert-Kennedy, better known as Woodbine Willie. In September 2010, Canon Tongue blessed and re-dedicated the war memorial outside St Paul's Church, Worcester, which has been fully restored with the re-engraved names of the 128 men of Worcester who died in the conflict. The memorial bears the wooden Calvary designed by Woodbine Willie himself, with the unusual caption he chose – 'Died for Us' rather than the more familiar 'Died for King and Country'.

It was a remarkable stroke of good fortune to learn from Christopher Fagan over a dinner at Winchester that he accompanied the veterans' tour to Gallipoli in 1967. It was on this tour that he met Kenneth Best. I felt therefore that nobody could be better equipped than Christopher to write the Epilogue – a task over which he took immense care and I am most grateful to him. Most appropriately, Christopher Fagan is also the chairman of the Gallipoli Association. This Association exists to honour the memory of all those who died in the campaign and continues to organise annual expeditions to the Peninsula. The Association also funds bursaries to enable students to travel out to Gallipoli and carry out research.

After the war was over, Kenneth Best was employed by

Cheltenham College, where he taught maths, carried out school chaplaincy duties, and became a housemaster. I am grateful to the former headmaster John Richardson, the school archivist, who permitted me to insert a notice in the alumni newsletter. Several former members of Boyne House, which was Best's house at the college, wrote to me with their reminiscences.

I have benefited considerably from my visits to the Army Chaplaincy Centre at Amport, near Andover, whose excellent museum should be more widely known. The curator, David Blake, referred me to some revealing primary sources, notably *Letters Home* by the Reverend Jack Blencowe, who sailed out to Gallipoli on the SS *Olympic* at the end of September 1915. Blencowe's letters to his mother give a clear insight into the appalling living conditions endured by the troops in those last three months of the campaign, especially during the November storms.

Michael Meredith, the curator of Modern Collections at Eton, kindly gave me access to the Macnaghten Library. Peter Woodward, a member of the politics faculty at Reading University, made some useful suggestions about the section relating to Cairo and Egypt, where Kenneth Best served when he first went abroad. My mentor, Patrick Wilson, cast his experienced historian's eye over the section devoted to British Army chaplains and Peter Costain, a great devotee of the campaign, kindly read sections of the edited diaries. I am also indebted to the support of Bill Marsh, treasurer of the Gallipoli Association. He gave me his copy of *With the 29th Division in Gallipoli*, comprising the diaries of the Reverend Oswin Creighton – one of the earliest books about the campaign to be published.

I am grateful to Liz Bowers, Head of Publications at the Imperial War Museum, for her help and advice, and also to Peter Taylor. Peter has provided an invaluable link with the publishers and prepared the many photographs reprinted from the comprehensive Imperial War Museum Photo Archives, where Alan Wakefield has kept me up-to-date with the latest additions.

My wife Patsy read sections of the book in the early stages and made some very constructive suggestions about the structure. Finally, I am once again indebted to Janet Easterling, whose impeccable presentation and attention to detail played a significant part in winning the approval of the publishers. She has thus compensated for all the all-too-apparent lack of computer skills on the part of the editor.

Gavin Roynon
Wargrave, April 2011

Kenneth Best with his father, Revd John Dugdale Best, Rector of
Sandon, near Chelmsford, 1910–1926. Both had been scholars
in mathematics, at Queens' College, Cambridge. This photo
was probably taken c. 1930. Photo: Peter Arnold
© the estate of Kenneth Best. Imperial War Museum.

Select Bibliography

Ashmead-Bartlett, E., *The Uncensored Dardanelles* (Hutchinson, London, undated)

Aspinall-Oglander, Brig.-Gen. C.F., *History of the Great War, based on Official Documents: Military Operations – Gallipoli,* vols I and II (London 1924–30)

Attlee, Clement, *As it Happened ...* (Heinemann, London, 1954)

Bean, C.E.W., *The Story of Anzac* (Australian Official History), (Sydney, NSW, 1921)

Bean, C.E.W. (ed.), *The Anzac Book* (Cassell, 1916)

Benstead, Charles R., *Retreat – A Story of 1918* (University of South Carolina Press, 1930)

Bernières, Louis de, *Birds Without Wings* (Vintage 2005)

Best, Revd J.K. *Memoir* in the *Gallipolian* (1971)

Best, Lieutenant Herbert, papers relating to (deposited with Imperial War Museum, London)

Bickersteth, John (ed.), *The Bickersteth Diaries* (Leo Cooper, London, 1988)

Blencowe, Peter and Susan (eds), *Letters Home – Jack Blencowe, 1909–1918*

Brown, Malcolm, *The Imperial War Museum History of the Great War* (Sidgwick and Jackson, London, 1991)

Buchan, John, *The King's Grace, 1910–1935* (Hodder and Stoughton, 1935)

Carlyon, L.A. *Gallipoli* (Doubleday, 2002)

Cecil, Hugh, *British Fiction of the First World War:* article relating to Ernest Raymond and George Blake in the *Gallipolian* (Autumn 2007 edition)

Chambers, Stephen, *Gully Ravine* (Battleground Europe Series)

Creighton, Revd O., *With the 29th Division in Gallipoli – A Chaplain's Experiences* (Longman, Green, London, 1916)

Darlington, Sir Henry, *Letters and Diaries from Helles* (London, 1936)

Falls, Cyril and George Macmunn, *Military Operations in Egypt and Palestine* (1928)

Farndale, General Sir Martin, *History of the Royal Regiment of Artillery, The Forgotten Fronts and the Home Base, 1914–18* (Dorset Press, 1988)

Gibbon, Frederick P., *The 42nd East Lancashire Division 1914–1918* (Country Life, 1920)

Gilbert, Sir Martin (ed.), *The Straits of War: Gallipoli Remembered* – A series of Memorial Lectures given annually at Holy Trinity Church, Eltham

Hamilton, General Sir Ian, *Gallipoli Diary* (London, 1920)

Hammerton, John (ed.), *I was There! Undying Memories of 1914–1918* Vol. 1 to 1916 (Amalgamated Press, Ltd)

Hargrave, John, *The Suvla Bay Landing* (Macmillan, 1964)

Hickey, Michael, *Gallipoli* (John Murray, 1995)

Holt, Tonie and Valmai, *Gallipoli – Holt's Battlefield Guide* (Leo Cooper, 2000)

Horden, Revd A.W., *War Diary of the Principal Chaplain* (National Archives, WO/95/2023)

Housman, A.E. (ed.), *War Letters of Fallen Englishmen* (Gollancz, 1930)

Jerrold, D., *The Royal Naval Division* (Hutchinson, London, 1927)

Keegan, John, *The First World War* (Hutchinson, London, 1998)

Latter, Major-General J.C., *The History of the Lancashire Fusiliers* (Gale and Polden, Aldershot 1949)

Liddell Hart, Basil, *The Real War* (Faber and Faber, 1930)

Liddell Hart, Basil, *History of the First World War* (Cassell, 1970)

Mackenzie, Compton, *Gallipoli Memories* (Cassell, 1929)

Madigan, Edward, *Faith Under Fire: Anglican Army Chaplains in the Great War* (Palgrave Macmillan, 2011)

McKernan, Michael, *Padre – Australian Chaplains in Gallipoli and France* (Allen & Unwin, 1986)

McPherson, John, & Barry Carman (eds), *The Man who Loved Egypt* – edited from 25 volumes of correspondence with Bimbashi McPherson (Ariel Books, 1983)

Moorehead, Alan, *Gallipoli* (London, 1956)

Moynihan, Michael, *God on Our side – The British Padre in WWI* (Leo Cooper, 1983)

Murray, J. *Gallipoli as I saw it* (London, 1965)

Nevinson, Henry, *The Dardanelles Campaign* (Nisbet, London, 1918)

North, John, *Gallipoli – The Fading Vision* (Faber and Faber, 1936)

Orr, Philip, *Field of Bones* (Lilliput Press, Dublin, 2005)

Parker, Linda, *The Whole Armour of God, Anglican Army Chaplains in the Great War* (Helion, 2009)

Pauncefort-Duncombe, Sir Everard, *Gallipoli Diaries* (papers held by Imperial War Museum)

Prior, Robin, *Gallipoli: The End of the Myth* (Yale University Press, 2009)

Quarterly Journal of Aviation History: *The Cross and the Cockade*

Raw, David, *'It's Only Me' – A life of Theodore Hardy, VC, DSO, MC* (Gatebeck, 1988)

Raymond, Ernest, *Tell England – A Study in a Generation* (London, 1922)

Rhodes-James, Robert, *Gallipoli* (London, 1965)

Rudenno, Victor, *Gallipoli – Attack from the Sea* (Yale University Press, 2008)

Snape, Michael, *The Royal Army Chaplains Department, 1796–1953* (Boydell Press, Woodbridge, 2008)

Steel, Nigel, *The Battlefields of Gallipoli: then and now* (London, 1990)

Strachan, Hew, *The First World War* (Simon and Schuster UK, 2003)

Sutton, F.A., *One-Arm Sutton* (Heinemann, London, 1933)

Taylor, A.J.P., *The First World War* (Hamish Hamilton, London, 1976)

Verschoyle, Lt. T., Inniskilling Fusiliers. Papers held by Imperial War Museum

Waite, Fred, *The New Zealanders at Gallipoli* (Whitcombe and Tombs, Auckland, 1921)

Wemyss, Lord Wester, *The Navy in the Gallipoli Campaign*

Westlake, Ray, *British Regiments at Gallipoli* (London, 1966)

Wilkinson, Alan, *The Church of England and the First World War* (SPCK, 1978)

Wilkinson, A.M. (ed.), *Reminiscences of Canon D.M.M. Bartlett* (Harrison and Son, 1969)

Williams, Jeffery, *Byng of Vimy, General and Governor General* (Leo Cooper, 1983)

Index

(KB in subentries refers to Kenneth Best;
page numbers in italic face denote photographs)

abbreviations, listed, 43
Achi Baba, 113, 133, 134, 136,
    137, 138, 159, 176, 188, 209
    bombardment of, 138
AE2 (submarine) 81
Agamemnon, 263
Alexandria, 21, 30, 39, 57, 151
    KB evacuated to, 180–5
    in KB's letters, 57
    KB in, 184–8
    origin of, 57*n*
    riots in, 26
Allen, Miss, 128
Allied Expeditionary Force
    Supreme HQ, 13
Alnwick Castle, 22–3
Andrews, Waggle, 126, 203–4,
    227, 228
Anglo-Egyptian Bank, 187, 235
Anson, Admiral, 165
Antwerp, 165
Anzac Cove, 37*n*, 106, 196
    chaplains pictured at, *213*
    evacuation of, 245, 247
Arabi, Col., 26
Aragon, 177
Aran, Gen., 266, 267, 268
Arcadian, 113
Ark Royal, 178*n*

Armistice, 3, 11
Army Quarterly, 248
Arnold House School, 9
As It Happened (Attlee), 37
'Asiatic Annie', 132
Asquith, Herbert, 34, 129*n*
Atatürk, Mustafa Kemal, 268, 288
Attlee, Clement, 37
Ausonia, HMT, 10, 23–4, 220, 223
Australia and New Zealand Army
    Corps (ANZAC), 17, 30, 31,
    36, 39, 107, 110*n*, *172*
    Australia and New Zealand
        Division of, 196
    and Gallipoli evacuation, 247
    landing of, at Anzac Cove, 106
Australian Light Horse, 165
Austria, 134
Austria-Hungary, 122*n*
Avon, RMSP, 14, 30
    KB's letters from, *see under* Best
        letters

Baden-Powell, Robert, 260
Baird (fellow serviceman), 217
Baker, Revd., 187
Baring, Evelyn (Lord Cromer),
    26, 27
Barrow, Bugler, 131

Bartlett, Canon Donald, 22–3
battery gun in action, *137*
Baylis (fellow serviceman), 170
Beardmore, Revd., 144, 148, 169, 213
Beelzebub, 150
Bentz, Lt., 156
Beresford, Admiral Lord Charles, 226
Bernières, Louis de, 41
Best, Cpl, 160, 208
Best diaries, 71–93, 95–8, 105–16, 117–18, 119–25, 126–94, 204–19, 221–40
   confused nature of, during Cyprus convalescence, 22
   on scraps of paper, 22
Best, Elsie (KB's sister), 51, 52
   KB's letters to, *see under* Best letters
Best, Lt. Herbert (KB's brother), 52, 53, 67–8
   KB's letters to, *see under* Best letters
Best, Revd. John Dugdale (KB's father), 9, 99*n*
   KB's letters to, *see under* Best letters
Best, Revd. Kenneth:
   agnostic years of, 4
   in Alexandria, 184–8
   Alexandria shopping expedition of, 185
   arrival in England of, 239
   arrival in Gallipoli of, 18
   on *Ausonia*, 10, 23–4, 223–4
   biographical note on, 9–13
   birth of, 9
   Cairo Rolls-Royce ride of, 187
   camera bought by, 66
   on *Carisbrooke Castle*, 24, 236–9
   certificate of commission of, *10*
   chaplaincy appointment of (WW1), 2, 9, 14, 30

chaplaincy appointment of (WW2), 12
Cheltenham College post of, 12, 273
at Cottonera hospital, 10, 24, 224–35
cricket played by, 56, 155, 192
Cyprus arrival of, 189
Cyprus convalescence of, 3, 22, 189–94
Cyprus convalescence ordered for, 185
Dardanelles' effects on, after 10 weeks, 145
day of funerals attended by, 207–8
death of, 13
deeds of heroism heard of by, 128
demobilisation of, 11
diaries and letters of, *see* Best diaries; Best letters
dysentery suffered by, 10, 23, 40, 216–23
education of, 9
enteric fever suffered by, 3, 10
enteritis suffered by, 22, 180–1
evacuation of, to Alexandria, 180–5
first military funeral conducted by, 15
first under-fire service conducted by, 19, 126
France ministry of, 3
frequent front-line visits by, 20
at Gallipoli, *see* Best diaries; Best letters
on Gallipoli Pilgrimage, 266, 267; *see also* Gallipoli Pilgrimage
on *Gascon* (hospital ship), 23, 218–23
lack of real action bemoaned by, 66

'land of shams' bemoaned by, 67

letters and diaries of, *see* Best diaries; Best letters

makeshift altar of, 19, 125

Malta convalescence of, 10, 24, 224–35

Malta police confiscate camera of, 229, 234

medical board appearance of, 24, 229

mess roles of, 56, 60

Military Cross awarded to, *264*, 267

citation, 11

Morse and semaphore learned by, 56

music loved by, 13

off-duty pursuits of, 15

photographs of (1914), *12*, *104*

post-convalescence return to Dardanelles of, 205

programme of, October 1914, 63–4

rheumatic problems of, 170

scorn of, towards fellow chaplains, 251

shellproof-pulpit suggestion made to, 127

singsong arranged by, 212

suspected lung infection of, 11

'unendurable' headache suffered by, 179

see also chaplains: role of

Best letters:

1914, 51–68

1915, 94–5, 98–103, 116–17

from 1st East Lancs Brigade, 21 May 1915, 125–6

from 5th Manchester Regiment:
9 May 1915, 116–17
11 May 1915, 118–19

from Abbassia Garrison, 28 Apr. 1915, 102–3

from Alexandria, 20 Aug. 1915, 203–4

from *Avon*, 52–7

to brother, 11 May 1915, 118–19

from YMCA, Cairo, 5 Oct. 1914, 58–63

on Christmas, 67–8

to family:
23 Sep. 1914, 54–9
5 Oct. 1914, 58
10 Dec. 1914, 67–8
28 Apr. 1915, 102–3
9 May 1915, 116–17
20 Aug. 1915, 203–4
23 Sep. 1915, 219–20

to father:
9 Sep. 1914, 51–2
16 Sep. 1914, 53–4
12 Nov. 1914, 63–6
6 Mar. 1915, 98–9
15 Mar. 1915, 100–1
21 May 1915, 125–6

from *Gascon*, 23 Sep. 1915, 219–20

from Heliopolis Camp, Cairo:
12 Nov. 1914, 63–6
10 Dec. 1914, 67–8
6 Mar. 1915, 98–9
15 Mar. 1915, 100–1

from Ismailia:
26 Jan. 1915, 75–9
16 Feb. 1915, 94–5

to mother:
10 Sep. 1914, 52
26 Jan. 1915, 75–9
16 Feb. 1915, 94–5

to sister, 23 Sep. 1914, 54–9

from Suez Canal Club, 16 Feb. 1915, 94–5

on Turks' invasion of Suez Canal, 16–17

Bieberstein, Baron Marschall von, 28

Birds without Wings (Bernières), 41
Birdwood, Maj.-Gen., 36, 39, 247
Birtwistle, Maj. 85
 Lt.-Col., 117, 124, 169, 171, 173
Blake, George, 263
Blandy (fellow serviceman), 178
Bolton, Geoff, 193
Bolton, Capt. H., 132
 burial of, 128
bomb-making, *136*
Bouvet, 40
Braithwaite, Gen. Sir Walter, 243
Breslau, 28, 121*n*
Britain:
 Dardanelles bombardment by, *see* Dardanelles
 Suez Canal share held by, 25; *see also* Suez Canal
 war declared by, 29
British and Irish military:
 1st Lancashire Fusiliers, 111
 1st Royal Inniskilling Fusiliers, 112, 135
 5th Manchester Regiment, 102, 117, 118, 140
  KB's letters from, *see under* Best letters
 10th Irish Division, 241, 265
 abbreviations for, listed, 43
 Aegean Squadron, 34
 Allied Expeditionary Force Supreme HQ, 13
 Army Service Corps (ASC), 117, 119
 British Expeditionary Force (BEF), 37, 241*n*
 Chaplains Department, 3, 250, 255; *see also* chaplains: role of
 Cumberland Howitzer Brigade, 206
 Devonshire Regiment, 8th Battalion, 259

East Anglian Division, 97
East Lancashires, 134
 1st/3rd Brigades, 9, 14, 30, 51, 94
 4th Brigade, 127, 140, 141, 142, 152, 153–4, 156, 158, 170, 206, 209, 215
 5th Brigade, 119, 133, 140, 144, 148, 152, 157, 163, 168, 169, 174, 211, 217
 6th Brigade, 172
 9th Brigade, 152
 87th Brigade, 129
 88th Brigade, 129, 152
 29th Division, 36, 39, 101, 107, 111, *131*, 139, 227*n*, 262
 42nd Division, 2, 9*n*, 17, 23, 29, 30, 101–2, *109*, 117, 224*n*, *245*, 262
 worries over sickness among, 149
Field Ambulance, 20
 1st, 121, 123, 133, 164
 2nd, 133, 164
 3rd, 117–18, 132
 7th, 142
 42nd, *140*
 87th, *131*, 133
 89th, 149, 262
 Lowland, 159, 214
and Gallipoli evacuation, *see* Gallipoli: evacuation of
Grenadier Guards, 4th Battalion, 11
King's Own Scottish Borderers (KOSB), 107, 114, 133
Lancashire Fusiliers, 18
 1st/8th Battalion, 124
Lincolnshire Regiment, 8th Battalion of, 256
Manchester Brigade, 146, 148, 158
Manchester Regiment:

8th Battalion, 158
9th Battalion, 21, 23, 99, 143, 152, 158, 165
10th Battalion, 71, 134, 140, 148, 156, 158, 208, 211, 214
Mediterranean Expeditionary Force, 39
Northumberland Fusiliers, 260
Plymouth Brigade, 120
private soldiers, daily wages of, 150*n*
respirator helmet used by, 209
Royal Air Force, formation of, 189*n*
Royal Bucks Hussars, 266
Royal Dublin and Royal Munster Fusiliers ('Dubsters'), 107, 115, 168, 176, 244–5, 244–5, 252
Royal Engineers, 85th Field Company, 265
Royal Field Artillery:
1st Brigade, 85*n*, 134, 186
5th Battery, 117, 135, 154, 155, 157
6th Battery, 117, 154–5
Royal Flying Corps, 189*n*
Royal Fusiliers, 260
Royal Marine Light Infantry (RMLI), 142
Royal Marines, 38, 165
Royal Naval Air Service (RNAS), 189
Royal Naval Division, 21, 36, 39, 139, 165–6, 214
Anson Battalion, 165
Collingwood Battalion, 21, 139, 165–6
formation and first assignment of, 165
Hawke Battalion, 165

Hood Battalion, 165, 166*n*
massive Gallipoli casualties suffered by, 165
Royal Welch Fusiliers, 260
Scottish Borderers, *see* British and Irish military: King's Own Scottish Borderers
Scottish Rifles, large casualty toll among, 159–60
South Lancashire Regiment, 6th Battalion, 37
South Staffordshire Regiment, 24
West Lancashires, 56
Westminster Dragoons, 54
Worcestershire Regiment, 20, 142
York and Lancaster Regiment, 24
13th Battalion, 11
14th Battalion, 11
94th Infantry Brigade, 11
British Legion, 265–6
Brooke, Capt. Sir Basil, *248*
Brooke, Rupert, 166*n*, 263
Brown, Capt., 84, 92
Browning, Maj. John, 157, 168, 173
Bruce (fellow serviceman), 187, 191
Bulgaria, 36, 228
Bulletin (Western Front Association), 261*n*
Burrows, R.A., 267
Bury, Lt., 168
Byng, Lt.-Gen. Sir Julian, 195, 242–3, 246, *248*
KCB awarded to, 247–8
Williams' biography of, 242
Byng of Vimy, General and Governor General (Williams), 247*n*

Cairns, Maj., 152, 172

Cairo, 14–16
  Australian and NZ troops arrive
    in, 15–16
  Kasrel Mil barracks, 62, 64
  KB's letters from, *see under* Best
    letters
  martial law declared in, 65
  Obelisk of On, 62
  War Cemetery, 15
Cameron, Capt., 193
Cape Helles, 18, 110, *131*, 132*n*,
    137
  evacuation of, 246, 249
Carden, Vice-Admiral Sackville,
    38, 40
Carisbrooke Castle, SS, 24, 236–9
Casal Paula, 230
Cecil, Hugh, 363
Central Powers, 228*n*
Challenor (fellow serviceman),
    173
chaplains:
  department for, *see* British
    military: Chaplains
    Department
  first VC recipient among, 260
  on hospital ships, 23
  KB's often virulent views on, 2
  KB's scorn towards some of,
    251
  legendary figures among, 2
  as non-combatants, 20, 250
  pictured at Anzac Cove, *213*
  pictured at burial, *153*
  rising numbers of, in British
    Army, 250
  role of, in WW1, 6–7, 250–64
  see also Best, Kenneth
Chapman, Mrs, 98
Chapman, Revd. S., 51
Cheetham, Sir Milne, 29
Cheltenham College, 12, 273
Chope, Capt., 31
Chunuk Bair, *197*

Church of England Missionary
    Society (CEMS), 64, 148, 185
Church Times, 254*n*
Churchill, Winston, 28, 33–6, 41,
    129, 165
  letter to Asquith from, re
    Dardanelles, 34–5
  persuasive eloquence of, 37
Clarke, Maj., 85, 90–1, 122, 132
Clauson, Sir John, 190, 191
Clauson, Lady, 190
Clauss (fellow serviceman), 151
Clayton, Revd. Philip ('Tubby'),
    2, 253, 257–8
Clegg, Lt., 129
Clegg, Percy, 176
Clifton, Harry, 226
Clowes, Revd., 124, 149
coalboxes, 149
Collingwood, Admiral, 165
Cooper, Leo, 247*n*
Copts, 65
Cornwallis, HMS, *248*
Corps Expéditionnaire d'Orient,
    42
Cottonera hospital, 10, 24, 224–7
Craston, Drummer, 148, 149, 151
Creighton, Revd. Oswin, 191,
    227, 262
Crimean War, 28
Cromer, Lord, 26, 27
Crookham, Revd. (fellow
    chaplain), 96–7, 98
Crosse, Revd. Ernest Courtenay,
    259
Cummings, Col., 105
Cyprus:
  KB arrives in, 189
  KB's convalescence in, 3, 22,
    189–94
  Surada Lake, 190
  Troodatissa Monastery, 191
  Troodos Monastery, 193
  Troodos Mountains, 190

Daily Telegraph, 266
Dale, Revd., *213*
Dardanelles, 34–42 *passim*
  beginning of British
      bombardment of, 34
  Commission, 120*n*
  Committee, 36*n*, 243–4
  effect of, on KB, 145
  first mines laid in, 28
  KB arrives in, 18, 110
  KB departs for, 105–6
  KB's post-convalescence return
      to, 205
  redolent of Greek legend, 263
  see also Gallipoli
Darke (Church of England
      Missionary Society), 185
Darlington, Sir Henry, 224*n*
Darwin Debating Society, 141
Davies, Gen., 249
Dean, Driver, 149
Dearsley (fellow serviceman),
      213, 218
Dennis, Karen, 261*n*
Derfflinger, 17, 105*n*, 194
devil, 93, 158
Dilley, Midshipman, 189
Dixon, Lt., 177
Djemal Pasha, 31
Douglas, Maj. Gen. Sir William,
      17, 21, 90, 105, *139*, 156, 168,
      177, 211–12
Drake, Admiral, 165
Drewry, Lt., 54
Dundas, Lt. Kenneth, 166
Dunlop, Dr Douglas, 27
dysentery, 22, 148
  scourge of ('Gallipoli Gallop'),
      244
  see also Best, Kenneth:
      dysentery suffered by

Earle, Staff Col., 115
Edge, Lt., 178–9, 182, 184

Edwards (fellow serviceman), 126
Egypt, 14–17, 25–30
  Alexandria, 21, 30, 39, 57, 151
      KB evacuated to, 180–5
      KB in, 184–8
      in KB's letters, 57
      origin of, 57*n*
      riots in, 26
  Cairo, *see main entry*; KB's
      letters from, *see* Best letters
  deemed formal Protectorate, 29
  Heliopolis, 14, 19, 36, 102
      KB's letters from, *see under*
          Best letters
  Ismailia, 16, 30, 32, 72
  Kantara, 28, 32, 88
  Lake Timsah, 31, 32, 73, 89
  Mongha Gardens, 187
  Obelisk of On, 62
  Port Said, 30, 31, 72, 98
  Serapeum, 16, 33, 85, 89–90
      corpses taken from canal at,
          96
  Suez Canal, *see main entry*
  Tel el Kebir, 72
  Toussoum, 16, 33, 88, 89–90
  Zagazig, 72
El Desire, 237
Elliott, Charlotte, 108*n*
England in Egypt (Milner), 26
Enver Pasha, 28, 41
EOKA (National Organisation of
      Cypriot Fighters), 265
Ermina, 23, 205

Fagan, Maj. C.F.F., 265, 267
Failes, Revd., 126
Ferguson, Sgt Maj., 170
Festubert, Battle of, 260
Finn, Father William, 107*n*, 251–2
Firle, Lt.-Com. Rudolph, 129
First World War, *see* World War
      One
First World War, The (Keegan), 40*n*

Fisher, Lord, 34, 35, 36
    resigns, 129
Fletcher, Revd (fellow chaplain),
        111, 130, 215
Foster, Revd., 178
Franz Ferdinand, Archduke, 27
French Army, 36, 39, 133, 154–5,
        167, 221, 248
    superior manpower of, 241
French, Sir John, 37
funerals/burials, 15, 16, 21, 23, 32,
        87, 91, 128, 130–1, 151, *153*,
        197, 256
    Mohammedan, 89
Furlong, Revd., 177, 211

Gaba Tepe, 124, 162
Gallagher (fellow serviceman), 90
Gallipoli:
    Achi Baba, 113, 133, 134, 136,
        137, 138, 159, 176, 188, 209
        bombardment of, 138
    Anzac Cove, 37*n*, 106, 196
        chaplains pictured at, *213*
        evacuation of, 245, 247
    appalling conditions in, 2
    Association, 269
    Attlee on, 37
    burial armistice during
        campaign at, 171
    Cabinet orders evacuation of,
        245
    Cape Helles, 18, 110, *131*, 132*n*,
        137
        evacuation of, 246, 249
    Chunuk Bair, *197*
    devastating weather saps
        morale at, 244–5
    evacuation of, 245–9
    Gaba Tepe, 124, 162
    'Gallop', *see* dysentery
    Gulf of Saros, 42
    Gully Beach, 122, 124, 133, 205,
        207, 209, 212

Gully Ravine, 20, 139, *245*, 262
Gurkha Bluff, 133, 135
    Hickey's book on, 37–8, 198,
        242*n*
    KB arrives in, 18, 110
    KB departs for, 105–6
    KB's post-convalescence return
        to, 205
    Kiretch Tepe Ridge, 200*n*, 244,
        267
    Kitchener opposes, then
        accepts inevitability of,
        evacuation of, 244
    Krithia battles in, 18, 20, 110,
        113, 136, 139, *139*
    Lancashire Bay, 111
    Marmara, Sea of , 38, 42, 81*n*
    Memorial, 268
    Monro recommends evacuation
        of, 243–4
    Monro's remit to lift stalemate
        at, 243
    news of heavy casualty toll
        from, 101
    Nullah, 114, 122
    Pilgrimage to, 265–9
    Rhodes-James's book on, 35*n*
    Sari Bair, 196, 241
    Saros, Gulf of, 42
    Sea of Marmara, 38, 42, 81*n*
    Suvla Bay, 37*n*, 166*n*, 195–202,
        199, 206, 234, 241, 242–3
        evacuation of, 246–7
        field kitchen at, *196*
        Thomas's vivid diary account
            of, 199–202
    unburied dead at, 3
    unexpected truce at, 245
    V Beach, *106*, 251, 267, 251
        cemetery at, 252
    see also Dardanelles; Turkey
Gallipoli (Hickey), 37–8, 198,
        242*n*
Gallipoli (Rhodes-James), 35n

Gallipoli Association, 269

Gallipoli – *The End of the Myth*
(Prior), 249*n*

Gallipoli Memorial, 268

Gallipoli Peninsula, 32

Gallipolian, 263

Garnet, Lt. Jerry, 51, 54, 60, 96,
207

Gascon, HMHS, 23, 218–23, 237
KB's letter from, *see under* Best
letters

Gaulois, 40

George V, King, 137, 250

German Army:
expert gunners in, 151
filter into Constantinople, 28
'first-rate' marksmen among,
151
mingle with British troops,
106
Turkish defences reinforced by,
38

Germany, Turks' secret alliance
with, 28

Ghali, Butros, 27*n*

Gibbon, Frederick P., 45, 101–2,
105*n*

Gibraltar, 11, 53, 55, 237

Gilbert, Martin, 34*n*

Glew, Revd., 227, 228

Gloucester Castle, 237

*God on Our Side – the British Padre
in World War I* (Moynihan),
250*n*

Godley, Maj.-Gen. Sir Alexander,
196

Goeben, 28, 121, 139

Goliath, 129, 130

Gorst, Sir Eldon, 27

Gough, Gen. Sir Hubert, 260

Great War, *see* World War One

Greece, 36
Mudros, 10, 23, 175, 180
Harbour, 39, 42, 183, 205

Lemnos, 23, 38, 39, 42, 118,
133, 135, 151, 177, 205
Australian Recreation Camp
in, 227

Gregory, Signalman, 96

Griffiths, Lt., 134

Gulf of Saros, 42

Gully Beach, 122, 124, 133, 205,
207, 209, 212

Gully Ravine, 20, 139, *245*, 262

Gurkha Bluff, 133, 135

Gurkhas, 72, 73, 83, 124, 163

Gurling, Jonathan, 254

Habsburg, Empire, 27

Hagar Qim, 231

Haig, Field Marshal Douglas, 7,
101

Hall, Revd., 111, 123

Hamilton, Lord George, 226

Hamilton, Gen. Sir Ian, 39, 40–1,
42, 102, 110, 113, 149, 176,
189*n*, 195, 198, 215, 241–2,
243
more divisions requested by,
241
mutterings about leadership of,
243
story circulates concerning, 212

Hammersley, Maj.-Gen., 197

Hankey, Sir Maurice, 35

Hardest Part, The (Studdert-
Kennedy), 5*n*

Hardy, Florence, 255

Hardy (fellow serviceman), 112

Hardy, Revd. Theodore, 2, 7–8,
253, 255–7

Hargrave, John, 195*n*

Hart, Bombardier, 88, 90

Hassall (fellow serviceman), 208

Hawke, Admiral, 165

Heliopolis, 14, 19, 36, 102
KB's letters from, *see under* Best
letters

Henry, Dr., 138–9, 141, 175
Hersing, Capt. Otto, 130
Hickey, Michael, 37–8, 198, 242, 247
Higgins (fellow serviceman), 92
Hilmi, Abbas II, Khedive, 27, 29
Hilton, Dr, 97
Hitchens, Canon, 155, 179, 191
Hood, Admiral, 165
Horden, Revd. A.W., 252
Hordern (fellow serviceman), 185
Hornby (fellow serviceman), 141, 175
Hugo, Col., 223
Hunt, Lt., 182
Hunter-Weston, Gen., 139
Huntsgreen, SS, 22–3, 194
Hussein Kamal, Prince, 29–30

Indian Army, 29*n*, 30–1, 159, 162
    Bikanir Camel Corps, 31
    padres in, 221
Indian Medical Services, 221
Inflexible, 40
Irresistible, 40
Isherwood, Lt.-Col., 181, 182, 184
Ismail, Khedive, 26
Ismailia, 16, 30, 32, 72
It's Only Me: A Life of Theodore Hardy (Raw), 255*n*, 256
Italy, 122, 127, 134

Jack Johnson shell (JJ), 161, 162
James, Lt., 117, 134
Jane's Fighting Ships, 138*n*
Joffre, Gen. Joseph, 36, 29, 39, 241
Johnson, Jack, 161*n*
Jonquil, 197

Kannengiesser, Col. Hans, 41
Kantara, 28, 32, 88
Keegan, John, 40*n*
Kemal, Mustafa, 32

Keyes, Commodore Roger, 40
khamseen (wind), 100
King, Gen., 51, 61, 64, 90, 187, 188
King, Revd., *213*
King's Own Malta Regiment of Militia, 231–2
Kinloch, Revd., 133, 144–5, 155
Kirby (fellow serviceman), 147, 169, 179, 210
Kiretch Tepe Ridge, 200*n*, 244, 267
Kitchener, Field Marshal H.H., 3, 33, 34, 129, 241
    29th Division released by, 39
    Gallipoli evacuation strongly opposed, then accepted as inevitable, by, 244
    Grand Duke's appeal to, 35–6
Kitchener's Army, 3, 172, 197
Knowles, Lt., 82, 92
Kressenstein, Friedrich Kress von, 32
Krithia, Second Battle of, 18, 110, 113
Krithia, Third Battle of, 20, 136, 139, *139*

Lancashire Bay, 111
Lancing College, 9
Lawford, Maj., 222, 224–5, 228
Lawrence, D.H., 255
Leach (fellow serviceman), 97
Lee, Gen. Noel, 138
Lemnos, 23, 38, 39, 42, 118, 133, 135, 151, 177, 205
    Australian Recreation Camp in, 227
Lesseps, Ferdinand de, 25, 98*n*
Letters from Helles (Darlington), 224n
Lewis, Kenneth, 96, 97
Lewis, Pte Neville, 131
Liddell Hart, B.H., 42n

Lilley (servant), 97
Limpus, Admiral Sir Arthur, 34,
    229, 230, 233
Limpus, Miss, 229, 233, 234
Limpus, Mrs, 74, 230, 234, 235
lines of communication (L of C),
    177, 216
Lisle, Gen. de, 242
Little (fellow serviceman), 71, 110
Lloyd George, David, 35
Lloyd, Trumpeter, 97
Longsdon, Cdr, 266
Loos, Battle of, 241
Lunnon, L.F., 266
lyddite, 21, 132, 149, 150, 151, 160
Lyddon (canal pilot), 93
Lyster, Pop, 265, 266
Lytham, 9, 51, 128
Lytham Standard, 172

McMenamin, Revd., *213*
McPherson, Bimbashi, 62*n*
Majestic, 130
Maloney, Dr, 138, 140
Malta:
    Casal Paula, 230
    Cottonera hospital, 10, 24,
        224–7
    Hagar Qim, 231
    National Museum, 228–9
    St John's Cathedral, 230
    Sliema Harbour, 234
    Valletta, 10–11, 228, 233
Man Who Loved Egypt, The
    (McPherson), 62*n*
Marmara, Sea of , 38, 42, 81*n*
Maude, Sir Stanley, 37
Mauretania, 183, 223
Maxwell, Gen. Sir John, 28–9, 39,
    91, 93, 105
McCrae (fellow serviceman), 188
Mellish, Claire, 262
Mellish, Revd. Noel, 2, 253,
    260–2

Merrinton, Revd., *213*
Methuen, Field Marshal Lord,
    226, 229, 236
Miller, J., 124
Milner, Lord, 26
Minerva, 55
Monro, Gen. Sir Charles, 243–4
More Rough Rhymes of a Padre
    (Studdert-Kennedy), 255*n*
Moreland (fellow serviceman), 88,
    150–1, 158, 167, 206
Morocco, 55
Moses, 217*n*
Motteux, Peter, 158*n*
Mount Olympus, Cyprus, 190
Moynihan, Michael, 250*n*, 263
Muavaneti-i-Millet, 129
Mudros, 10, 23, 175, 180
    Harbour, 39, 42, 183, 205

Nall, Maj., 96
National Museum, Malta, 228–9
New Zealand Memorial, 197
Newmarket, 182
Nicholas, Grand Duke, 35–6
Nightingale, Bombardier, 88, 97
Nullah, 114, 122

Obelisk of On, 62
Ocean, 40, 55, 90
    sunk, 90*n*
O'Connor, Revd., *213*
Ogden, Arthur, 124
Ottley, Lt.-Col. Glendower, 261
Ottoman Empire, 25, 29
Oxford Medical Mission, 257

Palmer, Rex, 265, 266
Parker, Lt.-Col. H.G., *140*, 181
Passchendaele, Battle of (3rd
    Ypres), 256, 263
Path of Glory, The (Blake), 263
Peel, Revd. Hon. Maurice,
    259–60

Phaeton, 39
Philip, Prince, 269
Philpott (batman), 105
Pilgrimage to Gallipoli, 265–9; *see also* Gallipoli
Port Said, 30, 31, 72, 98
Prendergast, Brig. Gen. D.G., 168, 174
Prior, Robin, 249

Queen Elizabeth (*Little Lizzie*), 36, 107*n*, 110, 119
recalled, 129
Queens' College, Cambridge, 9, 274

Ramadan, 187–8
Rancy, Sgt Maj., 93
Rankin (fellow serviceman), 72
Raw, David, 255, 256, 257
Rawlinson, Gen. Sir Henry, 195
Raymond, Revd. Ernest, 262–3
Real War, The (Liddell Hart), 42*n*
Red Sea, 30, 217*n*
Reed, Brig.-Gen., 195
Requin, 90
respirator helmet, 209
Rhodes-James, Robert, 35*n*
Richardson, Capt, 128
River Clyde, SS, view from, *106*
Robbins, Ven. Stephen, 262
Robeck, Vice-Admiral de, 40–1, 244
Robuste, 81
Rochdale, Lt.-Col. Lord, 168
Rooth, Lt.-Col. Richard, 252
Rosebery, Lord, 226
Rosser, Lt., 133
Rough Rhymes (Studdert-Kennedy), 254–5
Royal Army Medical Corps (RAMC), 16, 72, 110, 111, 174

Royal Edward, HMT, 22–3, 237
Royal Garrison Church of All Saints, Aldershot, 253
Royal George, 237
Russia, 29, 35, 228
Turkish–German alliance against, 28
Rye, Col., 149

St John's Cathedral, Malta, 230
Salem, Moses Mohammed, 57
Salonika Expedition, 241
Sanders, Limon von, 32, 41–2, 113
Saros, Gulf of, 42
Sassoon, Siegfried, 254, 263
Scharwenka, Xavier, 237*n*
Scorpion, 212
Scotian, 262
Scowcroft (fellow serviceman), 168
Sea of Marmara, 38, 42, 81*n*
Second World War, *see* World War Two
Serapeum, 16, 33, 85, 89–90
corpses taken from canal at, 96
Singapore, 29*n*
Smalley, Trumpeter, 33, 71, 86, 90, 96
Smith (fellow serviceman), 206
Somme, 3
Soudan, HMHS, 22, 181, 182
Spencer (fellow serviceman), 72, 88
Staveley, Capt., 246
Steinthal, Lt.-Col. W.M., 215, 216, 217
Stewart (fellow serviceman), 192, 239
Stopford, Sir Frederick, 195, 198, 241, 242
Studdert-Kennedy, Revd. Geoffrey ('Woodbine

Willie'), 2, 5, 7–8, 253–5, 258, 262
Suez Canal, 9, 16, 25–6, 30–1, 66, 75, 98*n*
  Britain a large shareholder in, 25
  construction of, 25
  in KB letter, 6 Mar. 1915, 99
  strategic importance of, 16, 30
  Turks advance on, 71
  Turks attack, 16, 31–3
Suez Canal Company, 25
Suez, Port of, 98*n*
Suez War, 98*n*
Suffren, 40
Sultan Hissar, 81*n*
Surada BI5N, SS, 188
Suvla Bay, 37*n*, 166*n*, 195–202, *196*, *199*, 206, 234, 241, 242–3
  evacuation of, 246–7
  Thomas's vivid diary account of, 199–202
Suvla Bay Landing, The (Hargrave), 195*n*
Swiftsure, 86, 90, 110, 138

Talbot, Very Revd. Albert Edward, 108–9
Talbot, Lt. Gilbert, 257–8
Talbot House/Toc H, 257, 258–9
  Journal of, 259, 260*n*
Talbot, Neville, 257–8
Taube, 154
  speed of, 154*n*, 161
Tell England (Raymond), 263
Tewfik, Khedive, 26
Thomas, Pte Harold, 198–202
Thorn (fellow serviceman), 98
Tirpitz, Admiral, 198
Toc H/Talbot House, 257, 258–9
  Journal of, 259, 260*n*
Tongue, Canon Paul, 253
Toussoum, 16, 33, 88, 89–90

Town and Country, 242*n*
Triumph, 130, 138*n*
Troodos (Troodatissa) Monastery, 191, 193
Tucker, Sub-Lt. Louis, 165–6, 167
Turkey, 27–30
  Dardanelles, *see main entry*
  Fisher proposes attack on, 36
  foreign diplomats banned from Istanbul by, 266
  Gallipoli, see main entry
  modern, 'coming-of-age' of, 42
  troops of, see Turkish Army
  war entered by, 28
Turkish Army:
  atrocities of, 17, 18, 106
  captured sniper from, *163*
  expert snipers/marksmen in, 2, 151
  fighting 'honourably and gentlemanly', 132
  Gaba Tepe casualties among, 124
  and Gallipoli evacuation, 246–9
  and Gallipoli Pilgrimage, 266
  Kantara outposts attacked by, 88
  KB's opinion of, 21, 177
  misinformation used by, 162
  renowned as brave, 103
  slaughter among, described by KB, 94–5
  soldiers of 'finest in world', 177
  Suez Canal attacked by, 16, 31–3
  see also Ottoman Empire; Turkey

Upchen, Pte, 233, 234
Ussher, Staff Capt., 152, 157

Valletta, 10–11, 228, 233
VE Day, 13

vessels:
  AE2 (submarine) 81
  Alnwick Castle, 22–3
  Aragon, 177
  Arcadian, 113
  Ark Royal, 178*n*
  Ausonia, HMT, 10, 23–4, 220, 223
  Avon, RMSP, 14, 30
    KB's letters from, *see under*
      Best letters
  Bouvet, 40
  Breslau, 28, 121*n*
  Carisbrooke Castle, SS, 24, 236–9
  Cornwallis, HMS, *248*
  Derfflinger, 17, 105*n*, 194
  El Desire, 237
  Ermina, 23, 205
  Gascon, HMHS, 23, 218–23, 237
    KB's letter from, *see under*
      Best letters
  Gaulois, 40
  Gloucester Castle, 237
  Goeben, 28, 121, 139
  Goliath, 129, 130
  Huntsgreen, SS, 22–3, 194
  Inflexible, 40
  Irresistible, 40
  Jonquil, 197
  Majestic, 130
  Mauretania, 183, 223
  Minerva, 55
  Muavaneti-i-Millet, 129
  Newmarket, 182
  Ocean, 40, 55, 90
    sunk, 90*n*
  Phaeton, 39
  Queen Elizabeth (*Little Lizzie*), 36, 107*n*, 110, 119
    recalled, 129
  Requin, 90
  River Clyde, SS, view from, *106*

Robuste, 81
Royal Edward, HMT, 22–3, 237
Royal George, 237
Scorpion, 212
Scotian, 262
Soudan, HMHS, 22, 181, 182
Suffren, 40
Sultan Hissar, 81*n*
Surada BI5N, SS, 188
Swiftsure, 86, 90, 110, 138
Triumph, 130, 138*n*
Vossische Zeitung, 247

Wade, Lt.-Col., 99
Walker, Col. C. E., 59, 135, 193
War Diary of the Principal Chaplain (Horden), 252
Ward, Archdeacon, 186–7, 193
'Waste' (Studdert-Kennedy), 254–5
Watts, Sub-Lt. Arthur, 166
Watts, Sub-Lt. John, 166, 167
Webster, Lt., 150, 163
Wells, H.G., 242
wells, nicknames for, 133
Wesley, Charles, 178*n*
Wesley, John, 178*n*
Western Front Association, *Bulletin*, 261*n*
Whitehead, Col., 208
Wilde, Cpl, 208
Williams (Australian serviceman), 172, 173
Williams, Jeffery, 242, 247*n*
Williamson, Capt., 218
Wilson, Maj. Gen. A., 31, 92, 93, 96
With the 29th Division in Gallipoli (Creighton), 262
Wolesley, Sir Garnet, 26
'Woodbine Willie', *see* Studdert-Kennedy, Geoffrey
Woods, Bombardier, 177

Woodward, Lt., 178
World War One:
  anniversary of declaration of, 190
  Festubert, Battle of, 260
  as historical watershed, 1
  Krithia, Second Battle of, 18, 110, 113
  Krithia, Third Battle of, 20, 136, 139, *139*
  Loos, Battle of, 241
  Passchendaele, Battle of (3rd Ypres), 256, 263
  see also Best diaries; Best letters; British and Irish military; Dardanelles; Gallipoli; Germany Army; Turkish Army
World War Two, 12
  Dunkirk evacuation during, 245
  atom bomb used in, 251

Xerxes, 263

Young Men's Christian Association (YMCA), 62, 71
  KB's letter from, *see under* Best letters
Ypres, Third Battle of (Passchendaele), 256, 263

Zaghlul, Saad, Pasha, 26–7